# TEACHING HEMINGWAY'S *A Farewell to Arms*

**TEACHING HEMINGWAY SERIES**
*Susan Beegel, Editor*

Teaching Hemingway's *The Sun Also Rises*
*Edited by Peter L. Hays*

Teaching Hemingway's *A Farewell to Arms*
*Edited by Lisa Tyler*

TEACHING HEMINGWAY'S

# A Farewell to Arms

EDITED BY LISA TYLER

*Kent State University Press*
*Kent, Ohio*

© 2008 by The Kent State University Press, Kent, Ohio 44242
All rights reserved
Library of Congress Catalog Card Number 2007021853
ISBN 978-0-87338-917-4

Manufactured in the United States of America

Library of Congress Cataloging-in-Publication Data

Teaching Hemingway's A farewell to arms / edited by Lisa Tyler.
    p. cm. — (Teaching Hemingway series)
Includes bibliographical references and index.
    ISBN 978-0-87338-917-4 (pbk. : alk. paper) ∞
    1. Hemingway, Ernest, 1899–1961. Farewell to arms.
    2. Hemingway, Ernest, 1899–1961—Study and teaching.
    I. Tyler, Lisa, 1964–
PS3515.E37F363 2007
813'.52—dc22        2007021853

British Library Cataloging-in-Publication data are available.

12  11  10  09  08      5  4  3  2  1

# Contents

# Acknowledgments

I MUST first acknowledge a very great debt to Susan Beegel, editor of the *Hemingway Review* and long a progressive force in Hemingway scholarship. Susan first recruited me to edit this book for a series on teaching Hemingway's novels, originally to be published by the University of Idaho Press. When the University of Idaho chose to dismantle its press after most of the essays in this collection had already been drafted, Susan stood by the project and helped steer it to its new home at Kent State University Press. She also signed on with KSUP as series editor, thoughtfully reviewed the manuscript, and gave me honest advice about editing.

Peter L. Hays, who edited Teaching Hemingway's *The Sun Also Rises*, the first book in the series, for the University of Idaho Press, also generously advised me.

Larry Grimes, who is editing a proposed third volume in the Teaching Hemingway series on *The Old Man and the Sea*, kindly invited me to participate in a panel on teaching *A Farewell to Arms* that he organized for the National Council of Teachers of English annual convention in Pittsburgh in fall 2005. It was exciting to have the opportunity to share with high school and college teachers some of what I had learned from the experience of editing this volume.

I am grateful to Will Underwood and Joanna H. Craig of Kent State University Press for their willingness to take us on. I am proud to have the book published by the press whose list includes such distinguished Hemingway scholarship as *Under Kilimanjaro*, edited by Robert W. Lewis and Robert E. Fleming.

As our manuscript's reviewer, Linda Patterson Miller deserves thanks here for her time, her careful reading, and her constructive suggestions.

I would also like to express my gratitude to Jim Tyler, who encouraged me to say yes to this project, assured me repeatedly that I could do it, and bore with great fortitude my many anxious moments. Rose Tyler remains, with her father, the single greatest joy in my life, and I am thankful that she tolerated the many times when I was working and she would have preferred for me to play.

Most of all, I am grateful to the contributors of this collection, who patiently waited while this book found its new home and while I figured out how to edit an anthology. As a community college professor who regularly teaches twelve or more classes a year, I am particularly appreciative of their kind patience with me.

# Introduction

*Lisa Tyler*

*A Farewell to Arms* is, in my estimation, Ernest Hemingway's finest novel. Such a claim flies in the face of received wisdom, which would now award that honor to his much more popular debut novel, *The Sun Also Rises.* Certainly *Sun* has garnered the lion's share of critical attention. Hemingway bibliographer Kelli A. Larson conceded in 1992 that *The Sun Also Rises* is "clearly the most analyzed novel of the last fifteen years," with *A Farewell to Arms* "a distant second" (21).

That has not always been the case. In his early (1952) influential study *Hemingway: The Writer as Artist,* Carlos Baker, one of the first scholars to study Hemingway's work and later the official biographer of Hemingway, devoted many pages to *A Farewell to Arms.* He drew on the book's opening sentence to examine its contrasts between the plains and the mountains, creating a geographical reading of the novel that influenced many midcentury critics of Hemingway's work. (For further discussion of Baker's work, see Gail D. Sinclair's essay in this volume.)

Of the period immediately following Hemingway's death, Susan F. Beegel observes, "The vast majority of critics at work in the academy during this period were white Anglo-Saxon Protestant males, who shared World War II as their most important historic memory. Indeed, many were combat veterans. Their favorite novel was *A Farewell to Arms,* Hemingway's romantic tragedy of love and duty in a theater of war" ("Conclusion" 275). Beegel notes that it was only in the 1970s that *A Farewell to Arms* faded in popularity, ceding first place to *The Sun Also Rises:* "Its lost-generation characters, alienated by World War I and self-anesthetized with alcohol, were familiar and appealing to an equally lost generation alienated by Vietnam and experimenting with drugs" ("Conclusion" 281).

Despite ebbs and flows in its popularity, however, *A Farewell to Arms* has always received scholarly attention. After all, while the novel may have lost ground in the 1970s, it was also in the 1970s that the availability of Hemingway's manuscripts led to increased attention to the artistic evolution of his fiction (Beegel, "Conclusion" 283) and to the publication of what remain two of the best book-length studies of *A Farewell to Arms.*[1] *Hemingway's First War: The Making of* A Farewell to Arms (1976), by Michael S. Reynolds, documented Hemingway's own war experience, distinguished between the autobiographical elements of the novel and those that were researched, and persuasively demonstrated the importance of Hemingway's reading to the construction of *A Farewell to Arms.* Bernard Oldsey's 1979 book, *Hemingway's Hidden Craft: The Writing of* A Farewell to Arms, also examined Hemingway's composition process.

Increasingly during the late 1970s and early 1980s, Catherine Barkley attracted scrutiny in light of the growing influence of feminism on literary scholarship. In 1978, Judith Fetterley roundly attacked what she perceived as Hemingway's pervasive misogyny: "the only good woman is a dead one, and even then there are questions" (71). Millicent Bell was equally disenchanted with Catherine: "She is a sort of inflated rubber woman available at will to the onanistic dreamer" (114). These charges went largely unanswered for many years and (I suspect) had the unfortunate effect of deterring many readers from even opening the book. Certainly anecdotal evidence would indicate that some college and university professors chose to drop Hemingway's work from their course reading lists, largely for perceived sexism, and openly disparaged him to their students.

In 1981, with the publication of Joyce Wexler's "E.R.A. for Hemingway: A Feminist Defense of *A Farewell to Arms,*" the tide slowly began to turn against feminist disparagement of Hemingway's novel and especially of Catherine Barkley. The most influential rereadings of Catherine's character were Sandra Whipple Spanier's two essays arguing that Catherine chooses to overcome her trauma by willing herself to love Frederic Henry. Spanier brilliantly defended Catherine as the "code hero" of Hemingway's novel.

With its letters, photographs, and journal entries, *Hemingway in Love and War,* Henry S. Villard's 1989 collaboration with James Nagel, spurred a renewed interest in Agnes von Kurowsky and the nature of her relationship with Ernest, which critics now generally concede was never consummated. That same year the *Hemingway Review* published a special issue exclusively on *A Farewell to Arms,* suggesting a resurgence of critical interest in the novel.

The publication of *Hemingway and Film* (Phillips), *Hemingway and the Movies* (Laurence), and *A Moving Picture Feast: The Filmgoer's Hemingway* (Oliver) during the 1980s focused attention on the many films based on Hemingway's writings, including both the 1932 and 1957 versions of *Farewell.* Also particularly popular in the 1980s were articles analyzing the influence of other writers upon Hemingway, including D. H. Lawrence and Norman Mailer (Balbert), Owen Wister (Price), and Shakespeare (Lockridge). Perhaps this trend was prompted at least in part by the publication early in that decade of *Hemingway's Library: A Composite Record* (Brasch and Sigman) and *Hemingway's Reading, 1910–1940: An Inventory* (Reynolds).

James Nagel's important 1987 article "Catherine Barkley and Retrospective Narration in *A Farewell to Arms*" calls readers' attention to the temporal distance between the narrated events of the novel and the time of the narration itself, reminding us that the only way we know Catherine at all is through the memories of a man who once loved her and is recalling his time with her long after she is dead. In the same vein, James Phelan's two 1990 articles on the novel introduce sophisticated narrative theory to critical study of *A Farewell to Arms.*

The 1986 publication of *The Garden of Eden* (with its own "crazy" Catherine B.) created new interest in Hemingway in general, but especially in *A Farewell to Arms.* Then in a highly controversial 1987 biography of Hemingway, Kenneth S. Lynn emphasized how Hemingway's mother "twinned" him with his older sister Marcelline, dressing them alike and holding Marcelline back from school a year so that they would enter school together. Lynn argued that this practice caused Hemingway more trauma than his 1918 wounding. The children's similar haircuts had their echo in *A Farewell to Arms,* a fact that, along with the publication of *The Garden of Eden,* has prompted scholars to reassess some of the details of Hemingway's work in a psychobiographical light. Mark Spilka, in *Hemingway's Quarrel with Androgyny* (1990), contended that Hemingway was uneasy with his own androgynous impulses and sometimes dealt with that uneasiness by becoming more noisily masculine. Carl P. Eby's 1999 work, *Hemingway's Fetishism: Psychoanalysis and the Mirror of Manhood,* offers a highly sophisticated psychoanalytic take on Hemingway's writings.

In the 1990s Jamie Barlowe-Kayes directed us to take a fresh look at Catherine Barkley, asking us to recognize the impossibility of fully coherent and stable readings of her as a character and of this complex text as a whole; Barlowe-Kayes advocates that we instead opt for destabilizing readings that no longer repress "the incoherent, problematic, unstable aspects of life into superficially coherent, stable fictional narratives" (32).

As the divergent readings of the character of Catherine Barkley might suggest, gender has played an increasingly important role in analyses of *A Farewell to Arms,* although such approaches have been very unpopular with earlier generations of scholars. Homoerotic and homosexual themes in the novel have received growing attention, for example, in Miriam Mandel's 1994 article examining Helen Ferguson's attachment to Catherine, and in Peter F. Cohen's 1995 article on the homoeroticism apparent in Frederic Henry's relationship with Rinaldi. Twenty-first-century approaches note the costs of masculinity for Frederic Henry (Herndl), the performativity of gender for Catherine (Traber), and the intersections of war and gender in not only *Farewell* but also Hemingway's other World War I writings (Vernon). Marc Hewson goes so far as to propose *A Farewell to Arms* as an example of what French feminist Hélène Cixous has termed *écriture feminine.* The novel's wordplay has become a more recent focus, prompting articles by Kleinman in 1995 and Harrington in 2001.

While it is impossible to predict where the future will take Hemingway's second novel, it is possible to make educated guesses as to likely developments. For example, the much-anticipated publication of the multivolume edition of Hemingway's collected letters is likely to reinvigorate the study of all his works for some time to come by offering new avenues of investigation. Publication of a scholarly edition of the complete manuscript from which *The Garden of Eden* was posthumously created might also spark renewed interest in *Farewell.* Perhaps the most obvious opportunity for scholars interested in *Farewell* would be investigations of its influence upon later generations of writers and their work.

The richness of the essays in this collection testifies to the wide-ranging nature of Hemingway's second, longer, and in my opinion aesthetically most complex novel. This collection is divided into five sections—Backgrounds and Contexts (with essays by Charles M. Oliver and Frederic J. Svoboda), Hemingway's Language and Style (J. T. Barbarese, Gail D. Sinclair, and Kim Moreland), Modernism and World War I (Ellen Andrews Knodt, Jackson A. Niday II and James H. Meredith, and Jennifer Haytock), Gender Issues (Amy Lerman, Peter L. Hays, and Thomas Strychacz), and Pedagogical Approaches (Mark P. Ott, David Scoma, and Brenda G. Cornell).

In "History and Imagined History," Charles M. Oliver examines the historical and biographical background of *A Farewell to Arms,* spelling out which aspects of Frederic's experience are autobiographical and which are purely fictional and based on Hemingway's extensive research. Frederic J. Svoboda, a veteran teacher of Hemingway's writings, suggests multiple contexts in which to teach *Farewell* and recommends a plethora of resources for classroom use.

Poet J. T. Barbarese devotes attention to Hemingway's legendary style and offers practical exercises for introducing that style to students unaccustomed to minimalism. Gail D. Sinclair walks students step-by-step through a close reading of individual paragraphs to help those new to literary analysis develop an appreciation for Hemingway and to prepare them to analyze literature on their own. Kim Moreland chooses one of the novel's classic passages—Frederic's discussion of the way certain words have changed in meaning because of their distortion during wartime—and shows how that key passage can unlock the meaning of the rest of the novel for students.

Ellen Andrews Knodt explores the question of modernist experimentation with point of view and argues for teaching this war novel *before* Fitzgerald's Jazz Age fiction and T. S. Eliot's *The Waste Land* to help students grasp the notion that World War I was the definitive experience of the Lost Generation. Captain Jackson A. Niday II and Lieutenant Colonel James H. Meredith, who have taught *Farewell* at the United States Air Force Academy, draw on the concept of distance—including geographical, chronological, and narrative distance—to lead their cadets to a greater understanding of the novel. Jennifer Haytock offers a detailed plan for teaching *Farewell* in a graduate seminar on war and American literature, including a proposed reading list and useful secondary sources.

Catherine Barkley and her development during the events Frederic narrates are the focus of Amy Lerman's essay, in which she presents a feminist argument for seeing Catherine as at least as central to the story as Frederic himself is. Peter L. Hays, a professor emeritus who taught the novel for many years, examines his own disquietude with the problematic Frederic Henry and the problems that uneasiness created for him when introducing the novel to students. Thomas Strychacz, who describes the experience of teaching *Farewell* at a women's college, asks his students to think about identity and masquerade in the novel and to explore the instability of its gender roles.

High school teacher Mark P. Ott explains how the Harkness model of pedagogy allows students to work out their own impressions of the novel through student-led discussion. David Scoma draws on a range of films for introducing the novel to increasingly reluctant readers with rapidly shrinking attention spans. Community college students in Brenda G. Cornell's classes become fledgling filmmakers—and active learners—through an innovative teaching method outlined in detail in her essay in this volume.

It is, I think, the collective hope of those of us involved with this volume that—through its authors' collective experience, intellectual rigor, practical advice, conversational tone, sample syllabi, and enthusiastic encouragement—it inspires future generations of teachers to return to this iconically modernist novel so that students once again have the opportunity to understand its artistry for themselves.

## NOTE

1. This introduction provides a brief and admittedly selective overview of the criticism of *A Farewell to Arms* during the last thirty years; for a more comprehensive checklist of work on the novel, see Monteiro.

# BACKGROUNDS AND CONTEXTS

# History and Imagined History

*Charles M. Oliver*

ONE OF the most interesting yet often misunderstood facts about Hemingway's *A Farewell to Arms* is that it was written not so much from personal experience as from research. The author was wounded badly while driving ambulances for the American Red Cross in support of the Italian army, and he apparently had a love affair with a nurse; that is more or less the extent of his personal life that went into the novel. The rest is a mix of research and imagination.

It is fairly easy to summarize Hemingway's actual experiences in northern Italy during World War I, the setting for the novel, because he was involved for such a short period of time. He arrived in Italy on June 4, 1918; was wounded on July 8; arrived at the American hospital in Milan on July 17; spent the rest of the summer and early fall recuperating from two operations; and was discharged from Red Cross service on January 4, 1919, leaving for home that day, barely six months after his arrival in Italy.

The author's description of the Italian army's retreat from Caporetto (chapters 28–30) is so vivid that even Italian soldiers who had been in the retreat themselves could not believe that Hemingway had not been there as well. But he had not. He was eighteen at the time, in Kansas City on his first newspaper job, and he read about the battle in the *Kansas City Star*'s front-page reports in late October and early November 1917, six months before he arrived in Italy. His rendering of the chaos during the retreat was accurate enough when he wrote about it ten years later that it could pass as a historical account. And Hemingway was fascinated by geography, so it doesn't take much to imagine that he studied the lay of the land throughout the battlefields of northern Italy. Yet he did not visit any of the important eastern fronts before he wrote the novel.

Although he did not observe the retreat from Caporetto, he did observe firsthand the chaos. Hemingway also wrote an article for the *Toronto Star Weekly* (March 13, 1920) titled "How to Be Popular in Peace though a Slacker in War." It was a slap at a group of Canadians who had avoided joining the army yet enjoyed telling war stories as if they had been there; if you read enough about the war, Hemingway tells them, then you can know enough to pretend you were there:

> Buy or borrow a good history of the war. Study it carefully and you will be able to talk intelligently on any part of the front. In fact, you will more than once be able to prove the average returned veteran a pinnacle of inaccuracy if not unveracity. The average soldier has a very abominable memory for names and dates. Take advantage of this. With a little conscientious study you should be able to prove to the man who was at first and second Ypres that he was not there at all. You, of course, are aided in this by the similarity of one day to another in the army. (*Dateline* 11)

Hemingway is clearly sarcastic in this article, but he knew from personal experience the importance of reading a "good history of the war." His thorough research of the battlefields of northern Italy produced in *A Farewell to Arms* a historical, yet fictional, account.

It is probably true that Frederic Henry's love affair with Catherine Barkley is based on Hemingway's own love affair with Agnes von Kurowsky, but there are few actual parallels. Hemingway did not meet Agnes until he was delivered, badly wounded, to the Red Cross hospital in Milan in July 1918, and she became his nurse. There were apparently daily visits from Agnes while he was recuperating during the summer, but she was assigned for duty in Florence and then Treviso for most of the fall and early winter. Hemingway visited her in Treviso on December 8, but that was apparently the last time they saw each other. He thought it was a love affair, but there is considerable doubt that she did; while he was nineteen years old that summer, she was twenty-seven. According to Bernice Kert in her book *The Hemingway Women,* and based on letters and diary entries, the affair was not consummated. Hemingway left for home in January and received a Dear John letter from Agnes dated March 7, 1919, telling him that whatever relationship they had had was over.

According to James Brasch and Joseph Sigman in their work *Hemingway's Library: A Composite Record,* Hemingway owned more than one hundred books on World War I. It isn't clear when the books were purchased, but the following five titles were published early enough to be useful as source material for *A Farewell to Arms:* Charles M. Bakewell's *The Story of the American Red Cross in Italy* (1920); Martin Hardie and Warner Allen's *Our Italian Front* (1920); Douglas Johnson's *Battlefields of the World War, Western and Southern Fronts: A Study of Military Geography* (1921); and two government monographs, *Report of the Department of Military Affairs, January to July 1918* and *The War in Italy, No. 18* (soldier's edition, published in September 1918).

*A Farewell to Arms* may be the most interesting of Hemingway's ten published novels precisely because it is so rich both as a good story and as history. Yet it is always difficult in reading Hemingway to tell the difference between what is real and what is made up. Even his letters are a mix of fiction and nonfiction. One of the nice things about good fiction, however, is that readers can be carried along by a good story without concern for what is real and what is not.

Frederic Henry's narration of his wounding in chapter 9 is no doubt taken from the author's memory of his own out-of-body experience during his wounding on July 8.

> I ate the end of my piece of cheese and took a swallow of wine. Through the other noise I heard a cough, then came the chuh-chuh-chuh-chuh—then there was a flash, as when a blast-furnace door is swung open, and a roar that started white and went red and on and on in a rushing wind. I tried to breathe but my breath would not come and I felt myself rush bodily out of myself and out and out and out and all the time bodily in the wind. I went out swiftly, all of myself, and I knew I was dead and that it had all been a mistake to think you just died. Then I floated, and instead of going on I felt myself slide back. I breathed and I was back. (54)

Hemingway was active with the American Red Cross for just thirty-four days—from June 4, 1918, when he joined Ambulance Section 4 at Schio in northern Italy, until July 8, when he was wounded along the Piave River while distributing candy and cigarettes to Italian soldiers. He spent the rest of the summer and fall at the American hospital in Milan or on crutches, recuperating from two operations on his leg and the removal of 227 pieces of shrapnel (Baker, *Life Story* 56).

He was apparently the first American to be wounded in Italy (an American had been killed earlier) and so became something of a hero both in Milan, where he was visited by officers of the Red Cross and several friends, and in Oak Park, where the Chicago papers picked up his story. He was home by the end of January 1919 and gave a talk to an assembly of Oak Park High School students on March 14, saying nothing that would take anything away from the hero's welcome home. He described his experience of being wounded by saying, according to the report that appeared the next week in the high school newspaper: "When the thing exploded, it seemed as if I was moving off somewhere in a sort of red din. I said to myself, 'Gee! Stein, you're dead' and then I began to feel myself pulling back to earth. Then I woke up. The sand bags had caved in on my legs and at first I felt disappointed that I had not been wounded" (*Hemingway at Oak Park High* 122).

Hemingway received two medals from the Italian government for his service with the American Red Cross: the Croce di Guerra and the Medaglia d'Argento al Valore.

## THE WAR

The war in Europe began on June 28, 1914, with the assassination in Sarajevo of Austrian archduke Francis Ferdinand. The fighting began a few weeks later. The Allies were made up of England, France, Russia, Belgium, Serbia, Montenegro, and Japan; the Central Powers consisted of Germany, Austria-Hungary, and the Ottoman Empire (which became the modern Turkish republic in 1923). Americans felt the war almost immediately: there were restrictions on travel, the stock market crashed and then closed, and the import of goods from European markets was disrupted. Nevertheless, America did not get into the war until April 6, 1917, three years after it started. Even after the sinking of the *Lusitania* off the Irish coast by a German submarine on May 7, 1915, which cost the lives of 1,195 passengers, including 128 Americans, President Wilson hesitated to involve American military personnel. It was nearly two years later, when Germany declared submarine warfare against Great Britain, that the United States finally broke off relations with Germany in February 1917 and officially entered the war on April 6.

Congress passed the Selective Service Act on May 18, 1917. Six million men volunteered, and another four million were drafted for military service. A small force of American soldiers under General John J. Pershing went to France in June, but it would be another year before significant numbers of troops were in Europe to help stop the German army's advance. By July 1918 one million American soldiers were in France; by the war's end four months later (November 11, 1918), there were two million Americans fighting in the war (*Concise Dictionary* 1026).

The Americans arrived in Europe in time to help stop major drives by the German forces that threatened Paris, including significant battles at Cantigny, Château-Thierry, and Belleau Wood. The Americans were involved in counterattacks at St. Mihiel and in the Argonne Forest and were prepared for counterattacks at Metz, in northeastern France, when the war ended.

There were more than 53,000 American soldiers killed in the war, compared to almost 300,000 killed in World War II and about 34,000 in Korea. Perhaps as important as the soldiers fighting was the American relief effort after the war. Millions of tons of supplies were sent to Central and Eastern Europe, where 200 million people needed help. The American Relief Administration also sent $134 million to Europe after the war, and supplies totaling another $1 billion. Between 1914 and 1923, the United States government sent to Europe $6 billion worth of food and supplies (*Concise Dictionary* 997).

## THE AMERICAN RED CROSS

Several charity organizations in the United States contributed money and personnel to help Europeans after the war. The American Friends Service (the Quakers), for example, sent several units to Germany to help feed children. They collected and distributed more than $9 million for the hunger relief efforts. The Jewish Joint Distribution Committee was formed in 1914 and by 1926 had spent $69 million on various European projects, mostly involving the provision of food and medicine. Other active groups included the YMCA and YWCA, the Federal Council of Churches, the Knights of Columbus, the National Catholic Welfare Council, and the Rockefeller Foundation.

The Red Cross was organized by Clara Barton in 1881; she had been a nurse in hospitals in Washington, D.C., during the Civil War, and the Red Cross provided its first disaster relief in the Spanish-American War (1895–98). During World War I, even before American troops entered the war, the American Red Cross operated hospital units, recruited doctors and nurses, and supplied and staffed ambulances for Allied armies. Hemingway volunteered in the spring of 1918, along with his friend Ted Brumback, who had worked with him at the *Kansas City Star.*

The American Red Cross spent more than $200 million in Europe between 1914 and 1923, most of it on medical relief for those affected by postwar epidemics, but a large portion of the money was spent on child care and refugee work; there were units of workers in twenty-four European countries in 1919. A medical unit of the Red Cross was involved in inoculating eight million people in Europe against various epidemics (most of this work done after the war), and $3 million' worth of Red Cross supplies was sent to Russian hospitals and clinics.

In his book *The Story of the American Red Cross in Italy,* which was in Hemingway's library, Charles M. Bakewell writes that the retreat from Caporetto made the need for medical supplies especially great because of the Italian army's failure to anticipate major losses. Bakewell states that "one of the most serious losses sustained in the retreat was that of hospitals and hospital supplies. Not anticipating any break, the hospitals had been put well towards the front. More than one hundred were lost, as were, in addition, two principal magazines of supplies, considerably more than one-third of the entire medical equipment of the war zone" (28). At one point during the retreat from Caporetto in *A Farewell to Arms,* Frederic Henry, whose ambulances were stuck in the mud, laments the fact that "all I had to do was to get Pordenone with three ambulances. I had failed at that" (212).

## Two Significant Battles

Two World War I battlefields held special significance for Hemingway in *A Farewell to Arms,* and some knowledge of both is essential for an understanding of the author's underlying tone in the novel. The battles were fought along the Isonzo River in northeastern Italy and along the Somme in northern France.

There were twelve battles fought in the Isonzo valley, the river of which now forms part of the Italian border with Slovenia; the battle at Caporetto was the twelfth, and certainly the most devastating because it started a massive retreat by the Italians across the Tagliamento and Livenza rivers, into the plains north of Venice. By the time the Austrian-German armies outran their supplies on the Venetian plains and were forced to stop, 30,000 Italians had been killed and 70,000 wounded (Bakewell 22).

Frederic sees some of the dead along the roads that he and his friends in the ambulance corps take as they become part of the retreating Italian army, but he doesn't provide readers with the entire picture; he is too close to it. The historic disaster that took place is in what is not said, or even known, by Frederic.

Knowledge of the geography of northeastern Italy—especially of the Veneto plains, south of the Dolomite mountains and between the Piave and the Isonzo rivers—was essential for both the Italian and German-Austrian armies during World War I. In his short duty with the Italian ambulance service, Hemingway never got farther east than the Piave River, where he was wounded on July 8, 1918. He had such knowledge of the territory, however, most of it from studying the maps later, that he would re-create in *A Farewell to Arms* the retreat from Caporetto with such accuracy that Italian historians (as well as the soldiers) were convinced that Hemingway had been there.

The retreat began on October 24, 1917, in the rain. Mario Morselli writes the following in his book *Caporetto 1917: Victory or Defeat?*

> The rainy weather had . . . a serious effect [on the advancing armies of Austria and Germany]. Usually the Tagliamento, a typical torrential stream, can be forded from the Cornino bridge all the way to the sea for about eight months of the year. However, by the time the Austro-German forces reached the river, its depth and width were such that, even with good bridging equipment, it could only be crossed with difficulty. The Tagliamento . . . was not the only water-course interfering with the advancing armies; once they reached the Venetian plains, there were several other rivers with their bridges destroyed and their banks overflowing. (26)

The Austrian-German Fourteenth Army, which was doing the attacking, was composed of 160 battalions, but only thirty-one engineering companies, and the engineers had the work, according to Morselli, of "installing radio stations, telephone and telegraph lines and repairing them" (26). No wonder the retreat was nearly as much of a disaster for the advancing Austrians as for the Italians. The Austrian-German army was virtually stopped at the Piave River. And the war ended a year later.

In reading *A Farewell to Arms,* it is even easier to miss the importance of the Somme battles in northern France; they are mentioned only in connection with the death of Catherine's fiancé. The first battle took place between June 24 and November 13, 1916, and the second between March 21 and April 5, 1918. The date of the first battle is crucial in the novel, because Frederic and Catherine meet for the first time in the late summer or early fall of 1916, which means that her fiancé had just recently been killed, blown to "bits," as Catherine informs Frederic.

The first battle was disastrous on both sides. The British and French armies fought to force the Germans out of a significant portion of occupied France. A total of three million men fought in that first battle on both sides, and one million were killed, wounded, or captured. The British forces attacked on the north side of the river, the French on the south. The German resistance was so enormous that the British lost 50,000 men on the first day. The gain for the British and French after four months of fighting was two hundred square miles of French territory and 80,000 German prisoners (Tucker 108).

No wonder Catherine seems "a little crazy" during her first meetings with Frederic. This knowledge of what Catherine has been through seems to negate the early criticism of her portrayal as a mere sex object. She has gone through far more trauma than he has at this point in the novel. Only Frederic's wounding, followed by his involvement in the retreat, his fear of being shot as a traitor by battle police at the Tagliamento, and his escape into the river, creates for him a balance with Catherine in their respective traumatic experiences.

Frederic's "separate peace" comes along with his discovery during the retreat from Caporetto, if not before, that war is hell and that nobody ever wins—though losing is worse. Thirteen years after the publication of *A Farewell to Arms,* Hemingway edited an anthology of war stories, *Men at War: The Best War Stories of All Time.* In the introduction, he writes that he "hates war and hates all the politicians whose mismanagement, gullibility, cupidity, selfishness and ambition brought on this present war [World War II] and made it inevitable." He adds, however: "Once we have a war there is only one thing to do. It must be won. For defeat brings worse things than any that can happen in a war" (xi).

Included in *Men at War* is Stephen Crane's complete short novel *The Red Badge of Courage* (1895), written by a man born after the war was over. The story features vivid details of the battles and casualties of the American Civil War. Crane, too, depended on research, especially Mathew Brady's photographs. War is the subject of *Men at War,* but the theme of the eighty-two stories taken together seems to be that at the human level, it is the chaos in war that always prevails.

Hemingway also included in *Men at War* a selection from Stendhal's *The Charterhouse of Parma* (1839), which he titled "A Personal View of Waterloo." War is never as clear cut or as clever as the generals (or their governments or the historians who follow) would have us believe. The individual soldier is nearly always confused in battle and never sure of the outcome until he hears about it later. Stendhal offers a battle scene that demonstrates the "essence" of this truth. There is the main character's detailed description of a battle in which he is forced to fight, of his retreat from the fighting, and of his discovery *only* when he reads about it in the Paris newspapers the next day that it had been the Battle of Waterloo and that his side had lost. By 1942 Hemingway had experienced enough of the chaos of war to appreciate Stendhal's novel more than ever.

## THE NOVEL

There is some confusion about when Hemingway began writing *A Farewell to Arms.* In a letter (dated March 17, 1929, from Paris) to his literary agent at Scribner's, Maxwell Perkins, Hemingway suggests that he began the novel in early March of the previous year. He had written 45,000 words on another novel, tentatively titled *Jimmy Breen,* which he never finished. In an inscription in Dr. Carlos Guffey's copy of *A Farewell to Arms,* however, Hemingway outlines his progress with the novel, stating that "This book was started in Paris in January." Dr. Guffey delivered both of Pauline Hemingway's sons, Patrick and Gregory.

Hemingway wrote the new novel during stops in several locations, beginning in Paris. His letters to Perkins and to other friends not only provide a running account of progress on *A Farewell to Arms* but also indicate that the letters' recipients already knew about the new novel. By January 22, 1929, he had finished the final typed copy of *A Farewell to Arms,* and he invited Perkins to Key West for fishing and to pick up the typescript. Perkins spent about ten days with Hemingway and left on February 9, taking the novel back to Scribners in New York.

Perkins wrote a letter to his boss, Charles Scribner (dated February 14, 1929), indicating his excitement with the new novel and stating that the title "is a bitter phrase: war taints and damages the beautiful and the gallant, and degrades everyone;—and this book which is a *farewell* to it, as useless and hateful, would be only grim reading if it were not illuminated with the beauty of the world, and of the characters, even though damaged, of some people, and by love" (Bruccoli 88).

Scribners paid Hemingway $16,000 for the serialization of the novel in *Scribner's Magazine.* Several exchanges of letters between Hemingway and Perkins show the author's struggle to keep in the book's four-letter words and a few descriptive passages that the editors at Scribners felt were not suitable for a family magazine. Several words were replaced with dashes: "We may drink——before Udine," for example, or "——the war." Hemingway won a few compromises, but Scribners was following the popular reaction to such language, and in 1929 readers were not yet ready for the greater freedom enjoyed by writers in the twenty-first century. Indeed, even the dashes did not stop the police in Boston from banning the June and July issues, parts 2 and 3 of the novel. According to a story in the *New York Times* (June 20, 1929), Boston's superintendent of police, Michael H. Crowley, barred the June issue of *Scribner's Magazine* from newsstands "because of objections to an installment of Ernest Hemingway's serial, 'A Farewell to Arms.' It is said that some persons deemed part of the installment salacious" ("Boston Police" 2). Crowley didn't define "salacious," but *Webster's New World Dictionary* defines it with the words "lecherous" and "erotically stimulating; pornographic." Crowley's complaint probably refers to the blanks Hemingway used, which still make clear the words he had in mind.

The *Times* story went on to say, however, that police action "was similar to locking the stable door after the horse had been stolen, because the June issue of *Scribner's* had been on sale since May 25." The Boston police superintendent certainly brought attention to the novel and no doubt increased the sales of both the serialization and, later, the book. Part 1 (in the May issue) had been sold in Boston, and copies of the June and July issues had been distributed to book stores and corner kiosks before the police began collecting and destroying copies, so the word was out, even in Boston.

The novel was published in book form by Scribner's on September 27, 1929, in an issue of 31,050 copies at $2.50 each. The first book edition is the same as the magazine version except that in a few cases words replace dashes.

Audre Hanneman notes in her Hemingway bibliography that *A Farewell to Arms* was reprinted twice in September, once in October, and three times in November. "By February 14, 1930, sales stood at 79,251." *Publishers' Weekly* reported on July 10, 1961, that the novel had sold 1,383,000 copies (Hanneman 23–24). And the work is still in print.

There was concern at Scribners that some of the novel's characters might have real-life prototypes, so the second printing contains the following disclaimer: "None of the characters in this book is a living person, nor are the units or military organizations mentioned actual units or organizations.—E.H." (This note was omitted after the second printing.) Despite these concerns, early reviews of the novel were generally favorable. Isabel Paterson in the *New York Herald Tribune* (September 27, 1929) wrote that Hemingway's "style and point of view are now sufficiently fixed as to be easily recognizable. . . . The public knows what to expect." Malcolm Cowley, for the same newspaper a few days later, wrote that Hemingway's "name is generally mentioned with the respect that one accords to a legendary figure" (74). T. S. Matthews, in a review titled "Nothing Ever Happens to the Brave" for the *New Republic* (October 9, 1929), wrote: "The writings of Ernest Hemingway have very quickly put him in a prominent place among American writers, and his numerous admirers have looked forward with impatience and great expectations to his second novel. They should not be disappointed: 'A Farewell to Arms' is worthy of their hopes and of its author's promise" (76). Clifton Fadiman in the *Nation* (October 30, 1929) wrote that "understatement is not so much a method with [Hemingway] as an instinctive habit of mind. (It is more or less an accident that it also happens to harmonize with the contemporary antiromantic tendency.) Consequently we believe in his love story" (83). John Dos Passos in *New Masses* (December 1, 1929) began his review by stating that "Hemingway's *A Farewell to Arms* is the best written book that has seen the light in America for many a long day" (95).

H. L. Mencken wrote in the *American Mercury* (January 1930) that "The virtue of [*A Farewell to Arms*] lies in its brilliant evocation of the horrible squalor and confusion of war—specifically, of war *a la Italienne*" (97).

There were also early reviews, however, that criticized Hemingway for writing "venereal fiction" or accused him of providing "vicarious [sexual] satisfaction" to readers (qtd. in Donaldson, *New Essays* 12). The *Bookman* ran a review by Robert Herrick titled "What Is Dirt?" (November 1929) in which the writer asks: "What is sexual evil? What 'contaminates' the adolescent or even the mature mind?" (86). Herrick compares *A Farewell to Arms* with *All Quiet on the Western Front*, both published in the same year. He concludes that "although the two stories present similar material, although both deal 'nakedly' with certain common physiological functions, one, I maintain, is literature and the other it would not be too strong to call mere garbage" (87). For Herrick, Hemingway's novel falls into the "garbage" category.

Herrick's review, plus a follow-up essay by M. K. Hare in the March 1930 issue of the *Bookman,* and an essay in criticism, "In Spite of Robert Herrick," by Louis Henry Cohn for his *A Bibliography of the Works of Ernest Hemingway,* became touchstones for later declarations for and against literary censorship, ideas still reverberating today in public schools with lists of books removed from library shelves.

Hemingway had no stomach for negative reviews or criticism, and Perkins was wise enough to send telegrams encouraging the author with general comments about the reviews, plus print-run and sales figures: "FIRST REVIEW SPLENDID STOP PROSPECTS BRIGHT" (September 28, 1929) and "ALREADY GETTING REORDERS STOP VERY FINE PRESS" (October 3, 1929). Perkins let Hemingway know that by October 15, 28,000 copies had been sold of a total 50,000 printed; that 57,000 had been sold by December 7; and that 59,000 had been sold by December 9 (Reynolds, *Hemingway's First War* 78–81).

The book created enough of a sensation to spawn the production of two film adaptations of the novel, a Broadway play, five radio dramatizations, and three television productions. Gary Cooper and Helen Hayes played lead roles in the first film in 1932; Rock Hudson and Jennifer Jones performed lead roles in the 1957 version. The radio productions included such leading actors and actresses as Orson Welles with Katharine Hepburn, Frederic March with Florence Eldridge, and Humphrey Bogart with Joan Fontaine.

Hemingway reported an advance of $750 for the Laurence Stallings Broadway adaptation, which had a run of three weeks in September 1930. He received $24,000 for the sale of the movie rights for the 1932 Paramount Pictures film (Bruccoli 121).

All this response to *A Farewell to Arms* was merely the beginning of what would become for Hemingway during the 1930s and 1940s a popularity unlike any experienced by an American writer before or since. He was in the news media almost daily, his experiences covered by reporters and photographers as if he were a Hollywood movie star. He was handsome, active, intelligent, and charismatic. Archibald MacLeish said of those years after *A Farewell to Arms* that "the only [other] person I have ever known who could exhaust the oxygen in a room the way Ernest could just by coming into it was Franklin Delano Roosevelt" (qtd. in Donaldson, *By Force* 2).

## APPENDIX: Chronology of *A Farewell to Arms*

| | |
|---|---|
| August 1914 | World War I begins in Europe. |
| April 6, 1917 | The United States enters the war. |
| June 1917 | Ernest Hemingway graduates from Oak Park High School. |
| July 21, 1917 | Hemingway celebrates his eighteenth birthday. |
| October 1917 | Hemingway becomes a reporter for the *Kansas City Star*. |
| October 24, 1917 | The Italian retreat from Caporetto begins. The *Kansas City Star* has the story on page 1 and carries stories about the retreat for several days. |
| May 23, 1918 | Hemingway and his friend Ted Brumback join other American Red Cross enlistees for a trip aboard the *Chicago* to Europe and the war. |
| June 4, 1918 | Hemingway is assigned to Schio, Italy, and to Red Cross Ambulance Section 4. |
| July 8, 1918 | Just after midnight, along the Piave River, Hemingway is wounded by a trench mortar shell while handing out cigarettes, chocolate, and postcards to Italian troops. |
| Summer–Fall 1918 | While recuperating in the American hospital in Milan, he undergoes two operations and the removal of more than two hundred pieces of shrapnel from his legs. |
| January 4, 1919 | Hemingway, discharged from American Red Cross, leaves Italy for the United States. |

| | |
|---|---|
| March 1928 | He begins writing *A Farewell to Arms* (there is a Hemingway inscription in a copy of the novel to Dr. Carlos Guffey, however, in which he says: "This book was started in Paris in January"). |
| January 22, 1929 | Hemingway completes the final typescript copy of *A Farewell to Arms*. |
| February 13, 1929 | Hemingway's agent, Maxwell Perkins, sends an offer of $16,000 for the serial rights to the novel for *Scribner's Magazine*. |
| May–October 1929 | *A Farewell to Arms* is published in *Scribner's* in six parts; the June and July issues (parts 2 and 3) are banned in Boston. |
| September 27, 1929 | *A Farewell to Arms* is published in book form by Charles Scribner's Sons in New York. |

# On Teaching Hemingway's *A Farewell to Arms* in Contexts

*Frederic J. Svoboda*

I TEACH Hemingway's works in some substantial way in five different courses: a 200-level topics course on midwestern writers, in which I use *In Our Time;* our 300-level survey of modern American literature, in which I usually use *The Snows of Kilimanjaro and Other Stories* or *The Sun Also Rises;* our 400-level course on the American novel, in which I usually teach *The Sun Also Rises;* a senior seminar on Fitzgerald, Hemingway, and the Lost Generation, in which I cover *In Our Time, The Sun Also Rises, A Farewell to Arms,* and a number of other short stories; and a 300-level course focusing on Hemingway, in which I handle the three novels mentioned immediately above as well as *For Whom the Bells Tolls* and *A Moveable Feast.* I teach this last course about every three years and supplement it with a number of films on Hemingway and his time.

Typical enrollments in these courses run from thirty to forty students, with the exception of the senior (400-level) seminars, in which there are usually about twenty students. The students vary somewhat by course level, as one might expect, but since the average UM–Flint student is about twenty-six, and since I tend by design to teach at hours when older students are likely to enroll, they tend to be quite mature in their experiences of the world, if not always in literary sophistication. (A couple of examples: Reading *A Moveable Feast,* a student vouched for the authenticity of the image of F. Scott Fitzgerald seeming to turn into a death's-head on taking a drink. "I've been tending bar for years," he said, "and I've seen that happen again and again." Reading *A Farewell to Arms,* a woman of about thirty-five, a nurse herself, commented on Frederic's desperate prayers and sense of loss at the novel's end: "I've seen that when people were dying in the cancer wards. I felt it too when the neonatologist told me my newborn daughter would not live.")

Many of these students arrive with only the popular image of Hemingway, but they are fairly fast studies, and they generally are willing to take time to be convinced by Hemingway's methods, even though those methods at first seem strange to them. If there is a problem for students, it is for the average undergraduate type, who tends to feel overwhelmed by the student brainpower being let loose upon the novels by older, more experienced students. (It is not unheard of for me in an upper-division course to begin a class session with, "Any questions?" and with that as a beginning, run a discussion that needs relatively little direction and lasts through a two-and-a-half-hour period.)

I tend to try to make my classes operate inductively, beginning with the examination of small things and over the course of a term building toward the large questions at work in the literature under consideration. As we go along, I lecture briefly on elements to be watched for in individual works, and I comment on biography, if only because it is one of the elements that most interests students early on. Since Hemingway himself builds from such tiny pieces as the vignettes of *In Our Time,* the method seems a particularly appropriate one, and it generally works well.

The all-Hemingway course that I teach at the 300 level might help to illustrate some of what happens in most courses in which I teach Hemingway. In this course I begin not with the first book but with the last. That is, I first assign *A Moveable Feast* rather than *In Our Time.* Thus the students get some background (admittedly slanted by Hemingway) on literary Paris in the 1920s, along with a somewhat fragmented narration that is, nonetheless, less daunting to them than the organizational scheme of *In Our Time.* (I also discuss a few examples of Hemingway's early poetry, crib an example of "cablese" from Malcolm Cowley, and show a film on the 1920s.) To a number of students, *In Our Time* is a puzzlement even after *A Moveable Feast.* We spend a fair amount of time discussing individual stories, discovering some of the ways in which Nick Adams may represent Hemingway without being a fully autobiographical character, and examining the book's organization, with its progressions from the early years of the century to the 1920s, from Michigan to Europe and back, from innocence to experience. Nick as the boy/man who never quite knows as much as he thinks he does comes in for some comment as well; he is a representative Hemingway protagonist.

*The Sun Also Rises* separates the sheep from the goats. Those who'll have trouble with Hemingway's methods clearly identify themselves here, while the canny readers have a wonderful time. The lyricism of Hemingway as well as the contrasts implicit in the novel's title and two epigraphs lead some students to comment that they never realized that they could enjoy an entire novel that contains no likeable characters. (Fans of Jake, Bill, Brett—and even of Robert Cohn—are quick to riposte.)

The concern with the use and misuse of language in *A Farewell to Arms* seems to engage much attention as we study it, perhaps because I use that idea to introduce the novel's place as a reaction to the Great War and as a parallel to such works as Erich Maria Remarque's *All Quiet on the Western Front* or the epic Hollywood silent film *The Big Parade*. The religious themes that we have already discussed in *In Our Time* and *The Sun Also Rises* seem better developed here, or at least by now the students are seeing them more clearly. Along these lines, the priest and Rinaldi rate considerable attention.

For many, the stories collected in *The Snows of Kilimanjaro and Other Stories* are relatively easy, particularly the title story and "The Short Happy Life of Francis Macomber." Perhaps because many of the students are parents, responses to "A Day's Wait" are quite positive, and the new images of Nick Adams in "A Way You'll Never Be" and "Fathers and Sons" elucidate the characterization and themes of *In Our Time*. "The Gambler, the Nun and the Radio" and "Fifty Grand" are often puzzles to students; when they're walked through these stories' complexities, they tend to like the first story and to have a sort of grudging admiration for the second. Many decide, even before I've identified the dates of composition of the stories, that "Snows" and "Short Happy Life" were written last. They can see the loss of purely focused narrative method in these two stories, but they appreciate their greater narrative flexibility.

That change in narration—and the love story and the linking of the Hemingway hero to larger human concerns—explains the relative popularity of *For Whom the Bell Tolls*. Students are particularly impressed by the grace with which Hemingway manages to move from one setting to the next, from one side of the war to the other, and from his own narration to the embedded narrations of Robert, Maria, and Pilar. (Some of the best readers feel that Hemingway here is writing "down" to his by-now wider audience, but most of them regard the novel as a success.) The positive, strong female characterizations, particularly of Pilar, come in for praise from the women in the class. (Interestingly, criticisms of Maria as immature and unrealistic are not often heard from my current students. They tend to see her near idolization of Robert Jordan as realistic for a nineteen-year-old who is recovering from the experience of her parents' deaths and her own rape and imprisonment.)

The theme of necessity that we have seen in earlier works, including *For Whom the Bell Tolls*, seems particularly to shape students' readings of *The Old*

*Man and the Sea.* Essentially, they have no negative criticisms to make of the book, even though we do take time to examine the slightly overplayed Christ imagery and the artist-versus-the-critics allegorical level of the work. By term's end, of course, they are skilled readers of Hemingway—and tired.

In discussing and evaluating such a course as this, students tend to appreciate the opportunity to explore the continuity and development of the author's methods and vision. They are interested by the window on a certain period of history that the works provide, and they seem to feel that Hemingway's time still is somehow continuous with our own—to feel that they too live in a modern, contingent world. The course ends with my discussion of other works that might be of interest to the new student of Hemingway, whether these are others of his works, criticisms and biographies, or works whose authors or subjects somehow paralleled his life.

As I mentioned above, in teaching *A Farewell to Arms,* I have found that the novel seems to come across most clearly to students when approached in multiple contexts. While Frederic Henry's first-person narration is not incredibly difficult, it seems to me to be easier to handle for students who have seen something of Hemingway's other works, likely because they already are primed for the narrator's omissions and unreliability. While the specific historical setting of the novel is not terribly difficult to explain, it does require some attention. Thus, in a course in which I teach only one work by Hemingway, I tend to choose another. I most often teach *A Farewell to Arms* in courses focusing on more than one of Hemingway's works.

My students may then have seen something of the Great War as they read *In Our Time* (including another treatment of some of the raw materials of *A Farewell to Arms* in "A Very Short Story"). They will have experienced the despairing reactions of the seemingly lost souls, for the most part veterans of the Great War, in *The Sun Also Rises.* They will already have become attuned to the Hemingway method of re-creating an experience in order to let the reader re-create the emotion evoked by the experience. Later, they will identify the 1926 "In Another Country" (in *The Snows of Kilimanjaro and Other Stories*) as an earlier attempt to deal with the emotional reactions to futility and loss that help to lend the novel so much of its power.

Concern with the use and misuse of language in *A Farewell to Arms* seems to engage much attention as we study it, perhaps because I use that idea to introduce the novel's importance as a reaction to the Great War and as a parallel to other works treating the war. Among other resources, I usually distribute to students a series of statements on the Great War by Hemingway; F. Scott

Fitzgerald; Gertrude Stein; cultural historians Modris Eksteins and Paul Fussell; and Sir Douglas Haig, British commander on the First World War's western front (see Appendix A). These help to give students a sense of the ways in which the novel's language derives from and comments upon concerns of its time, and how Hemingway's prose style was seen by many readers as more honest than what had come before. (To that end, the contrast between the language of *A Farewell to Arms* and that of Haig is particularly obvious; Fitzgerald's characterization of the war in *Tender Is the Night* as a great "love battle" also seems to the point and helps to explain the "unromantic" romance between Frederic and Catherine.)

In the context of language and truth telling, I often mention complementary works such as E. E. Cummings's *The Enormous Room* (1922), John Dos Passos's *One Man's Initiation: 1917* (1920) and *Three Soldiers* (1921), or Erich Maria Remarque's *All Quiet on the Western Front* (1929). Like Hemingway and other American intellectuals, Cummings and Dos Passos served as ambulance drivers. *The Enormous Room,* a work of great irony and power, chronicles Cummings's four-month internment by the French after he was found to have been insufficiently bloodthirsty in his opinions of the Germans. Dos Passos's works are full of the disillusionment and fear of the young man first facing battle—and the absurdities of day-to-day army life both during and after the war, in his latter work. Remarque's is probably the definitive novel of wartime combat and disillusionment and was later banned by the Nazis as a slander on the German fighting man. Of course, the literature of the First World War is extensive, and any number of other works treating the material and psychological costs of the war might be of interest to students of *A Farewell to Arms,* including Robert Graves's memoir, *Goodbye to All That* (1929); D. H. Lawrence's *Lady Chatterley's Lover* (1928); Henri Barbusse's harrowing memoir of combat, *Under Fire* (1917); Dalton Trumbo's equally harrowing novel of a blinded, incapacitated veteran, *Johnny Got His Gun* (1959); and, for a female point of view that may help to elucidate Catherine Barkley's emotions, Vera Brittain's wonderful and touching memoir of loss, *Testament of Youth* (1933). Any one of these works well as a subject for a student report, given enough lead time. (My advanced courses usually require at least one such report per student. These include a two- to three-page handout to the class detailing the work under discussion and its relevance to course concepts, as well as a five-minute oral presentation of the material, followed by questions and discussion. I usually assign these in the first week of the semester so that students have time to prepare.)

In discussing contexts for *A Farewell to Arms,* I pay some attention to other media. I often make mention of the 1925 Hollywood epic silent film *The Big*

*Parade* and of the 1932 Gary Cooper/Helen Hayes film of *A Farewell to Arms*, and I sometimes show excerpts from these, depending on class interest. (Both currently are available on VHS video; *A Farewell to Arms* is also available on DVD.) The war-fueled romance in *The Big Parade* is similar enough to that between Frederic and Catherine to provoke comment from students, and the film provides an effective visual sense of the war; like Frederic, the film's protagonist, rich boy Jim Apperson, is naive and sheltered before facing the wartime realities of life, love, and death. The 1932 film of *A Farewell to Arms* is interesting for its somewhat sanitized evocation of images of the war in Italy (in long shots the ambulances are obvious models), but also for the many ways in which it bowdlerizes Hemingway's story, including having the priest recite the marriage service in the background of one scene so that Frederic and Catherine's love is *not* illicit. This helps to illustrate for students some of the cultural limitations on treatment of subject matter that helped to make the novel shocking in its time and ties back in to the concerns with truth telling in relationship to the novel's use of language.

I often also use yet another film to provide context for *A Farewell to Arms*, particularly its critique of the use and misuse of language. The documentary film *The Moving Picture Boys in the Great War* (1975) discusses how America's pacifist views of the war were reshaped practically overnight by propaganda. It also contrasts sentimental romanticism with the realities of the war and thus parallels one of the tensions of the novel, in which romance seems far from romantic. These tensions also provide some hints regarding where the emotions of the novel's main characters are coming from—as well as intimations of the public's reaction to the novel when it appeared in 1929. The serious yet light tone of this documentary, dedicated to Erich von Stroheim, "the man you love to hate" for his portrayals of filmic Germans, makes it quite accessible to students at many levels. (This film is available on VHS but is now rare since it was a 1991 release.)

I also provide still images, for it is far easier for students to visualize the novel if they have some idea of what its settings might actually have looked like. To that end, I have found Giovanni Checchin's *Italiani sul Grappa: Documenti e fotografie inediti della Croce Rossa Americana in Italia nel 1918* (1984) invaluable for its many period photographs of the mountainous Italian front of the war and of Hemingway as a member of the ambulance corps. The Internet provides a quick source of images, whether students access them from the course Web site or I project them during a class session. My midwestern students, most not widely traveled, are interested to discover how many sites of the early twentieth century are largely unchanged, including much of Stresa, and Milan's Duomo,

Galleria, and La Scala. Even the hospital still exists, though it now serves as a bank. While Internet sites are notorious for the speed at which they may appear and disappear, among those I have found useful are "La Grande Guerra: The Italian Front, 1915–1918" at http://www.worldwar1.com/; "Battles: The Battle at Caporetto, 1917" at http://www.firstworldwar.com/battles/caporetto. htm; "StresaOnline" at http://www.stresaonline.com/stresa_lakemaggiore.php; "Memories from Stresa," for the site of Frederic and Catherine's escape, at http:// www.hemingwaysociety.org/virthem.htm#photos%20and%20other%20Images; "Cities: Milan" at http://www.itwg.com/ct_00002.asp; and Pierino Smanitto and Thea Bekers's "Milano—Italia" at http://www.smaniotto.net/milano_index_it.html. Search engines such as Google and Yahoo, of course, can be used to find similar sites if these have disappeared. Also, since I have traveled to some of the novel's locations, I always show a few snapshots: Svoboda in the Galleria and the Duomo; the train station at Stresa, essentially unchanged since Hemingway's time; the islands in Lago Maggiore; the arm of the lake leading north into Switzerland. Students seem to get a kick out of the "my professor actually went there" serious silliness of it all. My commitment to learning as much as I can about the novel reassures them that they are not wasting time by paying attention to it as well.

Regardless of the background I provide, however, at the very beginning the novel seems difficult to many students, for several reasons. While critics have celebrated the two opening chapters' effectiveness in tracing the course of the war over years, linking the novel's action to the cycles of life, and suggesting the ways in which man's war has perverted what is natural, often students are baffled by these chapters, probably because many of them aren't very sophisticated about literature. They do not expect a novel to begin with suggestion or indirection, especially a novel from an author whose popular image is so straightforwardly macho and simplistic as Hemingway's. I always warn students against judging Hemingway by images of him derived from popular culture, and in discussing these chapters I fall back on the idea of context. In these chapters Hemingway is providing context for the story to come and suggesting that his characters likely will not be immune to the natural cycles of life and death—and man's perversions of these cycles in war. (The image of caped infantrymen, looking "six months gone with child" because of their bulging ammunition pouches [4], is worth discussing in this respect.) Students who have read *The Sun Also Rises*—built around the contrast between human depravity and natural cycles of life and death and rebirth—have an advantage here, as do those who have read *In Our Time*, with its alternating vignettes and short stories giving a composite view of childhood and adulthood, natural beauty and war, America and Europe, love and violence.

I also have learned by experience that some very simple things need to be explained—geography and history, for example. We begin the novel in northeast Italy. The nearest large city is Venice, on the Adriatic Sea to the south. We are allied with the French and British, attacking generally northward into the Alps, fighting against the Austrians, allies of the Germans. Later we will be in northwestern Italy, recuperating in the industrial city of Milan and the nearby resort of Stresa, near neutral Switzerland. It's worth mentioning that on the railway journey from east to west we will pass through a number of northern Italian cities, notably, Verona, home to another pair of star-crossed lovers, Shakespeare's Romeo and Juliet.

Since we are in the Italian army, we are mostly speaking Italian, though Hemingway considerately has translated much of it into English for readers' convenience, leaving just a few Italian words here and there to give us the flavor of the language. I translate some of the words, although, as I explain, Hemingway has set them up to be clear from context, often providing the English synonym on the same page. I learned the importance of this many years ago when a significant number of students spent considerable energy—and class time—wondering who this man named "Tenente" was. Of course he is our protagonist, identified not as Frederic Henry but by his Italian rank of lieutenant. Others asked, "Will we ever know the narrator's name?" and I now generally let students know up front that it will be awhile—and mention that Stephen Crane did something similar in *The Red Badge of Courage*, identifying Henry Fleming only as "the youth" in the beginning of his novel as a way of suggesting that he is a generic, representative soldier. "Henry Fleming, Frederic Henry," I intone. "Similar names, right? Probably just a coincidence. Surely Hemingway couldn't have been picking up ideas from Crane." Students do get this point.

Somewhere along here in the discussion I mention what I see as Hemingway's other great debt to Crane. Crane wrote the story of a Civil War battle he never had seen, Chancellorsville, by paying close attention to histories of the war and veterans' accounts. Hemingway similarly builds a convincing account of the great Italian retreat from Caporetto out of the historical accounts, his few weeks at the front lines roughly a year after Caporetto had ended, and his own real wounding and convalescence. Neither author saw his battle; like *The Red Badge of Courage*, *A Farewell to Arms* is one of literature's great research papers. Of course there are other sources for the novel, including the George Peele poem from which its title comes, and this is worth discussing (see Appendix B). In case I overlook any of the above, I also provide a one-page summary of points for students to consider while reading (see Appendix C).

Frederic's affectless narration, dulled by his loss of Catherine (and of everything else he has valued) causes considerable comment. Once we have discussed the terms of the narration, most students quickly figure out how to read through the narrative surface to discover Frederic's hidden emotions. (This is particularly the case in some of the famous passages of the novel. The opening chapters' descriptions of the Italian landscape may at first be baffling, but in retrospect they make perfect sense as Frederic attempts to edge up to the novel's core subject matter: Frederic's description of his wounding, the discussion of how the world "kills the very good and the very gentle and the very brave," the explanation of how abstract words have lost their meanings, and Frederic's desperate prayers for Catherine as she is near death.) Some students never accept that Frederic might have felt anything beyond lust for Catherine, but most are willing to admit that a deep love may grow from just such a banal beginning as we see when Frederic and Catherine first meet in the garden. Even so, we tend to agree that Frederic is one of the less mature characters of his age (the mid-twenties) that we have seen, although Frederic as retrospective narrator of the novel may have achieved a somewhat deeper insight than he showed as events transpired. Along these lines I mention F. Scott Fitzgerald's very perceptive criticism to Hemingway that too much of the author's teenage view of Agnes von Kurowsky, the real-life prototype for Catherine, is coming through in the novel.

Catherine is read differently by different students. Some see the book as an epic story of the loss of an ideal love in which she is the more nearly ideal lover. Some respond to her best unromantic qualities, her courage and good sense. Others dislike her, finding her too clinging and conniving, feeling that she carries into the frozen garden of Switzerland the same manipulative qualities that she earlier showed as she let Frederic substitute for her dead lover. Indeed, with some contemporary critics, some students are willing to argue that she never really loved Frederic at all; that the whole "love story" is really a matter of the manipulation of the naive protagonist by the more artful Catherine.

Current events again have lent urgency to the novel, three-quarters of a century after its publication. Teaching it twice in senior seminars during the invasion and occupation of Iraq, I found that students clearly perceived the currency of the novel's concerns. The urgency of Frederic and Catherine's romance made particular sense to students who had friends and family members facing the prospect of separation from loved ones as national guardsman and reservists were deployed overseas with minimal notice. The novel's critique of the rhetoric of warfare seemed almost as important, paralleling media explorations of the justification for the war in Iraq. Along these lines, the "Shock and Awe" tagline for the bombardment of Baghdad came in for its critical share of discussion, as did the nonsensical press briefings of "Baghdad Bob," Iraqi minister of information Mohammed Saeed al-Sahaf. One could see from these examples how abstract words could become obscene to Frederic Henry, with meaning inhering only in "the concrete names of villages, the numbers of roads, the names of rivers, the numbers of regiments and the dates" (185).

The religious themes that students already have discussed in *In Our Time* and (particularly) *The Sun Also Rises* seem better developed here, or at least by now the students are seeing them more clearly, in context. Along these lines, the priest and Rinaldi rate considerable attention. Students debate the extent to which their admirable qualities can (in the case of the priest) or cannot protect them from the emotional devastation of the war (as seems to be the case with Rinaldi, who loses hope as the novel progresses). The priest seems more admirable as we move away from him and as Frederic's separation from much of the world and attachment to Catherine continue.

Biography engages students' attention, and I am careful to detail a number of ways in which Frederic Henry's experiences are and also are not those of the young Ernest Hemingway during World War I. Hemingway's experiences around the time of the novel's composition (particularly his father's suicide and his wife Pauline's cesarean delivery) are also of interest in classroom discussions of methods and sources. Here is where the continuing scholarly examination of the novel is most useful.

Finally, our attention is directed to the integrity of vision of *A Farewell to Arms,* which is in many ways a part of the integrity of vision of Hemingway's best works. That is, we read and understand the novel both as a self-contained work of art and within a multiplicity of contexts, some of which I have hinted at here.

## APPENDIX A: Statements on Language in *A Farewell to Arms*

From Paul Fussell, *The Great War and Modern Memory* (New York: Oxford University Press, 1975), 21:

> But the Great War took place in what was, compared with ours, a static world, where values appeared stable and where the meanings of abstractions seemed permanent and reliable. Everyone knew what Glory was, and what Honor meant. It was not until eleven years after the war that Hemingway

could declare in *A Farewell to Arms* that "abstract words such as glory, honor, courage or hallow were obscene beside the concrete names of villages, the numbers of roads, the names of rivers, the numbers of regiments and the dates." In the summer of 1914 no one would have understood what on earth he was talking about.

From Modris Eksteins, *Rites of Spring: The Great War and the Birth of the Modern Age* (Boston: Houghton Mifflin, 1989), 191:

In 1919 in a rector's address to undergraduates at St. Andrew's University, Douglas Haig continued to articulate the purpose of the war in the old, lofty terms, terms that, however, were also very much rooted in a bourgeois ethic of the nineteenth century: "In every stage of the great struggle from which we have at length emerged victorious, our courage was heightened and our resolve made stronger by the conviction that we were fighting, not only for ourselves and for our own Empire, but for a world ideal in which God was with us. We were doing battle for a higher form of civilization, in which man's duty to his neighbour finds a place more important than his duty to himself, against an Empire built up and made great by the sword, efficient indeed, but with an efficiency unredeemed by any sense of chivalry or of moral responsibility towards the weak."

That was one way of explaining the essence of the Anglo-French war effort. A decade later F. Scott Fitzgerald put the same idea in different language and more comprehensive terms. Dick Diver, the hero of *Tender Is the Night*, is touring the Somme battlefields and says: "This western front business couldn't be done again, not for a long time. The young men think they could do it but they couldn't. They could fight the first Marne again but not this. This took religion and years of plenty and tremendous sureties and the exact relation that existed between the classes. . . . You had to have a whole-souled sentimental equipment going back further than you could remember. You had to remember Christmas, and postcards of the Crown Prince and his fiancée, and little cafés in Valence and beer gardens in Unter den Linden and weddings at the *mairie,* and going to the Derby, and your grandfather's whiskers. . . . This kind of battle was invented by Lewis Carroll and Jules Verne and whoever wrote *Undine,* and country deacons bowling and *marraines* in Marseilles and girls seduced in the back lanes of Württemburg and Westphalia. Why, this was a love battle—there was a whole century of middle-class love spent here. . . . All my beautiful lovely safe world blew itself up here with a great gust of high-explosive love."

## APPENDIX B: The Original "A FAREWELL TO ARMS"

GEORGE PEELE, "A FAREWELL TO ARMS"

His golden locks Time hath to silver turn'd;
    O Time too swift, O swiftness never ceasing!
His youth 'gainst time and age hath ever spurn'd,
    But spurn'd in vain; youth waneth by increasing:
Beauty, strength, youth, are flowers but fading seen;
Duty, faith, love, are roots, and ever green.

His helmet now shall make a hive for bees;
    And, lovers' sonnets turn'd to holy psalms,
A man-at-arms must now serve on his knees,
    And feed on prayers, which are Age his alms:
But though from court to cottage he depart,
His Saint is sure of his unspotted heart.

And when he saddest sits in homely cell,
    He'll teach his swains this carol for a song,—
'Blest be the hearts that wish my sovereign well,
    Curst be the souls that think her any wrong.'
Goddess, allow this aged man his right
To be your beadsman now that was your knight.

## APPENDIX C: Handout for Students Beginning Hemingway's *A Farewell to Arms:* A Few Suggestions

As you read, be an active reader.

- Watch for the role of the past, both mythic and historical.
- Watch for references to other works of literature, either explicit or implicit.
- Do you see echoes of other works we have read so far?
- Watch for references to other arts, including painting, architecture, and opera.
- What other patterns develop that help you make sense of the novel?

Judge the characters.

- Watch for pairings and oppositions.
- Have we seen similar characters in other works by Hemingway or Fitzgerald?
- Who is Frederic Henry?
  How old is he?
  How mature is he?
  Does he change over the course of the novel?
- Who are Frederic's friends, and why are they his friends?
- Who is Dr. Rinaldi, and why does he like Frederic?
  What values does he learn as a surgeon and then teach to Frederic?
  How does he change over the course of the novel?
- What sort of man is the priest?
  What values does he represent?
  Does he change over the course of the novel?
- Who is Catherine Barkley?
  What are her values?
  Why is she attracted to Frederic?
  How mature is she?
  Does she change over the course of the novel?
- What is Frederic's relationship to the officers with whom he works and socializes?
- What is his relationship to the many enlisted men who work for him?
- Can you begin to see the officers and enlisted men as individuals, or do they blend together?
- What is the role of duty in the novel?
- Which characters believe in conventional religion, and which don't?
  What is the role of religion for the characters?
  What are the alternatives to religion?
- Which characters are capable of mature love?
  Is mature love necessarily identical to sexual love?
  Does one sort of love exclude the other?
  What other sorts of love do we see in the novel?
  Does love in this novel differ from love in other works by Hemingway and Fitzgerald?

Don't be thrown by the World War I European setting.

- For much of the novel we are in northern Italy, fighting with the Italian army against the Austrians. Italy was one of the Allies, along with Russia, England, and France. They fought against the Central Powers, which included Germany, the Austro-Hungarian Empire, and the Ottoman (Turkish) Empire. (A number of smaller countries also were involved.)
- When Germany began the war by attacking France in 1914, Italy was expected to be more or less its ally. Instead Italy entered the war on the Allied side in 1915.
- When the United States entered the war in 1917 after years of trying to mediate an end to the war, it fought on the side of the Allies.
- The Austro-Hungarian and Ottoman empires were destroyed by the war and broke into a number of smaller countries (eventually including Iraq). Italy was almost destroyed, and you'll "overhear" the Italian soldiers discussing the calamity of the war.
- Like Germany, Italy is a new country created from the unification of many smaller states during the nineteenth-century wave of nationalism.
- The Italians are trying to attack northward into the mountains that separate Italy and Austria. The Austrians are trying to attack southward down off the mountains onto the Italian plain that will lead them to the legendary city of Venice.
- Between Germany, Austria, Italy, and France is Switzerland, which was neutral in the war and thus a refuge to soldiers from either side.
- When Frederic is in the hospital, he is in the northern Italian city of Milan (Milano), quite a way to the east of the site of the battle. Milan is noted for its art (including da Vinci's *The Last Supper*) as well as its huge cathedral (the Duomo) and the adjacent late nineteenth-century shopping center (the Galleria) and nearby La Scala, the greatest opera house in Italy. The last three are within a block or two of each other. Go out the north end of the Galleria, and you're at the small square at La Scala. Go out the south end, and you're at the great square of the Duomo, with the Duomo to your left.
- An hour or so from Milan by train is Lago (Lake) Maggiore, which is surrounded by mountains. On its south shore is the resort town of Stresa. One arm of the lake goes north and crosses the border into neutral Switzerland.

*Here is some information on the main characters.*

- The first-person narrator of the novel is Frederic Henry, an American student of architecture who joined the Italian army medical services in 1915 and is supervising a section of ambulances. His rank is lieutenant, and you won't hear his name until you're a good way into the novel. Instead you'll hear him called Tenente—this is not his name, but the Italian word for lieutenant.
- Another young soldier in literature is Henry Fleming, protagonist of Stephen Crane's 1895 Civil War novel, *The Red Badge of Courage*. Through much of that novel Henry is known only as "the youth." The similarities in names and naming are probably just coincidences, right?
- Catherine Barkley is a member of the British Voluntary Aid Detachment (VAD), as was Brett Ashley in *The Sun Also Rises*. This is a sort of "instant nurse" position and doesn't have the prestige or level of training associated with a real nursing degree. Many VADs were well-off, sheltered young British women who wanted to help the war effort but weren't really prepared for the horrors they faced. Catherine's nickname is Cat—like Hadley Richardson Hemingway, Hemingway's first wife.

## APPENDIX D: Sample Syllabi

MAJOR NOVELISTS: ERNEST HEMINGWAY

Texts:
*A Moveable Feast* (1964)
*In Our Time* (1925)
*The Sun Also Rises* (1926)
*A Farewell to Arms* (1929)
*The Snows of Kilimanjaro and Other Stories* (1920s and 1930s)
*For Whom the Bell Tolls* (1940)
*The Old Man and the Sea* (1952)

*Class Sessions:* Classes will run as a mixture of lecture and discussion. We generally will move between close discussions of individual works to ensure your understanding of them; discussions of the larger patterns of Hemingway's life work; and examinations of his significance in American literature, history, and culture. You must attend regularly and be ready to participate in our discussions.

*Writing:* You'll be asked to write short individual papers (two to three pages) on at least five of the seven Hemingway works we will read. Please try to focus all these papers on one or two of the areas of concern in Hemingway studies that we'll discuss. These papers will be due on either of the days we discuss each book—your choice. While the papers will help prepare you for class discussions and will help me to follow your progress, at least some of them should eventually come together to become a longer examination of one important question. You'll also be asked to write several brief papers in class. These in-class papers will be related very directly to topics of class discussion.

*Exams:* Expect quizzes and several in-class writing assignments (based on short identification and short essay questions) to serve in the place of midterm exams. The take-home final will ask for a longer essay written on one of several questions. If you wish to do so, it will be possible to develop it from your earlier papers.

*Grading:* Your final grade will be based on all your activities for the course. I'll start by arriving at an average of your graded papers and exercises. I'll then adjust that grade on the basis of your attendance and performance in class discussions. Please feel free to consult with me at any time if you are unsure as to how you are doing.

A Tentative Schedule:

Day 1    Course Introduction: Hemingway's World—What It Was, What It Became
A few poems
Video selections: *The Great War and the Shaping of the 20th Century*
Day 2    Hemingway Looks Back on a Legend: *A Moveable Feast* (1964) through "Hunger Was Good Discipline"
Film: *The Jazz Age: 1919–1929*
Day 3    Hemingway Looks Back: *A Moveable Feast* to End
Day 4    Early Promise: *In Our Time* (1925) through "Soldier's Home"
Video: *Soldier's Home*

Day 5     Early Promise: *In Our Time* (1925) to End
          Films: *Hemingway's Spain: Death in the Afternoon; The Day Manolete Died*

Day 6     Early Fame: *The Sun Also Rises* (1926) through chapter 9
          Film: *Hemingway's Spain: The Sun Also Rises*

Day 7     Early Fame: *The Sun Also Rises* (1926) to End
          Slides: Paris and Pamplona's Fiesta

Day 8     Popular Success: *A Farewell to Arms* (1929) through Chapter 12 (End of Book 1)
          Film: *The Moving Picture Boys in the Great War*

Day 9     Popular Success: *A Farewell to Arms* (1929) to End

Day 10    Narrative Experimentation: *The Snows of Kilimanjaro and Other Stories* through "The Gambler, the Nun and the Radio"

Day 11    Mastering the Short Story: *The Snows of Kilimanjaro and Other Stories* to End

Day 12    The Great Novelist: *For Whom the Bell Tolls* (1940) through the Massacre in Pilar's Village (p. 125)
          Slides: Navacerrada Pass
          Film: *War in Spain: Prelude to World War II*

Day 13    The Great Novelist: *For Whom the Bell Tolls* (1940) to End

Day 14    Grace Note: *The Old Man and the Sea* (1952) to End
          Slides: Cuba
          Audio tape: Nobel Prize acceptance speech
          Last regular day of class

Day 15    Scheduled Final Exam Period: Take-Home Final Exam Due

Hemingway's Major Published Works:

| 1923 | *Three Stories and Ten Poems* (published in Paris) |
| 1924 | *in our time* (published in Paris) |
| 1925 | *In Our Time* (stories, many set in Michigan) |
| 1926 | *Torrents of Spring* (satiric novel set in Michigan) |
| 1926 | *The Sun Also Rises* (novel set in 1920s France and Spain) |
| 1927 | *Men Without Women* (stories) |
| 1929 | *A Farewell to Arms* (novel set in Great War Italy) |
| 1932 | *Death in the Afternoon* (nonfiction on bullfighting and aesthetics) |
| 1933 | *Winner Take Nothing* (stories) |
| 1935 | *The Green Hills of Africa* (nonfiction narrative of an African safari) |

1937    *To Have and Have Not* (novel set in Depression-era Key West)

1938    *The Fifth Column* (play of the Spanish civil war)

1940    *For Whom the Bell Tolls* (novel of the Spanish civil war)

1950    *Across the River and into the Trees* (novel set in post–World War II Italy)

1952    *The Old Man and the Sea* (novella set in Cuba)

1964    *A Moveable Feast* (posthumous memoir of life in 1920s Paris)

1970    *Islands in the Stream* (posthumous novel of World War II in the Caribbean)

1972    *The Nick Adams Stories* (posthumous short stories set in Michigan and elsewhere; many reprinted from *In Our Time*)

1981    *Selected Letters, 1917–1961*

1985    *The Dangerous Summer* (posthumous journalistic account of bullfighting in late-1950s Spain)

1986    *The Garden of Eden* (posthumous novel of 1920s France)

1987    *The Complete Stories of Ernest Hemingway: The Finca Vigía Edition* (includes some previously unpublished pieces)

Numerous drafts of stories and essays remain unpublished.

Continuing Questions in Hemingway Studies:

These will be explored during the course and should help guide your weekly papers.

1. What was Hemingway's early background? How did it influence his work? (Consider mother; father; Victorian/Edwardian values; childhood reading; life in Oak Park; summers in Michigan; early writing; journalism; World War I experiences, including wound; return from the war as hero; marriage to Hadley Richardson.)

2. How did Hemingway's work relate to that of his predecessors and contemporaries? How was he influenced? Whom did he influence? (Consider Sherwood Anderson, Gertrude Stein, Owen Wister, Ezra Pound, F. Scott Fitzgerald, Donald Ogden Stewart, Stephen Crane, Mark Twain, Henry James, Rudyard Kipling, Captain Marryat, W. H. Hudson, etc.)

3. How does Hemingway's work fit with conventional and experimental literary movements (e.g., realism, naturalism, modernism, existentialism)?

4. What is Hemingway's style or method? (Consider indirection, use of the devices of poetry, insistence, the iceberg, cablese, implication, juxtaposition, the re-creation of the moment in order to re-create the emotion of the moment.)

5. How did Hemingway transmute his experiences into fiction? How fictional is his fiction?

6. What are Hemingway's greatest achievements? Why is he an important writer? (Consider style, creation of a response to a seemingly hostile or indifferent world, creation of the "Hemingway hero," use of place, his time in world history, the international theme in American literature, the importance of the ordinary in American literature.)

7. How do Hemingway's works rank against each other? Do they decline or advance in quality throughout his career? Do his aesthetic principles remain the same?

8. How do Hemingway's works rank against the best works of other modern writers, both American and foreign (e.g., Anderson, Fitzgerald, Faulkner, Steinbeck, Dreiser, Irwin Shaw, Norman Mailer)?

9. How well have Hemingway's values held up? To what extent does he still speak directly to our concerns? To what extent must we view him as a historical figure in order to appreciate him? (Consider the existential view, compared to social values of the 1930s; returning to past values of honor and courage; pacifism; hunting; Hemingway as a Victorian and as a modern man.)

10. To what extent are Hemingway's times our times? To what extent do the concerns of the 1920s or 1930s mirror our concerns today?

11. Is Hemingway only a writer for and about men? Do his female characters lack depth and development, or are they fully realized? (Do we notice the imperfections of his female characters more than those of his male characters?) How does he deal with questions of sexuality and of gender?

12. Do the facts of his later life (marriages, illnesses, suicide) detract from our valuation of Hemingway? From our valuation of his work?

Net Resources:

This Web site has links to most of the Hemingway-related material on the Web: http://www.hemingwaysociety.org/virthem.htm

To subscribe to the Hemingway Listserv, which is sometimes quiet, sometimes quite active:
Address: majordomo@mtu.edu
Leave the subject line blank.
Send the message: subscribe heming-l

SEMINAR: FITZGERALD, HEMINGWAY, AND THE LOST GENERATION

Texts:

F. Scott Fitzgerald:

*The Short Stories of F. Scott Fitzgerald* (Ed. Matthew Bruccoli)

*The Great Gatsby* (1925)

*Tender Is the Night* (1934)

Ernest Hemingway:

*The Complete Short Stories of Ernest Hemingway: The Finca Vigia Edition* (1925)

*The Sun Also Rises* (1926)

*A Farewell to Arms* (1929)

*Class Sessions:* This is a seminar, in which students bear considerable responsibility for what happens in class. In general the course will run as a mixture of reading, student presentations, and discussion. We generally will begin with careful discussion of individual works to ensure your understanding and then move on to consider the larger patterns of the two authors' works and their importance in modern American literature and culture. (Completion of ENG 357, Modern American Literature, is helpful but certainly not necessary.) I'll add information as needed to clarify points. You are expected to attend regularly and to participate in class discussion, both in class and online.

*Student Presentations:* You'll be expected to do at least two presentations during the term, one before and one after the middle of the term. These will be both a written report of several pages, which will be distributed to members of the class, and an in-class presentation of that report, which will last about five minutes. Possible topics include but are not limited to:

- Chronology of modern literature and Fitzgerald's and Hemingway's works and lives
- Report on Fitzgerald and New York City
- Summary of and critical response to Fitzgerald's *This Side of Paradise*
- Report on H. L. Mencken and *The Smart Set*
- Report on the *Saturday Evening Post* during the 1920s
- Report on the *New Yorker,* 1920s to the present

- Summary of and critical response to Fitzgerald's *The Beautiful and Damned*
- Report on the flapper
- Report on Prohibition
- Report on women's suffrage
- Report on the movies in the 1920s
- Report on popular music of the era, including jazz
- Summary of and critical response to Fitzgerald's *The Great Gatsby*
- Summary of and critical response to Hemingway's *In Our Time*
- Summary of and critical response to Hemingway's *The Sun Also Rises*
- Summary of and critical response to Hemingway's *A Farewell to Arms*
- Summary of and critical response to Hemingway's *To Have and Have Not*
- Summary of and critical response to Hemingway's *For Whom the Bell Tolls*
- Report on *Esquire* during the 1930s
- Summary of and critical response to Fitzgerald's *Tender Is the Night*
- Report on the French Riviera as literary locale
- Summary of and critical response to Hemingway's *The Garden of Eden*
- Report on Hollywood and the two authors
- Summary of and critical response to Fitzgerald's *The Crack-Up*
- Summary of and critical response to Zelda Fitzgerald's *Save Me the Waltz*
- Report on Zelda Sayre Fitzgerald
- Report on Hadley Richardson Hemingway
- Report on Pauline Pfeiffer Hemingway
- Report on Sylvia Beach and Shakespeare and Company
- Summary of and critical response to Fitzgerald's *The Last Tycoon*
- Report on Gertrude Stein as literary influence on Hemingway
- Report on *Torrents of Spring* and Sherwood Anderson as literary influence on Hemingway
- Report on Paris in the 1920s, including Malcolm Cowley's *Exile's Return*
- Report on Hemingway's *A Moveable Feast*
- Report on Fitzgerald's family, childhood, and early adolescence, including St. Paul, Minnesota
- Report on Hemingway's family, childhood, and early adolescence, including Oak Park, Illinois
- Report on Fitzgerald's late adolescence, including Princeton University and army experiences

- Report on Hemingway's late adolescence, including *Kansas City Star* and Red Cross Ambulance Corps
- Report on the 1920s in American culture, including Frederick Lewis Allen's *Only Yesterday*
- Report on Hemingway and art
- Report on World War I

*Internet Site:* You should also participate via a threaded discussion on the class Internet site.

*Writing:* You'll be expected to comment at some length on each of our major readings, using the class Internet site's discussion board. I'll keep you informed of my evaluation of these. Keep hard or electronic copies for yourself. You also must respond to others' comments on each book so that we continue our in-class discussion online. I strongly suggest that you log on to the course Web site at least a couple of times per week. The comments and responses will help prepare you for class, let me follow your progress, and (perhaps) serve as building blocks for the final essay. There may be the occasional in-class writing or quiz. You'll also write one longer formal essay (ten to twenty pages) on a related subject of interest and, time permitting, present your work to the class.

*Grading:* Final grades will be based on all your activities for the course. You should miss no more than two class sessions. You should find ample feedback, but feel free to consult with me at any time if you're unsure about how you're doing in the course.

Tentative Class Sessions/Reading Schedule:

Day 1   Class introduction
        Video: *Winter Dreams* (PBS American Masters Video)
Day 2   Read selected short stories: "Head and Shoulders," "Bernice Bobs Her Hair," "The Ice Palace," "The Offshore Pirate"
        Report: Summary of and critical response to *This Side of Paradise*
        Report: Fitzgerald's family, childhood, and early adolescence, including St. Paul, Minnesota
        Report: Fitzgerald's late adolescence, including Princeton University and army experiences
Day 3   Read selected short stories: "May-Day," "The Diamond as Big as the Ritz"

Read: Fitzgerald's *The Great Gatsby,* chapter 1

Report: Summary of and critical response to Fitzgerald's *The Beautiful and Damned*

Day 4 Read selected short stories: "Absolution," "Winter Dreams"

Read: Fitzgerald's *The Great Gatsby,* chapters 2–5

Report: Summary of and critical response to *The Great Gatsby*

Report: The 1920s in American culture, including Frederick Lewis Allen's *Only Yesterday*

Day 5 Read selected short stories

Read: *The Great Gatsby,* chapters 6–9

Report: Hemingway's family, childhood, and early adolescence, including Oak Park, Illinois

Day 6 Read *In Our Time* through "The Revolutionist" (in *Complete Short Stories,* pp. 63–120)

Report: Summary of and critical response to *In Our Time*

Report: Gertrude Stein as literary influence on Hemingway

Day 7 Read *In Our Time* to end (in *Complete Short Stories,* pp. 121–81)

Report: *Torrents of Spring* and Sherwood Anderson as literary influence on Hemingway

Report: Paris in the 1920s, including Malcolm Cowley's *Exile's Return*

Day 8 Read *The Sun Also Rises,* book 1

Report: Paris in the 1920s

Video: *Pamplona and the Sanfermines*

Day 9 Read *The Sun Also Rises,* books 2–3

Slides: Pamplona, 1984

Day 10 Read *A Farewell to Arms,* books 1–3

Report: Hemingway's late adolescence, including *Kansas City Star* and Red Cross Ambulance Corps

Report: Summary of and critical response to *A Farewell to Arms*

Day 11 Read *A Farewell to Arms,* books 4–5

Report: Hollywood and the two authors

Day 12 Report: Summary of and critical response to Zelda Fitzgerald's *Save Me the Waltz*

Read and discuss Fitzgerald's *Tender Is the Night,* book 1

Report: Summary of and critical response to *Tender Is the Night*

Report: Summary of and critical response to Hemingway's *The Garden of Eden*

Day 13   Read *Tender Is the Night,* books 2–3
         Report: *Esquire* during the 1930s
         Report: Summary of and critical response to Hemingway's *To Have and Have Not*
Day 14   Read selected short stories
         Report: Summary of and critical response to Hemingway's *For Whom the Bell Tolls*
         Report: Summary of and critical response to Fitzgerald's *The Last Tycoon*
Day 15   Exam day (optional session)

# HEMINGWAY'S LANGUAGE AND STYLE

# Bert-and-Ernie Stylistics
## Introducing Hemingway through a Discussion of Hemingway's Style

*J. T. Barbarese*

The style is the man.
  —*Remy de Gourmont*

FOR CONTEMPORARY secondary school students and a startling number of college undergraduates, Hemingway's novels are often surprisingly hard to read. The elements of his writing commonly found objectionable by adult critics—the sexism, the anti-Semitism and racism (particularly evident in *The Sun Also Rises*), his "masculinism"—are easily enough handled, and with grace and dispatch, by the typical adolescent or postadolescent. At one point about a decade ago while teaching *A Farewell to Arms* to students attending an independent Quaker school in a major city—children of mostly affluent professionals—I realized that they were having little trouble dealing with the novel's potentially explosive sexism, its violence, and any of the overtly hot-button concerns that teachers preemptively worry about. These were students who had grown up in an atmosphere that celebrates nonviolence and sexual equality, yet the fact that this was a war story, and that Frederic's manipulation of the emotionally brittle Catherine in the opening chapters borders on abuse, and that Catherine herself seems to be portrayed in a sexist and stereotypical manner, as either crazy or vacuous, was not to them nearly as significant as Hemingway's style.

The reason for their discomfort is, I think, both subtle and interesting. The literary curriculum of secondary school children (no matter the school) feeds a young reader's hunger for rich language, varied dialects, colorful speech, and memorable metaphors, language that is musical and cadenced. In the ninth grade they would have read *The Lord of the Flies* and *Romeo and Juliet*; in the tenth, *I Know Why the Caged Bird Sings, Their Eyes Were Watching God,* and (in my case) *Adventures of Huckleberry Finn*. Whether this specific list is nowadays typical or not, it reflects a general attitude of American middle schools toward what is and is not "literary." Though these texts contain verbal environments that at face value are extraordinarily different in terms of point of view, genre, characterization, and plot, all in one respect are very much the same: each is a richly literary, writerly experience in which language is the star. The touchstones of literary style and verbal finish, certainly developmentally, might be the lushly euphuistic Alcott of *Little Women* or *Little Men*, or a passage like the following from a novel my students would have read in the tenth grade:

> She was stretched on her back beneath the pear tree soaking in the alto chant of the visiting bees, the gold of the sun and the panting breath of the breeze when the inaudible voice of it all came to her. She saw a dust-bearing bee sink into the sanctum of a bloom; the thousand sister-calyxes arch to meet the love embrace and the ecstatic shiver of the tree from root to tiniest branch creaming in every blossom and frothing with delight. So this was a marriage! She had been summoned to behold a revelation. Then Janie felt a pain remorseless sweet that left her limp and languid.
>
> After a while she got up from where she was and went over the little garden field entire. She was seeking confirmation of the voice and vision, and everywhere she found and acknowledged answers. (Hurston 10–11)

Janie Crawford's pear-tree epiphany is one of the more obvious examples of what most members of the profession teaching secondary school or Freshman English would call "great" writing. It is Hurston's highly wrought version of one of the crucial episodes in the literature of the rite of passage, the moment when youths begin to cross borders, test boundaries, and break rules. The language is richly figurative at both the level of speech and concept—the gate, for instance, is both object and symbol of all the thresholds Janie is about to transgress. Among all the other tasks it fulfills successfully, even luridly, is probably the one so obvious we overlook it: *it sounds and looks like literature*. Hurston's narrative is luxuriantly metaphorical as it probes Janie's imagination, borne up on verbs like "creaming," "frothing," and "panting." Until they reach at least the middle grades of secondary school, students are encouraged—with the best will in the world—to think of literature, and to write it, in exactly such terms and in such ways: as thickly metaphorical, densely hypotactic, and ostentatiously literary. I would also add eminently *teachable*: students' experiences of the literary must be consonant with their teachers' (and parents') trained predispositions and sense of what good writing is.[1] In the usual case, the grammar and the punctuation are unexceptionable, and the point of view is stable, and though characterization increasingly "rounds out" as children move up, wherever irony appears—irony being a perennial problem for young readers—it is often either spontaneously tamed in context or presented via teacherly intervention as maintenance-level sarcasm.[2] The more notable exceptions (I'm thinking of suddenly unconventional classics such as *Adventures of Huckleberry Finn* and *Alice in Wonderland*) can be finessed or taught as exceptions justified by the tenets of realism, naturalism, fantasy, or even biography—if in fact they are still taught at all.

Given all this, is it any wonder that the attentive but unwary adolescent, raised on the conventional curriculum, experiences something like a trauma on coming upon the following?

In the late summer of that year we lived in a house in a village that looked across the river and the plain to the mountains. In the bed of the river there were pebbles and boulders, dry and white in the sun, and the water was clear and swiftly moving and blue in the channels. Troops went by the house and down the road and the dust they raised powdered the leaves of the trees. The trunks of the trees too were dusty and the leaves fell early that year and we saw the troops marching along the road and the dust rising and leaves, stirred by the breeze, falling and the soldiers marching and afterward the road bare and white except for the leaves. (Hemingway, *Farewell* 3)

How do you teach students trained to hear the cadences of Shakespeare and prepared to see the natural world painted in figurative terms—"Night's candles are burnt out and jocund day / Stands tiptoe on the misty mountain tops"—or in the densely sexualized metonymic terms of a Hurston that writing like this is not just the "inspired baby talk" famously parodied forty years ago by Dwight MacDonald and more recently by Woody Allen? How do you get them to recognize rather than dismiss, in the determinedly childlike cadences of the narrator and the childish responses of Catherine, the serious intentions of a serious writer? Hemingway doesn't *sound* like literature to readers, young or old, who have grown up on a steady diet of what is supposed to be literary.

Many of the problems in comprehending Hemingway's fiction ultimately come down, or so I found in my teaching of *A Farewell to Arms,* to an inability to penetrate not the *what* but the *how* of his narrative. My students were equipped with the basic tools of novel reading before we began, including a multipage in-house study guide used to generate homework assignments and vocabulary quizzes, and so it was clearly not a question of content alone. While there are moments of occasional difficulty—in chapter 2, for instance, where the Italian colonel's finger counting is a crude masturbation joke aimed at mocking the priest's sexual celibacy—most of my students had already experienced texts of modestly greater difficulty, from the vocabulary of *The Scarlet Letter* to the structural complexity of *The Grapes of Wrath* and that tonal minefield, *Sister Carrie*. But the problems with Hemingway appear with the opening sentences of chapter 1, and the obvious way to begin seemed to be to occupy the position of the reader on the other side of the desk.

And the obvious questions were, in fact, painfully so. "In the late summer of that year" are the first seven words of the novel. Well, *what* year? Why does the narrator say "that" year, and why does so much of the language point *forward* to what is unspecified and remains so for pages and pages?[3] Who is this narrator? (We find out his full name on page 84, in book 2, chapter 13, about a third of the way in, after he is wounded; his last name is mentioned on page 25.) After the initial burst of frustration come the other questions. Is Hemingway trying to make things hard to make himself look important? (Yes and no. Don't confuse Hemingway with his narrator.) What "house," "village," "river," and "mountain"? Why that particular run of nouns and in that order? Why the sudden coloring—which, from the perspective of a reader of any age, erupts into the narrative—only of "pebbles" and "water"? Marching troops and dusty roads one can see, but why the aggressive repetition of the word "dust" or some cognate (three times), which runs right up against those middle school language arts teachers' and my sixth-grade nun's cautions against overusing the same word, cautions that send students fleeing to *Roget's*? But none of this— the repetition of the words; the loss of punctuation after compounds, which my students aptly but incorrectly called "run-ons"; the vague deictic gestures; the stripped palette—is as confounding as the domination of coordinate conjunctions. "It's all 'and' 'and' 'and'!" one student cried in ecstatic exasperation. Who cares whether or not those opening five paragraphs are, according to the copybook insights of critics (and parroted by the latest generation of authors of ponies like *SparkNotes*), a structural echo of a five-act play (i.e., *Romeo and Juliet*)? Or whether the soldier's ballooning capes foreshadow the pregnancy of Catherine? Or whether it seems always to be raining? "If we wrote like that," the kids said, "you'd flunk us."[4]

Teaching *A Farewell to Arms* therefore became a problem not so much of content as of form, which is the delivery system for content. Though the students had their own copies of the novel, it seemed essential to isolate the opening paragraph and concentrate on its formal operations, so the initial discussions began with an examination of the opening paragraph, which I reproduced as a separate handout. (Though secondary school students are beginning to understand that, with age, learning gets lonelier, all reading still in a sense goes on collectively: even alone, readers ask the same questions and supply each other with answers.)

Once the opening paragraph's content was cracked and spread out, it would be possible to move to the next and the one after that.

Yet it is one thing to know that you're confused, another to know why. At this point it seemed useful to pause and look back, drawing on what the students had already read in order to demonstrate how emphatically different was the book they were reading and why it was making such outrageous cognitive demands. The texts already under their belts from their years as ninth and tenth graders made an impressive list, from which two comparison texts emerged. The first was a summer reading selection, Dreiser's *Sister Carrie,* the opening paragraph of which was a suggestive point of comparison with Hemingway:

> When Caroline Meeber boarded the afternoon train for Chicago, her total outfit consisted of a small trunk, which was checked in a baggage car, a cheap imitation alligator-skin satchel holding some minor details of the toilet, a small lunch in a paper box and a yellow leather snap purse, containing her ticket, a scrap of paper with her sister's address in Van Buren Street, and four dollars in money. It was in August, 1889. She was eighteen years of age, bright, timid, and full of the illusions of ignorance and youth. Whatever touch of regret at parting characterized her thoughts it was certainly not for advantages now being given up. A gush of tears at her mother's farewell kiss, a touch in her throat when the cars clacked by the flour mill where her father worked by the day, a pathetic sigh as the familiar green environs of the village passed in review, and the threads which bound her so lightly to girlhood and home were irretrievably broken. (3)

It is instantly clear how much more information Dreiser gives the reader, and how immediately present in the paragraph that telling is, than does Hemingway—or rather, Hemingway's narrator. Dreiser's Carrie comes fully arrayed according to the conventions of traditional exposition: she is provided with a name, a date in history, a place to live, a time of day, useful emotional information (a "touch of regret at parting characterized her thoughts"), and sketchy but useful character referents—the mother's farewell kiss, for instance. The difference in point of view, though, between Dreiser's third-person limited and Hemingway's first-person narrator, argued for if not a different example then at least another one: "You don't know about me without you have read a book by the name of *The Adventures of Tom Sawyer;* but that ain't no matter. That book was made by Mr. Mark Twain, and he told the truth, mainly. There was things which he stretched, but mainly he told the truth. That is nothing. I never seen anybody but lied one time or another, without it was Aunt Polly, or the widow, or maybe Mary. Aunt Polly—Tom's Aunt Polly, she is—and Mary, and the Widow Douglas is all told about in that book, which is mostly a true book, with some stretchers, as I said before" (Twain 7). The same points were made through *Huckleberry Finn*'s opening paragraph: traditional exposition gives the reader a place to stand in the story. We instantly know who is speaking as well as useful contextual information (friends, relatives, tone of voice, dialectic patterns).[5]

If Hemingway's novel seemed significantly, if not completely, more available to my students, or at least sufficiently readable to bring us to the tragic rainy ending, the fact was that it was only that way because I had demystified the style for them. Yet this was a problem for me: Hemingway's style is supposed to make us nervous. His books are written for the reader with an active intelligence to penetrate, not peruse, and to encounter, not just appreciate; with Hemingway, as with all the modernists, reading is more than just looking at the words. Hemingway's style, in other words, is one of the best reasons for reading Hemingway. Moreover, many circumstantial objections to his work—Frederic/ Hemingway's sexism, for instance—are more easily managed once a reader is willing to recognize in the style itself a deliberately adopted linguistic stance toward a particular subject matter, and not just a stunt to confound the critics or impress his audience. But how to demonstrate Hemingway's method? I asked my students to assume that Hemingway's editor at Scribners decided to rework that opening paragraph for Hemingway; then I asked them further to assume such a reworked version still exists and could be read by us—all the while reminding them that no such alternate paragraph actually exists. The demonstration took the form of the following reworking, which I constructed based on their questions about the lacunae that Hemingway leaves and that his readers are forced to fill as they make their way through that opening paragraph:

The Phantom Reworking: In the late summer of 1915, an Italian lieutenant named Rinaldi and I, a volunteer ambulance driver born in Illinois and serving in the Italian army, were billeted in a house near a town called Gorizia, in a village that faced the Tagliamento River across an adjacent plain that led toward the Alps. In the bed of the river, whose waters run clear, swift, and blue in the channels, were pebbles and boulders, dried out and whitening in the sun. When the Italian troops marched past our house and down the road, the dust they raised powdered the leaves of the trees first and then the trunks. I remember that the leaves fell early that year and that the troops marched along the road, raising dust and leaves which, stirred by the breeze, would fall as the troops passed and left the road bare and white except for those leaves.

The Original: In the late summer of that year we lived in a house in a village that looked across the river and the plain to the mountains. In the bed of the river there were pebbles and boulders, dry and white in the sun, and the water was clear and swiftly moving and blue in the channels. Troops went by the house and down the road and the dust they raised powdered the leaves of the trees. The trunks of the trees too were dusty and the leaves fell early that year and we saw the troops marching along the road and the dust rising and leaves, stirred by the breeze, falling and the soldiers marching and afterward the road bare and white except for the leaves.

Just about each sentence in the thankfully lost revision drew a comment, either from me or from the students. Despite the restoration of information that secures the reader's sense of place in the narrative—the names and the dates and carefully punctuated periodicity—many students instantly recognized the cost from the stylistic point of view of their increased comfort level. For instance, Hemingway's narrator interposes nothing so hackneyed as the reworking's whimsical, overmodulated, and cheeky first-person singular; the source text supplies only the rather more impersonal first-person plural. The revision faces us toward the Tagliamento River, but the original's lack of geographical precision is part of the point: Frederic Henry's sense of place, like his sense of intimacy, is unfocused and desperately self-centered. The Italian troops in my reworked version are marching "past our house and down the road," but north or south, or in either direction? The preposition might imply southerly movement, but the original denies us secure knowledge: the more one says, the more one is forced to add, and Hemingway's commitment was to less, not more. Then there's that raised dust: the solution of my reworked version is illogical unless one can envision road dust that starts powdering from the top down. The problem, of course, arises from a stricter tracing of Hemingway's third and fourth sentences than the off-handed Frederic Henry would have attempted. Other alternatives tested on site were in some sense clearer, but always the cost of clarity was either in characterization or, as the students came to hear as the passage was read and reread to them, in cadence.[6]

Having established a literary or aesthetic justification for the way Hemingway wrote, the next step is to take the lesson further; this involves a basic course in stylistics. Faced as I was with a classroom of high school juniors, the idea seemed tricky at the time. Even the most basic stylistics requires knowledge of grammar: there is no sense in discussing the lay of any landscape, pasture, or paragraph unless there are agreed-upon features that have been homologized through a shared critical or technical vocabulary. The terminology that stylisticians use, moreover, might pose a developmental hurdle greater than Hemingway's prose. My solution was a modified approach that drew on their expected knowledge of grammar and supplemented that knowledge with two carefully chosen terms known to even the most amateur stylisticians.

"Paratactic" and "hypotactic," respectively, identify a difference in the way sentences are constructed. The terms can be illustrated in complex or simple ways, though the simplest illustration, for me, came directly from experience. My then four-year-old daughter had been standing outside on a spring day when it began to rain and, entering the house, had said, "It's raining and I came inside." Her four-year-old's explanation was not only perfectly clear but clear in the way that the paratactic style, whether Homer's or Hemingway's, is inevitably clear: it lays out its meanings in *parallel* constructions and leaves them unconnected: like parallel lines, parallel constructions never meet unless a connection is supplied from without. My daughter's statement consisted of two clauses, both simple sentences connected by that conjunction favored by paratactic stylists everywhere—the word "and." Grammatically, what Julie had given was a description of the world in the form of a compound sentence. One side gave the world's situation; the other, her instantaneous and unstudied reaction.

Now imagine that this four-year-old had come up to her father and said, "*Because* it's raining, I came inside." What is the difference? Well, not much, most of my students said, or at least not until you look at the actual language. Her original delivery of the information is textbook parataxis: it leaves the external and the internal, the natural situation and the human reaction, disconnected. In order to connect them, an intelligent outside observer or listener (her father, Hemingway's reader) must intervene and do the job of interpretation. The second, though, is different in a manner so subtle as to suggest how some radical differences may be couched in modest dress. The second statement ("Because it's raining, I came inside") differs mainly in the addition of one modest word: the deployment of the subordinate conjunction "because" irreversibly changes the cognitive environment by imposing a cause-and-effect relationship on our experience of natural phenomena. The fact that it is raining, the second example says, produced my reaction, which was to come inside.

One of the things we begin to do automatically as we get older is impose order and reason on the world, a habit that is reflected in—some might say imposed on us by—language itself. The mind begins to think in terms of *connected* relationships among and between things and to subordinate one relationship to another; the instrument the mind uses is the subordinate conjunction, which enforces overt connections that can be logical, temporal, or geographical. This shift is from the paratactic, or simple, to the hypotactic, or complex, syntax, and it signals the overcoming of a particularly important developmental threshold in our lives. It is why speakers who speak or write paratactically—my four-year-old, Hemingway's narrator—sometimes sound like children.

This modified and admittedly compromised stylistic vocabulary therefore asks the student to use the words "paratactic" and "hypotactic" as classroom synonyms for "simple" and "complex." From there, it became obvious that the next step was an actual guide to stylistic difference, which took the following form:

| CATEGORY | PARATACTIC | HYPOTACTIC |
|---|---|---|
| *Syntax* | | |
| sentence types | simple, compound | more compounds, compound-complex |
| conjunctions | coordinate, *Fanboys* | subordinate |
| *Vocabulary* | | |
| palette | simple, "primaries" | richer, ornate, Latinate |
| diction | terse, concise | wordier, "talky" |
| *Modification* | | |
| specificity by adjectival clumping | relatively rare | rather common |
| specificity by repetition | rather common | relatively rare |
| *Figurative Language (in Hemingway)* | | |
| open figures of speech? | sparse | generous |
| embedded | not usual | routine, instinctive |
| *Tone or "Feel" of the Passage* | | |
| | disconnected | connected |
| | haphazard | sense of a controlling vision |
| | ironic | |

Certain aspects of this guide are applicable to stylistic difference generally. One can expect to find greater syntactic simplicity in a paratactic environment, say a passage from Homer, than in a comparable hypotactic example, such as a passage from Virgil; the fact that the distinction is descriptive and not evaluative, moreover, is usually an opportunity for a teacher to invite the student to reflect on his or her own style—not to critique or correct it but simply to position it within a formal category and thus take a measure of its effectiveness or at least gain some sense of the worldview it represents. My own conviction, one I share with my students, is that the paratactic stylist and the hypotactic stylist see the world in vastly different ways; while one is not better than the other, each reveals the idiosyncratic contours of thoughts and emotions just as powerfully as a Rorshach test or any other psychological discovery tool.

The word "simplicity" is, moreover, a term that refers to some qualities of the way an utterance is constructed, not to the actual cognitive or metacognitive situation of the reader, as is obvious from the example of Hemingway, whose very simplicity is a complex problem for readers to solve. The dominance of coordinate over subordinate clauses, a feature of Hemingway, may not always be the *only* signal of paratactic style, but it does tend to produce a greater number of simple or compound constructions in contrast to styles dominated by the habit of subordination—for instance, Poe's "The Fall of the House of Usher," or the following scene from Hawthorne:

The stigma gone, Hester heaved a long, deep sigh, in which the burden of shame and anguish departed from her spirit. O exquisite relief! She had not known the weight, until she felt the freedom! By another impulse, she took off the formal cap that confined her hair; and down it fell upon her shoulders, dark and rich, with at once a shadow and a light in its abundance, and imparting the charm of softness to her features. There played around her mouth, and beamed around her eyes, a radiant and tender smile, that seemed gushing from the very heart of womanhood. A crimson flush was glowing on her cheek, that had been long so pale. Her sex, her youth, and whole richness of her beauty, came back from what men call the irrevocable past, and clustered themselves, with her maiden hope, and a happiness before unknown, within the magic circle of this hour. And, as if the gloom of the earth and sky had been but the effluence of these two mortal hearts, it vanished with their sorrow. All at once, as with a sudden smile of heaven, forth burst the sunshine, pouring a very flood into the obscure forest, gladdening each green leaf, transmuting the yellow fallen ones to gold, and gleaming adown the gray trunks of the solemn trees. The objects that had made a shadow hitherto, embodied the brightness now. The course of the little brook might be traced by its merry gleam afar into the wood's heart of mystery, which had become a mystery of joy. (*Scarlet Letter* 138)

Every feature of the hypotactic profile is present in Hawthorne's description of Hester letting her hair down: the sentences are highly intricate periodic constructions in a landscape of ornate Latinate diction ("exquisite," "irrevocable," "transmuting," etc.); front-loaded adjectival constructions ("a radiant and tender smile," "sudden smile of heaven"); densely embedded figures of speech, including personifications ("Her sex, her youth, and whole richness of her beauty . . . *clustered themselves*"); and none of the ritual repetitions found in Hemingway.

Thus, the purpose of the prospectus is really twofold. First, it introduces conventional stylistic terminology by reducing that terminology to a central distinction in the way stylistic emphasis and difference are achieved. Second, it stipulates within the larger stylistic realm a particular role or spot for Hemingway by pointing to something in his work that we refer to as Hemingwayesque. For, as visual a writer as he is, there are simply fewer metaphors per the typical Hemingway page than in, say, a contemporary like Fitzgerald or his predecessor Hawthorne. Arguably, in *A Farewell to Arms,* the reduced load of metaphorical utterance is the outcome of the point of view: the host of the narrative is Frederic Henry, a blunt-thinking ambulance driver with a war-coarsened sensibility whose treatment of the woman who loves him is blockheaded and perhaps inexcusable. It would be useless to expect of Frederic the descriptive ability of, say, a Nick Carraway. To explain why would entail a much longer conversation taking in much of the history of American modernism along with Hemingway's associations with Stein, Cézanne's painting, Pound's imagism, and the traditions of American journalism.

Students may point out, of course, the moments in *A Farewell to Arms* where metaphors are in view. But in the long run there are few such moments. Most are "open" metaphorical opportunities where the comparison is announced by a simile, as in chapter 1. Less usual are moments like this, from page 44 of the book: "I saw arched stone bridges over the river where tracks turned off from the road and where we passed stone farmhouses with pear trees candelabraed against their south walls." To make the point, I set Frederic's actual description beside an alternative: "I saw arched stone bridges over the river where tracks turned off from the road and we passed stone farmhouses with pear trees standing *like* candelabras against their south walls" (emphasis added). The use of the simile generously focuses attention on a similarity between two elements (trees and candelabras); the use of similes creates what I called open or explicit comparisons or figures of speech. Hemingway, in contrast, uses the vehicle of the comparison (a candelabra) as the main verb in the second clause and embeds the comparison in the passage.[7]

At this point the students have been nearly through the novel itself and the range of routine assessment—twice-weekly quizzes on the reading, one major test—that will culminate in the writing of the usual final essay. Having spent so much of their attention on style, however, in my initial deployment of this methodology mere common sense seemed to argue for something different from the normal outcome—different from, say, a full-blown research paper (which they would have experienced as sophomores), a creative assignment (e.g., writing a new ending), or something in between (the personal-experience take on Hemingway's characters). The last possibility has always seemed suspiciously self-serving to me: many students are actually incapacitated by their teachers' invitations to address their own (generally limited) experience, and high-minded attempts to lighten their workloads only increase it, partly because most high school kids are at the outset and not the end of that experience. The creative outcome, moreover, seemed age inappropriate (and with certain groups, an invitation to disaster). While a research assignment struck me as right for the grade level and the book, the question was how to integrate research and analysis into several weeks' concentration on style. Given where the course was headed—through Nella Larson's *Passing* to Fitzgerald's *Gatsby*—it might make sense to give style an emphasis strong enough to carry over into subsequent discussions. As it turned out, the stylistics exercise was repeated with Fitzgerald, the emphasis removed, logically, from paratactic to hypotactic analysis and discovery.

The result was a combination of traditional stylistic analysis with the creative approach. With the book and discussions of the book complete, attentions are turned back to the very first paragraph of the novel. After reviewing the major terminology and the significant grammatical concepts of coordination and subordination, the students receive the following assignment descriptor:

Your next written assignment will be a stylistic analysis of Hemingway: Step 1:

(a)   Select a passage of significant length from *A Farewell to Arms*. With respect to length, if you're doubtful, undecided, or apathetic, you can choose one of the following passages to analyze: pages 37–38, beginning with the words, "The sun was going down and the day was cooling off" to the end of the paragraph; the last paragraph on page 44 that continues to page 45; page 87, the only full paragraph; pages 101–2, ending where the dialogue begins; pages 113–14, beginning with the long (and rare) subordinate temporal clause at the bottom of the page; pages 226–27, the first two paragraphs of chapter 31; page 225, the last paragraph; page 249, beginning with the words, "That night at the hotel"; or pages 320–21, the stream-of-consciousness monologue. These are suggestions only.

(b)     Transcribe your selection on a typewriter or word processor verbatim onto a sheet of paper. Do not make a photocopy of your passage.

Step 2:

This step is divided into two tasks. Once you have selected a passage, proceed to analyze it.

(a)     Identify three ways in which your passage fits the description of paratactic style. Count conjunctions, modifiers, and articles; compute the proportions of coordinate to subordinate constructions; note the incidences of the active and the passive voices; in short, anything that signals the presence of the paratactic—repetition for emphasis, a cluster metaphor, vivid visual moments—ought to be a focal point for analysis.

(b)     Rewrite a significant portion of your paragraph in the hypotactic style, linking coordinate clauses. Your analysis should occupy no less than a full page of handwritten text.

Step 3:

Imitate Hemingway's style as closely as possible, using your object text as your model. You are free to take your imitation in any direction that suggests itself. You may, for instance, elect to try to extend or change or advance the book's meaning in a new direction by rewriting the ending or writing an additional chapter; you may want to do a piece of isolated interpretive writing by imitating only the style and ignoring wholly the themes of *A Farewell to Arms;* or you may want to try a full-scale send-up of Hemingway, prodding his style for its implicit humor. The choice is entirely yours. Your imitation should occupy no less than a full page of handwritten text.

The assignment is then modeled in front of the class, using the opening paragraph of the book as the target passage. The emphasis on transcription, which many students may consider busywork, comes out of a lifetime of personal experience in which accidental memorization of certain passages has led to a certain expertise. The step that most found either completely absurd or suspicious is, not incidentally, 2a. In order to model it, I instruct students to read the passage silently and then reread it aloud—possibly for the sixth or seventh time since beginning the study of the novel; they are then charged to look for what they view as key grammatical elements and/or signals of stylistic importance. The following are the results of an in situ run-through of part 2a of the assignment:

- The passage contains twenty-five instances of *the,* two *a*'s, fifteen *and*'s, four *in*'s and five *-ing* endings, all present participles.

- The paragraph contains 126 words.
- There are no subordinate conjunctions of any kind (*because, when, if, since*).
- There are no relative clauses (*which* or *that* clauses).
- There are few adjectives (fewer than ten), one of which is a color (*white*).
- There is not one possessive pronoun or noun (i.e., no apostrophe-plus-*s* endings, only prepositional phrases).
- There are five sentences in total.

Excruciatingly obvious, of course, but the demonstration accomplishes several objectives. It establishes a staging area for the remainder of the demonstration by stipulating the knowledge and application of basic grammatical terms, and it permits instructors to extend the identification of grammatical terms into syntactical structures (and perhaps along the way do a quick-and-dirty grammar review). If the demonstration is undertaken using a comparison passage, by the way, it may be both more interesting and more dramatic.[8] Normally I would turn the group's attention (in the bad old days, by using a prepared overhead, and nowadays a PowerPoint demonstration, of the originally distributed example) to something we had looked at earlier—that passage from *Sister Carrie* or *Huck Finn* or "The Fall of the House of Usher."[9] Step 2b had already been demonstrated weeks earlier with the bogus reworking of the opening paragraph.

The final step of the assignment, though, is the moment when most of the students discover not only how to write like Hemingway but, as one of them put it, to discover which side of the stylistic ledger, paratactic or hypotactic, one naturally occupied. Several students find this to be a moment of truth in their experiences as writers and are charmed to realize that they were instinctively more hypotactic or paratactic than not and that the difference is actually quantifiable. Others use it as a form of (predictable) self-justification or congratulation, their executions of the final stage of the assignment sounding as they always have. And occasionally, the assignment inspires an imitation so extraordinary that it can find its way into institutional writing archives or literary magazines.

In the long run, no literary pedagogy can for very long exclude some attention to writing at the atomic or elemental level of the writing itself; this is especially the case with authors like Hemingway, whose superficial difficulties must be evaporated in analysis in order to carry on discussions of the political, social, and historical concerns of greater moment and interest. It makes little sense, for instance, to exclude Hemingway from a book list on the basis of the sexism of his novels until it is clear that the attitudes of his characters—whether Nick Adams, Jake Barnes, or Frederic Henry—are carefully crafted literary instrumentalities susceptible to analysis, imitation, and reproduction, if necessary. What turned out to be profitable for a fairly affluent independent secondary school audience, moreover, has proven to be equally so with audiences of college undergraduates and, in a radically altered form, for graduate students interested in investigating precisely how content is delivered—their own, or that of others.

## NOTES

1. In what follows I will be using the terms "hypotactic" and "paratactic" in the sense in which they appear in traditional formalist analyses of literary style, notably in the work of R. S. Crane. The latter, or paratactic, environment generally is recognized by "arrangement[s] of sentences, clauses, phrases, or words in coordinate conjunctions" and is marked by excessive polysyndeton (i.e., chains of compounds linked with coordinate clauses and essentially overcoordinated). The contrasting hypotactic style "refers to writing that uses subordination to reflect logical, causal, temporal or spatial relations" (Harmon and Holman 366, 254).

2. The Man in the Yellow Suit in Babbitt's *Tuck Everlasting,* for instance, is exposed both by his obvious deviousness and the very fact that he is the only character in the book without a (Christian) name, facts that children love to point out as evidence of his wickedness while simultaneously overlooking the obvious ironies: he is not only the savviest character in the book but the one possessed of the most typically American outlook toward opportunity.

   More profound examples would be the depictions of Hagrid in *Harry Potter and the Chamber of Secrets,* who is gently condemned at the end of the book by Ron for his inability to spot evil, and the fascinating evolution of Mary Lennox in *The Secret Garden* from orphaned spoiled brat to the savior of Colin Craven. In each case the earlier tonal or thematic ironies are either resolved by or dissolved in the context and thus allow the reader (a young adult) to identify more comfortably and experience less sense of cultural friction with a character.

3. The first time a date is mentioned is on page 20, which tells us that the year 1915 has already passed: "Have you done nursing long?" Frederic asks Catherine. "Since the end of '15," she replies. The references to baseball while Frederic reads the sports page in the hospital in Milan would reveal, but only to someone reading with a baseball encyclopedia, that at page 136 the year is 1917, when Babe Ruth was still pitching for the Red Sox (and went 24–3) and the White Sox beat the Giants in the World Series. The only point in the novel where Frederic explicitly dates events is on page 308, near the end of the narrative: "It was March, 1918, and the German offensive had started in France."

4. Harmon and Holman, who use Hemingway as an exemplar in their definition of parataxis, conclude the entry by noting, "As a rule parataxis is found . . . more in juvenile or uncultivated utterance than in the mature [or] sophisticated" (366).

5. The difference in point of view, in fact, between the first-person Frederic and the third-person omniscient Dreiser proved useful later, for other reasons that illuminated a problem with Frederic's laconic narrative habits. The fact that the point of view is Frederic Henry's becomes a means of introducing students to narrative reliability or, in this case, unreliability. The fact that Catherine comes across as a "ditz," as one student noted, is as poor a reflection

of Frederic's judgment as it is of Catherine herself in as much as her ditziness may actually be his own male-projected version of her. The "masculinist" affect, in other words, belongs to the character, not necessarily the author.

6. "With the leaves falling early that year, the troops marched along the road and raised dust and leaves that, stirred by the breeze, kept falling as the soldiers marched, until the road was bare and white except for those leaves." But this is just as limp. Note the sudden burst of punctuation.

7. The demonstration of differences between open and embedded metaphors produced the exercise in the appendix, one I would recommend highly because the students found it to be so much fun.

8. An example that worked beautifully was Woody Allen's parody of Hemingway's style in "A Twenties Memory." A more polemical and hostile one can be found in MacDonald's *Against the American Grain* (167–71).

9. Comparative results using Dreiser's *Sister Carrie:* Total word count: 155. The passage uses nine *the*'s, eight *a*'s, six *and*'s, six *in*'s, and two *-ing* endings (one of which is a gerund). Note the three subordinate conjunctions (two instances of *when* and one of *as*) in the same number of sentences (five). Note, too, the presence in this passage of a name (Caroline Meeber), date (August, 1889) and a specified place (Chicago, Van Buren Street).

## APPENDIX: A Figuration Exercise

Here are some open figures. See how artfully you can embed them in closed sentences that have the same meaning:

Example:         (Open) He ate like a pig last night.
                 (Closed) He pigged out.

1. He always behaves like a clown in company.
2. The soda can made a sound like a fizz when she opened it.
3. The door of the spaceship opened like an iris and the robot stepped through.
4. The old car snorted like a pig getting up the hill.
5. He manipulated the group like a snake charmer into believing in his absolute sincerity.
6. He made his way like King Kong into the room.
7. She stunned them into silence with her Medusa-like stare.
8. The kids surrounded Santa like a swarm of bees.
9. The boy puffed his cheeks until they looked like apples.
10. She spoke to him like a mother and made him submit.

# Hemingway's Road Map
## A Cartography for Teaching *A Farewell to Arms*

*Gail D. Sinclair*

LET'S FACE it, Ernest Hemingway is not William Faulkner, and for those who teach students other than upper-level English majors or graduate students, we can express sincere gratitude for that. This is not to say Hemingway isn't deep or that he doesn't have subterranean layers demanding profound contemplation. More precisely, what I wish to imply is Hemingway's accessibility, even his work's great capacity to produce an enjoyable experience for the less highly trained sojourner into the literary landscape. *A Farewell to Arms* is an excellent novel for introducing Hemingway to this level of reader. The work is a perfect choice for reluctant adolescent males whose more physically oriented interests likely override the relatively passive act of literary participation. Hemingway's protagonists exhibit the conventional qualities of maleness through their connection to war, boxing, big game hunting, and deep-sea fishing. Even as remote as these subjects may be to contemporary youths, they more easily dovetail with the male realm than might other canonical American literature likely encountered in a classroom setting. What makes *A Farewell to Arms* an even more perfect selection is its ability to also engage a young female audience through Frederic Henry and Catherine Barkley's romantically tragic love story. Once these readers are actively engrossed in the novel's plot, diving past surface events to instruct them in the more embedded artistic and literary qualities becomes an easier task. At its core, *A Farewell to Arms* contains all the quintessential thematic and stylistic elements with which students would contend in any of Hemingway's writing, possibly exempting the posthumously published works. Through informed instruction, readers should come away from this novel with a good road map and skills to approach with equal finesse *The Sun Also Rises, For Whom the Bell Tolls, The Old Man and the Sea,* and his best-known short stories, and they will be prepared to make the journey with a clear sense of Hemingway's aesthetics.

## CREATING THE MAP

Before delving into the specific plot, style, and thematic elements of *A Farewell to Arms,* I think it is important to validate why students ought to study Hemingway. To do so, we must establish the qualities his writing possesses and make particular note of the ways in which he adds to the American literary canon. This could involve a comprehensive discussion of modernism, existentialism, and various other theoretical concepts, but at the high school or early college level such debate would likely turn off any reluctant readers, at least in the introduction to the work. Instead, I like to focus initial conversation upon the famous Hemingway style, and how it distinctively marks his writing and creates a modern aesthetic mirroring his attitudes toward the post–World War I milieu in which he creates and sets many of his most famous works.

Discussing biographical details is certainly interesting given the aura surrounding Hemingway's personal life, but such knowledge is not essential beyond knowing that his first professional job was as a reporter for the *Kansas City Star.* There, his news editor, C. G. Wellington, molded the young writer's prose by insisting on strict adherence to "one hundred and ten rules for writing vigorous journalism" (Lynn 68). Put succinctly, those rules covered three basic guidelines:

1. Use short sentences.
2. Avoid slang or other overused phrasing.
3. Use simple language devoid of excessive adjectives.[1]

Hemingway affirms the significance that early instruction had in developing his writing principles by declaring, "Those were the best rules I ever learned for the business of writing. I've never forgotten them. No man with any talent, who feels and writes truly about the thing he is trying to say, can fail to write well if he abides by them" (Lynn 68). Throughout his career Hemingway preaches the value of these rules, and he maintains adherence to them in his work. Pointing out examples where the author practices this conviction makes a fun and useful opening activity in establishing the famous Hemingway style.

To begin that examination in *A Farewell to Arms,* I like to have students first look at a passage from Hemingway's short story "Soldier's Home" as a general introduction to style.[2] In this piece he places a young war veteran, Harold Krebs, at the psychological center; we can find an encapsulated version of several important Hemingway characteristics more developed in the subsequent novel, but they are easier to perceive here. The story provides a passage so obviously illustrating many of Hemingway's writing principles that even the least observant students cannot miss some of them. An overhead projection of the following paragraphs, minus the italics, works well to model several stylistic issues that also provide an entrée to thematic discussion:

> Nothing had changed in the town except that the young girls had grown up. . . . *He liked to look* at them from the front porch as *they walked* on the other side of the street. *He liked to watch them walking* under the shade of the trees. *He liked* the round Dutch collars about their sweaters. *He liked* their silk stockings and flat shoes. *He liked* their bobbed hair and the way *they walked.*
>
> When he was in town their appeal to him was not very strong. *He did not like* them when he saw them in the Greek's ice cream parlor. *He did not want* them themselves really. They were too complicated. There was something else. Vaguely *he wanted* a girl but *he did not want to have to work to get* her. He *would have liked to have* a girl but *he did not want to have to spend* a long time getting her. *He did not want to get* into the intrigue and the politics. *He did not want to have to do* any courting. *He did not want to tell* any more lies. It wasn't worth it. *He did not want any consequences. He did not want any consequences* ever again. *He wanted to live* along *without consequences.* (*Complete Short Stories* 112–13; emphasis added)

I begin by asking students to point out what they observe in the passage. After I model what to look for by underlining just a few words and phrases, classes eagerly join in, and the usual responses catch the most obvious examples: repetitive use of sentence length and word choice, simple subject/predicate construction, "feeling" verbs rather than action verbs, the author's focused observation on the male protagonist's responses rather than action—in this case the contrasting like/dislike.

At this point the exercise usually produces a sense of incredulity that this is the prose of a Nobel Prize–winning author, whose conscious style would no doubt draw criticism in the composition classes they have experienced. We then discuss whether or not this sample actually exhibits a sophomoric or a

highly developed artistic style, given its repetitive phrasing and verbal simplicity. More sophisticated students may recognize the tone being established and
point out Harold Krebs's lack of active participation and the third-person narrative technique Hemingway uses to create it. This moves us to discuss the way
in which prose style provides clues toward theme. We point to Hemingway's
use of matter-of-fact language devoid of didactic interjection and how such
conscious choice conveys Krebs's remote, emotionally truncated thoughts and
withdrawal from overt action. I lead them to an understanding that this simplistic, emotionless language vividly displays the aftermath of war's psychological
trauma and its subsequent inertia. They come to recognize the author's dramatic
rhetorical restraint and verbal manipulation not as a sign of immature writing,
but as an obvious intent to underscore the young ex-soldier's passive observation rather than active participation in his postwar civilian life. This moves us
naturally to a discussion of the opening passages of *A Farewell to Arms* and
their impact. I conclude this exercise by asking students as they begin reading
the novel to pay attention not only to what the words reveal of surface action,
but also to how they are used, what is said or left unsaid, and what we must
supply beyond the text to fill in the gaps and make meaning.

Immediately in paragraph 1, chapter 1, of *A Farewell to Arms,* the Hemingway minimalist techniques we have already discussed become evident. He
uses controlled language in this opening passage to maximize artistic effect
and quickly establish his thematic template. The verbally and emotionally un-
adorned opening is uncluttered by excessive description or interpretive slant.
I direct students once again toward discussing Hemingway's methodology
here, his painting of the opening with sparse brushstrokes and without undue
attempts to color the reader's emotions. They can start finding other representative passages on their own, and you can lead them to describe how he writes
of a country and a people in the midst of war without imposing a sentimental
tone suggesting the conflict's disruptive influence. Like Krebs's emotional withdrawal, the result here is also an authorial detachment where Frederic Henry,
the novel's narrator, simply reports. Again, I might put the following paragraph
on an overhead projector and identify stylistic aspects. Here I use parentheses
to show where adjectives exist or don't, and italics to identify the rather bland
verb choice:

> In the (late) summer of that year we *lived* in a ( ) house in a ( ) village that
> *looked* across the ( ) river and the ( ) plain to the ( ) mountains. In the ( )
> bed of the ( ) river there *were* pebbles and boulders, (dry) and (white) in the

( ) sun, and the water *was* (clear) and swiftly *moving* and (blue) in the ( ·) channels. ( ) Troops *went* by the ( ) house and down the ( ) road and the ( ) dust they *raised* powdered the ( ) leaves of the ( ) trees. The trunks of the ( ) trees too *were* (dusty) and the ( ) leaves *fell* early that ( ) year and we *saw* the ( ) troops *marching* along the ( ) road and the ( ) dust *rising* and ( ) leaves, *stirred* by the ( ) breeze, *falling* and the ( ) soldiers *marching* and afterward the road (bare) and (white) except for the ( ) leaves. (3)

One way to highlight the impact these choices create is to insert vivid adjectives in the parentheses and substitute active verbs for the italicized ones. You can model a sample sentence such as the one below and have them create their own examples showing emotional bias.

The (brutish) soldiers carrying (heavy machine) guns and ammunition belts *slung* over one shoulder *descended* upon the (sleepy little) village where only women, those (too young), or those (too infirm) to be *dragged* into the war remained to witness the (sudden invasion).

Changes in tone become obvious, and students see how Hemingway could have—but chose not to—overtly lead readers toward strong responses. A quick discussion of word connotation makes the point about conscious choice and language's power to affect the reader's response.

This paragraph also elicits an important discussion about how on the surface this anti-didactic, antiromantic approach mirrors the realistic vein of his more immediate literary predecessors such as Stephen Crane or Mark Twain and is an early example of the modern approach that Hemingway helps develop. In a survey course, you no doubt would have already presented those earlier authors and literary characteristics. If this is not the case, providing simple definitions of terms such as "realism" and "naturalism" is enough to establish a sense of the type of literature Hemingway grew up reading and respecting. A few questions make clear the idea that Hemingway is reporting the visual and sensory facts of the scene, not painting an emotional subtext through intentionally coercive language. I will discuss later how the paragraph's lack of emotional or authorial interjection relays by subtle means volumes more beneath its surface than the few short sentences reveal about war's far-reaching ramifications.

The opening paragraph relies on easy universal symbolism to establish the tone, and I always take a moment to discuss the concept of understood symbols as literary shorthand. You could create a quick list from ones students already know:

| *Symbol* | *Meaning* |
|----------|-----------|
| day | light, life, good |
| night | death, darkness, evil |
| spring | birth, renewal |
| summer | life, maturity, vitality |
| fall | approaching death, old age |
| winter | death |
| cross | Christ, Christianity, resurrection |

This exercise could be carried as far as you wish, but the important point is for students to both recognize certain objects or concepts as having deeper representative meaning and understand that authors' literary use of these may signal thematic agendas readers could otherwise miss.

If you wish to use supplementary information to support central Hemingway concepts, a plethora of critical evaluations and a good number of biographies are available (see list of works cited and selected bibliography). However, having taught high school English for twenty-one years in three different states, I am aware of the often-limited resources at hand, though increasingly the Internet makes accessing information easier even in remote locations. Gale Research Group has long been a staple for abridged collections, and its series, *Literary Masters*, has a well-done volume on Ernest Hemingway. Michael Reynolds, a highly acclaimed Hemingway scholar and biographer, includes in this comprehensive but easy-to-use text sections on biography, career, publications, critical reception, authorial philosophy, background teaching material, and a bibliography including Internet sites. *Ernest Hemingway: A Literary Reference,* edited by Robert Trogdon, is also a compilation along the same lines, somewhat less easy to use but much more financially accessible than the expensive Gale series.[3]

Hemingway studies in the last twenty-five years have undergone dramatic changes brought about by the publication of several posthumous works that don't fit easily into the traditional critique. In addition, shifts in analysis have occurred, especially in gender studies, that greatly enlarge our sense of this author. Non-academics and novitiates to Hemingway's work might be best served, however, by first developing a basic sense of the author. While Carlos Baker's work is now decades old, it is nevertheless still useful and accessible for establishing patterns in the early writing. His bedrock essay, "The Mountain and the Plain," explicates Hemingway's understatement of complex emotional and symbolic imagery in *A Farewell to Arms,* especially that presented in the opening paragraph and chapter.[4] Baker points out what Hemingway accomplishes in the novel's opening: "It helps to establish the dominant mood (which is one of doom), plants a series of important images for future symbolic cultivation, and subtly compels the reader into the position of detached observer" (*Writer as Artist* 94). You can draw students' attention to images Hemingway uses in these first lines: the dust, the falling leaves, approaching autumn, the marching soldiers indistinguishable one from another and seen only at a distance, the far-off mountains, and the up-close plain. They become road signs students can identify throughout the novel denoting complicated emotions or themes revealed later only through a steady building of scenes. These "important images for future symbolic cultivation" immediately help students establish some of Hemingway's most prominent concepts, set the tone of the novel, and open themselves up to the work of deeper analysis from the simple but suggestive text.

Yet another point of discussion elicited from the opening paragraph might be the novel's relationship to T. S. Eliot's wasteland imagery, specifically his modernist representation of impending doom coupled with stoic endurance. I read or reread to the students lines 329–59 and 386–95 from *The Waste Land,* emphasizing the sterile, godless landscape of empty cisterns and a chapel whose only inhabitant is the wind. Mirroring that scene, the initial aridity in *A Farewell to Arms* serves as backdrop for the troops' steady stirring of dust when their marching creates an ash-coated landscape reminiscent of the funereal phrase "ashes to ashes, dust to dust." Such description underscores war's proximity to death. The opening exercises on style prepare students to see Hemingway's surrealistic rendering of automaton-like soldiers drifting through a disinterested landscape. I ask the class to keep this in mind as they follow Frederic and Catherine's plight/ flight and to forecast what they believe the central characters' struggle will be. At a later point in explicating the novel you will be able to facilitate discussion about how the subtle, nihilistic opening tone persists and demonstrates natural forces' indifference to and disengagement from human activity.

Another essential discussion that should come early in teaching Hemingway is his adherence to a stylistic philosophy labeled the iceberg principle. I quote for students Hemingway's own definition put forth first in the 1932 publication of *Death in the Afternoon.* He explains, "If a writer of prose knows enough about what he is writing about he may omit things that he knows and the reader, if the writer is writing truly enough, will have a feeling of those things as strongly as though the writer had stated them. The dignity of movement of an ice-berg is due to only one-eighth of it being above water" (192). Later in 1958 he revisits his theory in an interview for the *Paris Review.* Hemingway reiterates, "I always try to write on the principle of the iceberg. There is seven eighths of it underwater for every part that shows. Anything you know you can eliminate and it only strengthens your iceberg. It is the part that doesn't show" (Plimpton 84).

Finally, in the posthumously published *A Moveable Feast* he offers yet another justification for this intentional style. "You could omit anything if you know that you omitted and the omitted part would strengthen the story and make people feel something more than they understood" (75). Through our already-detailed explication of chapter 1, students can begin identifying Hemingway's iceberg principle by pointing to omissions of all but the bare descriptive essentials, either emotional or physical. And in referencing his own definition, we can discuss what readers sense without needing to be told directly.

While still examining the crucial opening paragraph and setting the stage for deeper inspection of the novel, it is important to establish yet another of Hemingway's bedrock stylistic and thematic practices. This, again, is an easy concept for students to identify throughout the novel, and this exercise can build their analytic confidence. Characteristically, the places his protagonists inhabit physically, mentally, and spiritually divide themselves dichotomously into "good" places and "bad" places, or what Baker calls "Home" and "Not-Home" (*Writer as Artist* 101). If you've used Baker's "The Mountain and the Plain," you will have already examined his discussion of these geographical locations as Hemingway's first set of oppositional extremes. On some occasions the author presents the mountains as treacherous, and on others they offer sanctuary, but the concept of antithetical regions remains steady. Starting with these obvious divisions, and assuming the students have read the novel prior to this exercise, you can help them create two columns on the board showing safe and happy abodes in opposition to those where one is fearful because of physically or emotionally dangerous terrain. They can see how this contraposition heightens Hemingway's thematic emphasis, and they can also add to my abbreviated list below by identifying other locales throughout the novel exhibiting the same patterning.

| *Good Places (Safety):* | *Bad Places (Danger):* |
|---|---|
| snow-covered mountain | rain-drenched, muddy plain |
| Abruzzi (natural retreat for hunting) | large cities (drinking and whoring) |
| Switzerland (amnesty) | Italy (death for desertion) |
| hospital room (pleasant sexual experience) | red velvet and mirrored hotel room (potentially unsavory sexual experience) |
| Catherine and Frederic alone together | Catherine and Frederic separated |

Students will no doubt find evidence from time to time of Hemingway's symbolic shifts in this paradigm, and these can also open up discussion about deeper meaning behind those contrasting uses.

One easily identifiable symbol Hemingway variously employs is water, particularly natural bodies of it. Before students even begin reading the novel, I ask them to make note of when Hemingway mentions water and what its function might be at those points. The rapidly flowing stream whose source is the mountain runs through the dust-laden valley, bringing "clear and swiftly moving" blue water in its channels, but later overabundance produces danger and disease. The Tagliamento River facilitates Frederic Henry's lifesaving desertion from the army, and Lago Maggiore provides the lovers safe exit from the war, but both also threaten potential disaster if they are not successfully navigated in the escape attempts. Students can point out other such references and discuss what experiences occur in relation to that proximity. As in Hemingway's earlier short story "Big Two-Hearted River," where the stream's swiftly flowing current is trout laden and restorative but the swamp at its edge lurks dangerously, water's symbolic function in *A Farewell to Arms* can be both healing and dangerous, and I bring students around to a discussion of this.

Another concept central to Hemingway, tangentially connected to symbolism and fairly easily taught in *A Farewell to Arms,* is his use of objective correlative. We've already established rain as an important signal, and again I ask students before they begin reading to note its frequent occurrence and impact. During examination of the opening paragraphs, I offer T. S. Eliot's definition of objective correlative as "a set of objects, a situation, a chain of events which shall be the formula for that *particular* emotion."[5] We become trained through a sort of operant conditioning that when a set stimulus appears, it will elicit a predictable psychological response. In this opening chapter Hemingway begins such pairing of water to emotional reaction. We take a close look at his description of summer's far-off nighttime fighting bringing "flashes from the artillery" seeming more like distant heat lightning than dangerous activity, and the observation that "the nights were cool and there was not the feeling of a storm coming" (3). However, as fall approaches, students can identify the mood shifts where narrative tone conveys the changing atmosphere. Frederic relays this opening scene to us with the backward-looking vision of one who has survived to tell the story and knows how it ends. His narrative informs us:

> There was fighting for that mountain too, but it was not successful, and in the *fall* when the *rains came* the leaves all *fell* from the chestnut trees and the branches were *bare* and the trunks *black with rain*. The vineyards were

*thin* and *bare-branched* too and all the country *wet* and *brown* and *dead with the autumn.* There were *mists over the river* and *clouds on the mountain* and the trucks *splashed mud* on the road and the troops were *muddy* and *wet* in their capes; their rifles were *wet.* (4; emphasis added)

Once again, students can easily see on an overhead projection Hemingway's mood painting as he establishes the link between rain and disaster. Almost immediately it becomes a signal for "things [going] very badly." Hemingway silhouettes the drenched and muddy soldiers against the mountain backdrop as they march across the plain. In profile with their guns, belts, and ammunition protected under their capes, the soldiers look "as though they were six months gone with child" (4). This odd and contextually disjunct description can easily lead students to a discussion of Hemingway's foreshadowing. If they've been asked to make note of this passage, by the end of the novel they will connect it to Catherine's pregnancy and subsequent death in the rain, when she, too, will be "gone with child," first referencing her pregnancy and, finally, her resulting death during the act of giving birth. This observation helps solidify the point that Hemingway's unusual textual description has definite thematic intent.

Beyond simply acting as an objective correlative for disaster, in Hemingway's work rain most often functions as a reminder of humankind's fatalistic existence in the post–World War I landscape. Chapter 1's brief final paragraph foregrounds his symbolic triune of rain, death, and human insignificance to natural order. Frederic reports, "At the start of the winter came the permanent rain and with the rain came the cholera. But it was checked and in the end only seven thousand died of it in the army" (4). I point out the word "only" and ask students to respond. They react strongly to the implication that this many deaths are treated as seemingly unimportant. You can lead them to see how Hemingway's style effectively heightens the drama of war's efficiency as a killing machine rather than minimizing such a statistic, as the sentence's matter-of-fact tone seems to do. These losses do not matter in the grand scheme of nature, which is precisely Hemingway's point, but they have poignancy in the humanistic sense where each individual is significant and "every man is a peece of the *Continent,* a part of the *maine,*" as the sixteenth-century poet John Donne wrote. Hemingway juxtaposes Donne's philosophy, "any mans *death* diminishes *me,* because I am involved in *Mankinde*" (*For Whom the Bell Tolls* epigraph), against contrasting natural indifference both in *A Farewell to Arms* and in his later war novel, *For Whom the Bell Tolls,* taking its title directly from Donne's poem. An important aspect that you will want to lead your students toward is Hemingway's thematic emphasis on "man alone" against nature's principles and the idea that he must come to recognize a dramatic contrast between the grand desire for self-preservation and a universal indifference wielding ultimate power through inevitable death. At the novel's end the students will observe Hemingway's skillful contrast between these two forces. Catherine Barkley's demise is tragic for the young lovers and emotionally wrenching for the involved reader, yet the tone suggests this death is relatively insignificant against the greater backdrop of nature, with its indifference to human loss.

Close examination of the five-paragraph opening establishes central Hemingway style, tone, symbols, and theme. I outline these in Appendix A, and I find it useful to share such information with classes as they begin the task of explication. One can trace these same literary qualities in the gamut of works published during his lifetime, though their accessibility in this novel in particular is what makes it such a wonderful introduction to an inexperienced Hemingway reader. This stylistically conscious author will consistently simplify his prose, disengage emotionally in his telling of the story, and use imagery and symbolism to more subtly lead the reader to what lies buried beneath the surface text. Students can plumb the iceberg's depths with the pick and ax of literary analysis you've put in their hands. Tracing Hemingwayesque qualities first embedded in chapter 1 through the rest of the novel then becomes an exciting journey offering positive rewards. On their own, with the map Hemingway provides in the opening chapter, and with the interpretive skills you have taught them, students will hopefully have a pleasant experience unearthing the buried literary treasures Hemingway and *A Farewell to Arms* offer.

## THE JOURNEY

Now that you have initiated the students into Hemingway and set the stage for their journey into *A Farewell to Arms,* it's time to get on the road! With their guides and the notes they have taken during your orientation session in chapter 1, they should be ready to assume positions as map readers themselves.

I start chapter 2 with a reminder of Hemingway's dichotomous concept of good and bad places already established through our initial discussion. Students can see this idea continued as Frederic Henry contemplates destinations for an army leave. The priest offers his mountain town of Abruzzi, saying that there the young soldier can enjoy both solitude and acceptance "like a son" of the priest's family. Instead, Frederic chooses Milan, Florence, Rome, Naples, and the cities' cafés, bars, and whorehouses. We examine Frederic's response to his choice in the following paragraph:

> *I had wanted to go to Abruzzi. I had gone to no place* where the roads were
> frozen and hard as iron, where it was clear cold and dry and the snow was
> dry and powdery and hare-tracks in the snow and the peasants took off
> their hats and called you Lord and there was good hunting. *I had gone to no
> such place* but to the smoke of cafes and nights when the room whirled and
> you needed to look at the wall to make it stop, nights in bed, drunk, when
> you know that was all there was, and the strange excitement of waking and
> not knowing who it was with you, and the world all unreal in the dark and
> so exciting that you must resume again unknowing and not caring in the
> night, sure that this was all and all and all and not caring. Suddenly to care
> very much. (13; emphasis added)

Though the young soldier's disgust seems clear, some students will miss it
and suggest that he feels pleasure. I lead them to an examination of the next
page, where the cities' magnetism, though having immediate gratification, is
not what calms his soul. Frederic acknowledges the priest's wise advice, saying, "He had always known what I did not know and what, when I learned it,
I was always able to forget. But I did not know that then, although I learned
it later" (14). What I want students to make note of here is how Hemingway
expresses, and will again and again through his characters, the necessity of order, cleanliness, security, and the light certain places provide, as well as how
those qualities offer a healing balm for his protagonists' troubled souls. Seeking out these good places and avoiding those that are not become essential for
Hemingway characters' efforts toward survival in their chaotic modern world.
As mentioned earlier, students can continue throughout the novel to point to
contrasts between realms of sanctuary and places of danger and how these affect the characters' lives.[6]

Examination of Catherine and Frederic's relationship provides another characteristic trait closely associated with the "Home" and "Not-Home" concept you
will want to point out in Hemingway's writing. His central characters live in a
world of "them" versus "us," where the insiders might be called initiates. The
females in this category generally bear emotional scars, and Catherine Barkley
shares a sisterhood in that respect with Brett Ashley of *The Sun Also Rises* and
Maria of *For Whom the Bell Tolls,* who have also lost loved ones to war's violence and must put themselves back together after such traumatic experiences.
Similarly, Hemingway's male victims carry both psychological and physical
manifestations of their injuries. Frederic Henry belongs to the fraternity of
wounded soldiers like Nick Adams of *In Our Time* and Jake Barnes of *The Sun
Also Rises,* whose external scars indicate the deeper emotional wounds they

have suffered. Frederic and Catherine represent just such damaged goods, and like other Hemingway protagonists, they rely upon the protective cocoon of good places and their relationship with each other to provide sanctuary from the world outside. I have students emphasize throughout the novel where that concept of the exclusive "us" exists as a shield against those who are dangerous outsiders threatening the safety of the inner sanctum.

Debunking the view that Hemingway provides no strong, positive female figures has been one area of active criticism in the past decade or two in conjunction with the feminist movement's revisionist examination of "dead-white-male" texts and their rebuttal of traditional white-male critique. Sandra Whipple Spanier believes that "Catherine Barkley not only is a strong and fully realized character, she is the one character in the novel who exemplifies in the widest range the controls of honor and courage, the 'grace under pressure' that have come to be known as the 'Hemingway code.'"[7] Many contemporary critics strongly support this argument, though the old mind-set persists, and less-informed readers still cling to their sense that the author celebrates the male realm and that female intrusion is generally antithetical to male autonomy, if not deadly. Moving away from such polarized gender divisions, students can find evidence to place Catherine in a position of strength even surpassing those qualities found in Frederic Henry. Women in the class usually revel in this view, so oppositional to the male-dominated Hemingway studies with which they are more likely familiar, and these students are happy to seek illustration and support for such a conclusion in passages where Catherine guides Frederic toward calmness, acceptance, understanding, and even philosophical epiphany. If they see her only as the typical Hemingway "dream girl" without any backbone of her own, I point out how she is also an initiate living in war's brutal aftermath, how she can willingly create her own momentary sense of reality blocking out a more complicated and devastating existence, and how she guides Frederic to do the same. In dying, Catherine eases Frederic's pain by declaring, "Don't worry darling. I'm not a bit afraid. It's just a dirty trick" (331). Her stoicism models the hero's ability to comport himself with grace in the face of ultimate powerlessness, thus gaining the only ascendancy he can generate. Frederic must go on living alone with his existential angst and the absurdity of life, but through Catherine's example he now has the chance to absorb the lesson—that dignity in the endeavor is all one can ultimately claim as victory. Students who have been reluctant to accept Catherine as the stronger figure can usually at least concede this.[8]

One of the essential themes I want a class to glean from its study of *A Farewell to Arms* is Hemingway's dissatisfaction with the old romantic notions of battle. An excellent lead-in for this would be to read and discuss the tone of Rupert Brooke's 1915 poem, "The Soldier":

> If I should die, think only this of me:
>     That there's some corner of a foreign field
> That is forever England. There shall be
>     In that rich earth a richer dust concealed;
> A dust whom England bore, shaped, made aware,
>     Gave, once, her flowers to love, her ways to roam,
> A body of England's, breathing English air,
>     Washed by the rivers, blest by suns of home.
>
> And think, this heart, all evil shed away,
>     A pulse in the eternal mind, no less
> Gives somewhere back the thoughts by England given,
> Her sights and sounds; dreams happy as her day;
>     And laughter, learnt of friends; and gentleness,
>     In hearts at peace, under an English heaven. (Brooke 74)

The poem's emphasis is clearly upon the honor given to the fallen, and as a group we discuss that stance as typical of pre–World War I patriotic idealism. Brooke, like so many of the men of his generation, supported the venerated concept of honor achieved through battle. Dying onboard ship heading for Gallipoli, one of the most horrific British engagements in the war, he did not live to experience personal involvement. Had he been part of this campaign and survived it, as many did not, there seems little doubt his views would have been dramatically altered. You can powerfully demonstrate reasons for this radical shift by showing the BBC film *All the King's Men*, which chronicles the battle of Gallipoli and its devastating aftermath.[9] If you are unable to use the film, its post-narration provides a strong sense of the causes for the emotional shift:

> Young men of the British ruling class flung themselves into the First World War with patriotic fervor and an eagerness to prove themselves noble in combat. . . . This was a generation of bright young men who saw the war as something in which death itself would be heroic. Many were handsome, intellectual, athletic, ambitious. . . . Colossal blunders were frequent in World War I, and they destroyed a big part of the generation of 1914. The poets who survived sang songs far different from the heroic stanzas of Rupert Brooke.

Siegfried Sassoon could now write with undisguised contempt for those who believe in the nobility of war:

You smug-faced crowds with kindling eye,
Who cheer when soldier lads march by,
Sneak home and pray you'll never know
The hell where youth and laughter go.[10]

I also like to add to this the final stanza of Wilfred Owen's poem "Dulce Et Decorum Est," circa 1917:

If in some smothering dreams you too could pace
Behind the wagon that we flung him in,
And watch the white eyes writhing in his face,
His hanging face, like a devil's sick of sin;
If you could hear, at every jolt, the blood
Come gargling from the froth-corrupted lungs,
Obscene as cancer, bitter as the cud
Of vile, incurable sores on innocent tongues,—
My friend, you would not tell with such high zest
To children ardent for some desperate glory,
The old Lie: *Dulce et decorum est*
*Pro patria mori.* (Sweet and fitting it is to die for your fatherland.) (Owen 541)

This poem's tone clearly establishes the dramatic philosophical shift the war's horrific legacy created. Having experienced battle trauma firsthand as Owen, Sassoon, and other poets had, Hemingway identified with this attitude and became one of the postwar literati working to dismantle what they saw as the past's dangerous romantic rhetoric.

This purpose is especially evident in one of the book's most famous passages, where Frederic rejects the patriotic language employed by those seeking to drag in a fresh crop of soldiers to fuel the war machine. He muses:

I was always embarrassed by the words *sacred, glorious,* and *sacrifice* and the *expression in vain.* We had heard them, sometimes standing in the rain almost out of earshot, so that only the shouted words came through, and had read them, on proclamations that were slapped up by billposters over other proclamations, now for a long time, and *I had seen nothing sacred,* and the *things that were glorious had no glory* and the *sacrifices were like the*

> *stockyards* at Chicago if nothing was done with the meat except to bury it. There were many words that you could not stand to hear and finally only the names of places had dignity. . . . *Abstract words such as glory, honor, courage, or hallow were obscene* beside the concrete names of villages, the numbers of roads, the names of rivers, the numbers of regiments and dates. (184–85; emphasis added)

Students should easily be able to interpret this passage, like the ones from Sassoon's and Owen's poems, as oppositional to those representing earlier romanticized views of war. I then ask them to find other passages in the novel that convey like sentiments. This makes an excellent collaborative project for groups of four to five students. I find that a hunt for specific items often becomes a quest drawing in competitive natures, and students usually actively participate in locating antiromantic quotations to which I would otherwise lead them. Specifically, they should find Catherine's preconceived view of her lover's death when she reveals, "I remember having a silly idea he might come to the hospital where I was. With a sabre cut, I suppose, and a bandage around his head. Or shot through the shoulder. Something picturesque," as opposed to the reality that instead he is blown "all to bits" (20). They should also point to Frederic's wounding, not in some heroic feat, but, as he sardonically reports, "while we were eating cheese" (63). Further, I would draw their attention, if they don't see it on their own, to Frederic's near-death experience forcibly moving him into the realm of initiates. This, students should be brought to see, signals the moment where his philosophical attitude takes a dramatic shift. Both he and Catherine now view the war as a propaganda trap to draw young men into sacrificing themselves for abstract values. Discussion of the title's significance, as well as a play on words about which "arms" (human arms or war armaments) are surrendered, is appropriate and effective here also, and students will come up with many other passages to substantiate this theme's validity.

One unsurprising outcome of romantic disillusionment is a loss of religious faith, seemingly no longer valid in a war-torn modern landscape. This, too, is a concept students can trace through *A Farewell to Arms.* I emphasize Hemingway's use of momentary pleasure-seeking activities as substitutes for traditional worship experiences. Drink, sex, sport, and communion with nature become just such replacements, and students can point to many occurrences supporting this conclusion. More importantly, Hemingway uses physical and spiritual union between man and woman as the strongest chance for fleeting joy in this temporal world. True solace from the actual or psychological war can come only from a joining of kindred souls. Catherine and Frederic create this bond through their burgeoning relationship and their initial emotional liberation from the war. Later Frederic converses with Count Greffi about the concept of love as replacement for religious foundations. The count emphasizes this world as the only known certainty and believes that we must extract the most joy we can from it. He leads Frederic through a question-and-response conversation based on his existential view of life's value:

> C. G. "What do you value most?"
> F. "Someone I love."
> C. G. "With me it is the same. That is not wisdom. Do you value life?"
> F. "Yes."
> C. G. "So do I. Because it is all I have."

Count Greffi continues a few lines later:

> C. G. "Perhaps I have outlived my religious feeling."
> F. "My own comes only at night."
> C. G. "Then too you are in love. Do not forget that is a religious feeling."
> F. "You believe so?"
> C. G. "Of course." (262–63)

This passage substantiates the importance of love's momentary ability to stave off loneliness, godlessness, and death. Hemingway's central characters will not find lasting happiness in a relationship with another, but they nevertheless seek that momentary escape.

We can also deduce further meaning from the conversation. The dialogue underscores Hemingway's support of existentialism and its emphasis upon this life, not any possible realm beyond death. Finally, we have a good example of his use of rapid-fire conversational style, where distinction between speakers becomes blurred by lack of authorial interjection, and the exchange of ideas comes at almost breakneck speed for the characters and the reader. Students will no doubt have already noticed this technique, and you can point to how Hemingway uses such banter as the iceberg's exposed tip while hinting at the crucial buried philosophical and thematic underbelly remaining unspoken but ominously present.

Having established the idea of love as an antidote to modern malaise, you should now stress Hemingway's emphasis on its transitory nature. I point out his explanation in *Death in the Afternoon*: "If two people love each other there can be no happy end to it" (122). In the introduction to a 1948 edition of *A Farewell to Arms* he further adds, "I believed that life was a tragedy and knew it could only have one end" (xi–xii). As the author predicts, Frederic and Catherine's safety is ultimately elusive, and no examination of Hemingway or this novel could avoid one of its most fatalistic statements:

> If people bring so much courage to this world *the world has to kill them to break them,* so of course *it kills them. The world breaks every one* and afterward many are strong *at the broken places.* But *those that will not break it kills. It kills* the very good and the very gentle and the very brave *impartially.* If you are none of these you can be sure *it will kill you too* but there will be no special hurry. (249; emphasis added)

Herein lies the crux of Hemingway's "one man alone against the world" philosophy. I like to pair this quotation with the one coming very near the end, just before Catherine's death when Frederic wrestles for the last time to grasp what she already knows, that death is "just a dirty trick," one they cannot overcome except through their private display of personal courage. I have students discuss the passage occurring moments after the child's stillbirth and just before Catherine's death. Here Frederic poses the novel's most fatalistic statement: "Now Catherine would *die. That was what you did. You died.* You did not know what it was about. You never had time to learn. They threw you in and told you the rules and the first time they caught you off base *they killed you.* Or *they killed you gratuitously* like Aymo. Or gave you the syphilis like Rinaldi. But *they killed you* in the end. You could count on that. Stay around and *they would kill you*" (327; emphasis added). The next paragraph's image, Frederic's memory of putting into the fire a log swarming with ants and watching them meet the doom he has imposed, becomes the novel's metaphor for life's fatalistic stranglehold and an important point of class discussion concerning existentialism. Frederic's experience thinking it would be "a splendid chance to be a messiah and lift the log off the fire" (328), but final realization that he is no savior, nor does he expect one to rescue him, can begin to demonstrate Hemingway's nihilistic view: all life and all love stories involve the ability to stave off death only momentarily. Students will be troubled by this pessimistic philosophy, but I emphasize Hemingway's chief focus. His hero in training must act with dignity, and if he can do so knowing that life will inevitably kill him, then he has performed with the "grace under pressure" that all Hemingway heroes seek.

Hemingway leaves his protagonist with the inevitable loss necessarily wrought upon humanity. This character has reached at least one plateau of understanding, however, and the keenness with which he comes to treasure moments lived intensely makes the loss ever more poignant. I would suggest that Frederic Henry is still a very young man at novel's end, and as such I encourage students to recognize him as an exemplar of early Hemingway protagonists. These men feel bowed down by the loss of loved ones and belief systems, and a lack of stability. They are searching for models to help them cope and to form strategies for doing just that. If students go on to read works like *For Whom the Bell Tolls* or *The Old Man and the Sea,* they will encounter protagonists still searching but able to find in their intimate connection with another human being some profound moments of love's transcendent power. While connection to others is still transitory and life still ends in death, these later novels demonstrate Hemingway's more hopeful if perhaps less realistic stance as a maturing author.

## THE DESTINATION

Ernest Hemingway's name is synonymous with American literature and significant contributions to the modern canon's themes and style. As one of his most critically acclaimed texts, *A Farewell to Arms* rests squarely in the author's philosophical and artistic context but also extends to the historical milieu of the tumultuous early twentieth century. The novel provides a great reading experience—both accessible and appropriate—for the high school and early college populations and also gives students a substantial introduction to the traditional Hemingway they will most likely encounter at this level. In *A Farewell to Arms* Hemingway embeds all the essential qualities that have made him famous as a stylist, an artistic theorist, and a modernist in his own right. An ability to understand these characteristics makes movement to other Hemingway works a logical step but also paves the way for easier comprehension of his contemporaries' artistic and thematic aesthetics. Taking up the metaphor of the road map and the journey, teachers can use this war novel simply as an excursion into the single text or more broadly as a starting point to a complete voyage through Hemingway and the modern literary landscape. Finally and most significantly, the novel creates a space for itself as a timeless universal piece transcending the writer and the time frame to represent literature at its best.

## NOTES

1. Biographer Kenneth Lynn reports, "Wellington had compelled him to write in short sentences, to stay away from slang phrases that had lost their freshness, and to cultivate a plainness of expression all but devoid of adjectives" (68).

2. I might even suggest having students read the whole story because you can then use it as a reference point to several other important Hemingway elements more easily identified there first. I will point to these later in this chapter.

3. Other general sources include Charles Oliver's *Ernest Hemingway A to Z;* Arthur Waldhorn's *A Reader's Guide to Ernest Hemingway;* and, on a more advanced level, Scott Donaldson's *The Cambridge Companion to Ernest Hemingway.*

4. This essay is printed in both *Hemingway: The Writer as Artist* and *Twentieth Century Interpretations of* A Farewell to Arms. The latter is a useful source for teaching *A Farewell to Arms* because it provides a compilation of the best early Hemingway critics. The pieces are short and easily digestible and offer a good range of traditional issues and analysis for the novel. The thinking is not cutting edge but is accessible to and appropriate for young readers and for instructors not deeply versed in more contemporary literary criticism. Countless other articles and books are dedicated to understanding Hemingway's craft. Among them are Charles Fenton's *The Apprenticeship of Ernest Hemingway: The Early Years,* Joseph DeFalco's *The Hero in Hemingway's Short Stories,* Jackson Benson's *Hemingway: The Writer's Art of Self-Defense,* Sheldon Grebstein's *Hemingway's Craft,* and Susan Beegel's *Hemingway's Craft of Omission.*

5. This description, plus further explanation of the concept, comes from Harmon and Holman's *A Handbook to Literature* (327). The reference book is a valuable source for literary terminology.

6. "A Clean, Well-Lighted Place" demonstrates these concepts and works well as a subsidiary piece to emphasize many of Hemingway's standard themes.

7. Both this article, "Catherine Barkley and the Hemingway Code," and a second one also by Spanier, "Hemingway's Unknown Soldier: Catherine Barkley, the Critics, and the Great War," make an excellent argument for Catherine as the code hero in *A Farewell to Arms.*

8. If you teach this novel at the high school level, you would probably not offer additional critical reading for your students. If this more feminist approach to Hemingway analysis interests you, Broer and Holland's *Hemingway and Women: Female Critics and the Female Voice* is an excellent source for expounding such analysis, though not exclusively for this novel.

9. This works well as an activity you can do after the unit introduction and while you are giving students time to begin the reading, or you can use it in conjunction with discussion of Frederic's desertion. The film portrays British troops initially eager to prove their manhood in battle, and it follows these soldiers' horrific fate as well as the ramifications for those back home in England. One note of caution: there is a near-rape scene between a British soldier and a captured female enemy, and a rather graphic sexual encounter between a British woman and an ex-soldier. No nudity is shown, but the second scene in particular is perhaps inappropriate for a young audience. At the very least, they should be warned of it before viewing.

10. Battle figures suggest that 225,000 Allied troops either died, were wounded, or went missing, along with 300,000 Turkish casualties. The film calls such numbers "slaughter on an industrial scale."

## APPENDIX A: A Quick Guide to Hemingway's Technique and Theme in *A Farewell to Arms*

I. Hemingway Style
A. Journalistic approach
   1. Mechanics
      a. Short sentences
      b. Simple word choice
      c. Plainness of expression
      d. Avoidance of slang
      e. Avoidance of excessive adjectives
      f. Rapid-fire exchange of dialogue
      g. Repetition
   2. Tone
      a. Authorial detachment
      b. Characters' emotional distancing
B. Iceberg theory
   1. Surface text represents one-eighth of meaning
   2. Submerged (implied) text represents seven-eighths of meaning—reader must fill in this portion
C. Dichotomous contrasts
   1. Mountain/plain
      a. Safety/danger
      b. Escape/entrapment
   2. Good places/bad places
      a. Order/chaos
      b. Light/dark
      c. Security/danger
   3. Home/Not-Home
      a. Physical
      b. Psychological
      c. Spiritual
   4. Us/them
      a. Insider/outsider
      b. Participant/observer
   5. Initiated/uninitiated
      a. Experienced war/haven't experienced war
      b. Wounded/not wounded

D. Symbolism
    1. Reliance on standard or universal symbols for disaster and death
        a. Fall
        b. Winter
        c. Rain
    2. Objective correlative—set symbol elicits expected emotional response
        a. Mountain—homelike qualities, security
        b. Plain—entrapment and danger
        c. Rain—fear and sense of impending doom
II. Hemingway Themes
A. Naturalism
    1. Natural indifference
    2. Human insignificance
B. Humanism
    1. Sense of individual importance
    2. Desire for self-preservation
    3. Reliance on self—no expectation of divine intervention
C. Antiromanticism
    1. Dispelling precepts of war as romantic
    2. Dispelling patriotic rhetoric
D. Existentialism
    1. Loss of belief in God the Father
    2. Loss of belief in country as symbolic father
    3. Emphasis on human existence—the here and now, not life beyond death
E. Hero paradigm
    1. Code hero—models how to live in godless, chaotic world
        a. Simplistic life
        b. Nonintellectual
        c. Usually isolated from others
        d. Closer to nature
        e. Exhibits grace under pressure
    2. Code hero in training—tries to learn from code hero model
        a. Complex emotions
        b. Usually prone to thinking too much
        c. Usually social
        d. Uses nature as escape from life
        e. Seeks to develop grace under pressure

F. Anti-fatalism/nihilism
    1. Union with others
        a. Physical oneness has concrete temporal value
        b. Oneness becomes a spiritual substitute
    2. Celebration of temporal values
        a. Good food and drink
        b. Good places
        c. Good company
        d. Good activities/sport

## APPENDIX B: Syllabus for Teaching *A Farewell to Arms*

Day 1    Background Information: Discussion of Modern Period
    I. Discussion of industrialization
        A. Shifts from rural to urban
        B. Faith in modernization/science as answer to human strife
    II. Brief discussion of World War I and its devastating effects
    III. Look at T. S. Eliot's *The Waste Land* (suggested passages)

Day 2    Biographical Background (supplementary film could provide this)
    I. Personal history
    II. Career history
    Read "Soldier's Home"
    (Days 1 and 2 could be interchanged)

Day 3    Stylistic Background
    I. Journalistic training
    II. Literary progenitors (this could be left out)
    Discuss "Soldier's Home" (see chapter for details)

Day 4    Begin Novel Examination—Chapter 1
    I. Examine stylistic techniques (see chapter for examples)
        A. Language
        B. Authorial absence (lack of didacticism)
    II. Discuss tone
    III. Discuss symbolism, imagery, objective correlative
    IV. Themes

V. Discuss cues of things to come
Students should begin reading the novel and keeping track of elements you ask them to note (see suggestions in this chapter).

Day 5   Begin viewing *All the King's Men* (first thirty to forty minutes)
   I. Prewar romantic sensibility
      A. Discuss Rupert Brooke's poem
      B. Make comparisons between poem's attitude and film's opening tone and philosophy
   II. Hints at shift in war stance
If the film is not available, you can simply discuss some of these issues. You might also look to a film like *Saving Private Ryan*, which shows the horrors of war and yet still seems to cling to the more romantic view of death as honorable. Discuss contrasting representations.

Day 6   Continue Novel Examination: Book 1, Chapters 2–12
   I. Central events
      A. The wounding
      B. The developing relationship
   II. Central themes
      A. Ideas about war—antiromantic examples
      B. Religion—loss of faith; sex and alcohol as substitutions
      C. Love—sexual versus emotional

Day 7   Continue Viewing Film (next thirty to forty minutes)
   I. Discuss nonchronological modern storytelling approach
   II. Discuss emerging war experience as catalyst to philosophy

Day 8   Continue Novel Examination: Book 2, Chapters 13–24
   I. Developing relationship
      A. Them/us
      B. Sex as substitution for religion
   II. Characterizations of Catherine and Frederic

Day 9   Finish Viewing Film (last section of film)
   I. Postwar cynicism: Antiwar poetry (see examples in chapter)
      A. Siegfried Sassoon
      B. Wilfred Owens
   II. Summarize shift in attitudes about war

Day 10   Continue Novel Examination: Book 3, Chapters 25–32
  I. Language as propaganda
  II. Desertion—baptism/rebirth in river
  Exercise: Look at the examples students have been accumulating of contrasts (them/us, good/bad places), foreshadowing, recurring symbols.

Day 11   In-Class Writing Assignment: You could have students respond to the idea of desertion from the military. I would seek their response not only to Frederic's desertion but also to more current circumstances like the war in Iraq. You can ask questions like, "Are there ever circumstances where desertion is acceptable?" to get them started.

Day 12   Continue Novel Examination: Book 4, Chapters 33–37
  I. World/nature as antagonistic
  II. Sanctuary
      A. Places of escape
      B. Love as escape

Day 13   Continue Novel Examination: Book 5, Chapters 38–41
  I. Use of sensory pleasure
  II. Fatalism
  III. Grace under pressure

Day 14   Review Major Elements of the Novel Using Study Guide

## APPENDIX C: Additional Activities and Writing Assignments

1.  View a war film and write an analysis of what impression of war is offered. Does the film bolster traditional values of honor and glory, question such attitudes, or present mixed signals? Pay attention to when the film was made. What in society at the time might have contributed to the film's viewpoint?

2.  Read an additional Hemingway story and make note of the style, theme, and techniques employed. Which are similar to those used in *A Farewell to Arms?* What differences can you find, such as new themes, shifts in philosophy, or different types of characterization?

3.  Rewrite the ending of the novel to allow Catherine and the baby to live. Discuss what this change would do in terms of the overall effect. Would

it strengthen or damage the novel? What changes would it make in our sense of Hemingway? Defend your argument.

4. Many critics see Catherine as a weak character controlled by Frederic. Write a defense of her as the stronger of the two.

5. *In Love and War* (1996), starring Sandra Bullock, is a film loosely based on Ernest Hemingway's war experience, wounding, and falling in love with a nurse. Read a biographical account of these events, compare them to the events portrayed in the movie version, and then compare both to how Hemingway has fictionalized the events in *A Farewell to Arms*.

6. Contrast Stephen Crane's Henry Fleming in *The Red Badge of Courage* to Ernest Hemingway's Frederic Henry. Pay special attention to the attitudes these men exhibit at the end of the novels.

7. Assume the role of the priest, and counsel Frederic Henry.

8. Choose a favorite passage in the text. Discuss its implications, as you believe Hemingway meant them thematically, and add to that your own feelings and response. (It works well to ask this of the entire class. Have them choose at least three passages, in case someone else chooses theirs. The variety of quotes you will get is always surprising, and they always hit the central ones you would want to emphasize as well.)

9. Write a transcript of Frederic Henry's trial for desertion.

10. Defend this novel as one of the must-reads for high school students. Be sure to give strong, clear arguments to support your case.

# *A Farewell to Arms,* World War I, and "the stockyards at Chicago"

*Kim Moreland*

FROM A pedagogical perspective, *A Farewell to Arms* is an incredibly elastic text that works well in a variety of teaching contexts. I have taught it successfully, for example, in a course on the twentieth-century American novel, two major authors courses (one focusing on Hemingway and F. Scott Fitzgerald, and the other focusing on Hemingway and Martha Gellhorn), and a graduate seminar on literature of World War I—all at George Washington University, a private university located in Washington, D.C., where students typically matriculate immediately after graduating from high school, with average SAT scores of 1975 for admitted freshmen (2006). I have also taught it in a course focusing exclusively on Hemingway at the Campus on the Mall, the Smithsonian Institute's educational outreach program, the audience of which is comprised in my experience not of traditional college students but typically of young adults who work on Capitol Hill, middle-aged attorneys and government workers, high school English teachers, and retired people—all attending the not-for-credit sessions because of personal interest in the subject matter.

Each of these contexts invites a somewhat different approach to the novel. In the twentieth-century American novel course, *A Farewell to Arms* serves as a wonderful example of literary modernism. In the Hemingway and Fitzgerald course, it provides a way to explore the different manners in which these two writers address World War I, the defining event of their generation, in their fiction—Hemingway directly (using both autobiographical material and historical research), and Fitzgerald (who didn't "get over") indirectly, as in the odd middle section of *This Side of Paradise* (composed almost exclusively in epistolary form with interpolated poems), and in the battlefield tour that Dick Diver leads for his friends in *Tender Is the Night* (wherein World War I becomes the objective correlative for the Divers' marriage). In the Hemingway and Gellhorn course, it provides a way to explore the different styles of these two writers in their war fiction (Hemingway largely eschewing interiority, while Gellhorn employs it in a tour-de-force fashion) and their war correspondence; it also offers an opportunity to discuss the ways in which the respective male and female protagonists—Frederic Henry and Catherine Barkley in *Farewell*, and Jacob Levy, Colonel John Smithers, Kathe Limpert, and Dorothy Brock in *Point of No Return*—respond to the different pressures of their different wars, World War I and World War II, respectively. In the World War I course, it offers a definitive American perspective (along with John Dos Passos's *Three Soldiers* and his *Nineteen Nineteen,* which is the middle volume of his trilogy *U.S.A.*) that is compared to the perspectives provided in works by English writers (like Robert Graves in *Goodbye to All That* and Siegfried Sassoon in *Memoirs of an Infantry Officer,* which is the middle volume of his trilogy *Memoirs of George Sherston*) and German writers (notably Erich Maria Remarque in *All Quiet on the Western Front*). And in the Hemingway course, it offers an opportunity to compare Hemingway's early, middle, and late works, including those that were posthumously published, and thereby to discover both continuities and changes in his perspective, style, and subject matter.

One could also teach *Farewell* in a course focusing on narrative, using it as an example of a retrospective narrative wherein the distance between the actions narrated and the narrator's present time is significant; here, questions about the oft-noted idealized portrait of Catherine might be analyzed with reference to the passage of time between her tragic death and Frederic's recounting of their love story. The novel could, more narrowly, be taught in a course on first-person narratives, wherein questions of Frederic's narrative reliability would also loom large, or even in a course on autobiographical fiction (alongside novels like D. H. Lawrence's *Sons and Lovers,* Fitzgerald's *This Side of Paradise,* James Joyce's *Portrait of the Artist as a Young Man,* and Sylvia Plath's *The Bell Jar*) in which the vexed relationship of history (personal as well as cultural in the case of autobiographical novels) and fiction would be explored.

No matter the course, however, an issue that inevitably must be addressed is that of war as an arena for male self-realization—that is, as the situation in which man realizes himself, indeed makes himself real *as* a man by means of a defining male experience. This subject offers rich opportunities for exploration and discussion. Among many questions that it raises are the following, which may involve students in historical research as well as in theoretical approaches such as cultural studies and gender studies: To what degree does modern technological war, as represented by World War I, inhibit the possibilities of male self-realization? Does technology make individual heroic action superfluous, even absurd? Does such a war justify desertion? Is all technological war meaningless, or is World War I particularly so, and if so, why? Can man realize himself in love as well as—or instead of—in war?

And what of the changing role of women in war? Women, here in the role of nurses and VADs (members of the Voluntary Aid Detachment), move increasingly close to the front, as in the early scenes of *A Farewell to Arms,* when Frederic first meets Catherine at the British hospital in Gorizia, Italy, where the women must be "on very special behavior," not leaving the hospital grounds since "the Italians didn't want women so near the front" (25). Does the presence of women at war threaten the possibility of war as a defining *male* experience? If war has ceased to be a meaningful locus for male self-realization, then what other arenas remain?

In this chapter, I will explore the ways in which these questions play out in the context of the classroom, offering one possible point of entry into the novel and explaining the ways in which it enables a pedagogically effective means of discussion and discovery. The passage that I have chosen as my point of entry is the following:

> I was always embarrassed by the words sacred, glorious, and sacrifice and the expression in vain. We had heard them, sometimes standing in the rain almost out of earshot, so that only the shouted words came through, and had read them, on proclamations that were slapped up by billposters over other proclamations, now for a long time, and I had seen nothing sacred, and the things that were glorious had no glory and the sacrifices were like the stockyards at Chicago if nothing was done with the meat except to bury it. There were many words that you could not stand to hear and finally only the names of places had dignity. (184–85)

Among the most famous lines in Hemingway's *A Farewell to Arms,* this passage is a required stop—along with Frederic Henry's declaration of "a separate peace" (243)—in the teaching of the novel. But in the classroom this passage can be far more than a stop, instead offering a point of entry into the major questions of the novel if the passage is sufficiently explored and unpacked. And the beauty of this approach is that students typically can make important discoveries themselves in a guided class discussion of this passage.

Rather than beginning the discussion with questions about the abstract meaning of the passage, an approach, after all, that Frederic abjures in the passage itself, I instead ask the students what they can tell me about stockyards in order to establish their basic function. I then ask more specifically about "the stockyards at Chicago." Here, a bit of information about Hemingway's early life is relevant, and it is readily available in Michael Reynolds's highly readable *The Young Hemingway* (the first volume in his definitive five-volume biography). I note that Hemingway grew up in Oak Park, a suburb of Chicago, and that he could ride the commuter train into Chicago for a nickel. I mention his frequent visits to the city, initially with his father to the Museum of Natural Science and with his mother to the Chicago Art Institute and the opera. As he grew older, he made visits with his sister Marcelline and also alone. After his return from World War I, he lived in 1921 with friends in Chicago for about a year, writing copy and helping to edit the weekly trade journal *Co-operative Commonwealth*. This brief biographical information establishes for the students Hemingway's deep familiarity with Chicago.

Given Frederic's insistence on "the concrete names of villages" (185), it becomes clear that "the stockyards *at Chicago*" (emphasis added) must have a particular significance. I cite the first line of Carl Sandburg's famous 1914 poem "Chicago"—"Hog Butcher for the World"—and ask them what they know about the meatpacking industry in Chicago. Typically several students have either read or know about Upton Sinclair's 1906 novel and publishing phenomenon *The Jungle*, which is set in Chicago, and they are able to speak about Sinclair's horrifying portrait—the filthy conditions of the stockyards, the animals' suffering during the messy and chaotic slaughter, the efficient and dangerous technology, the anonymity occasioned by the application of mass production processes, the dangers to employees occasioned by animals and machinery alike, the risk to the American public who consumed the tainted meat. If students are not aware of Sinclair's portrait, then a brief lecture provides the necessary information. I then speak a bit about Sinclair's career as a muckraking journalist and about the regulations passed governing the meatpacking industry, new laws occasioned by public outrage at the conditions represented in Sinclair's novel—outrage of which Hemingway would certainly have known, given his experience of Chicago and in journalism. I then cite the following passage from *The Jungle*:

> That day they had killed about four thousand cattle, and these cattle had come in freight trains from far states, and some of them had got hurt. There were some with broken legs, and some with gored sides; there were some that had died, from what cause no one could say; and they were all to be disposed of, here in darkness and silence. "Downers," the men called them; and the packing house had a special elevator upon which they were raised to the killing beds, where the gang proceeded to handle them. . . . It took a

couple of hours to get them out of the way, and in the end Jurgis saw them go into the chilling rooms with the rest of the meat, being carefully scattered here and there so that they could not be identified. When he came home that night he was in a very somber mood. (67)

While this discussion and the citation of the passage above may seem like a rather long detour from Hemingway's own novel, I immediately return the students to it, still by way of the stockyards, asking about the significance of Frederic's hypothetical conclusion, "if nothing was done with the meat except to bury it." Having explored the human and animal cost already, the students readily describe the sense of waste evoked by these lines, the sense of useless-ness and even absurdity of the whole enterprise. This bit of cultural history of course has a contemporary significance for students, given the outbreaks in the past decades of foot-and-mouth disease and mad cow disease (Sinclair's reference to downer cows is particularly resonant), and the still more recent outbreaks of bird flu—all of which have resulted in the mass destruction of animals in attempts to contain the diseases. Often, students will describe the visceral impact of the powerful televised images of huge piles of burning ani-mal carcasses, the flames fed by gasoline or other accelerants.

Having unpacked the various connotations of this resonant phrase, we return to the novel, where we discover that Frederic presents the long passage as an objective correlative for World War I, a relationship that I emphasize visually by depicting it on the blackboard, as follows:

World War I = Stockyards at Chicago

The novel itself presents a horrific vision of that particularly horrific war—one whose cause was opaque, whose conduct was governed largely by the imper-sonal forces of technology adapted to military purposes, and whose conclusion was a function of attrition rather than victory in glorious battle. Catherine Bark-ley comments in an early conversation with Frederic that she had imagined her now-dead fiancé with a "picturesque" wound, "a sabre cut, I suppose," but that instead "they blew him all to bits" (20)—an economical acknowledgment that this war was different from wars of the past, indeed different from the war that had been expected in 1914. Teachers interested in gaining background on World War I would benefit from David Fromkin's recent *Europe's Last Summer: Who Started the Great War in 1914?* which provides a highly detailed explora-tion of the still murky causes of World War I and would prove useful for an overview of the war's complicated origins, and Paul Fussell's classic *The Great*

*War and Modern Memory,* which offers a brilliant and eloquent exploration of the literary meanings and uses of this most literary war.

Given the contrast that Catherine draws between her fiancé's actual death and the sabre cut she had expected, I ask the students if Frederic might be implying the second term of a contrast when he describes World War I as "like the stockyards at Chicago if nothing was done with the meat except to bury it." What is the implied second term, the absence of which exerts a palpable pressure in this critical passage? What had Frederic expected of this war, in contrast to his felt experience? If his description is taken with utmost seriousness, then what would its opposite be? Is there any circumstance where an animal is killed and the death is imbued with powerful meaning? Where neither the animal nor the man is anonymous? Where individual valor and skill rather than technology determine the outcome? Where ritual and ceremony govern the proceedings, which are enacted by an artist of sorts before an appreciative audience rather than revealed by a muckraking journalist to a horrified public? Prompted by such questions, the students are quickly able to identify the bullfight as the absent term, if for no other reason than their knowledge of Hemingway's cult of personality, where the bullfight is inevitably part of the nexus of terms used to describe him.

At this point, I provide students with some information about the significance of the bullfight for Hemingway, with references to *The Sun Also Rises* (which some of them may have read) and *Death in the Afternoon* (which none is likely to have read). I note Hemingway's insistence that the bullfight is not a sport but a tragedy—that is, an ancient drama whose significance is derived from ceremony and ritual, resulting in catharsis for the audience. I cite these lines from *Death in the Afternoon:* "The aficionado, or lover of the bullfight, may be said, broadly, then, to be one who has this sense of the tragedy and ritual of the fight so that the minor aspects are not important except as they relate to the whole" (9).

The absent second term thus completes the subtextual binary opposition, setting the "stockyards at Chicago" in contrast to the bullfight. Here I find it useful to point out that structuralist theory demonstrated the importance of the binary opposition as a structural device in texts, while deconstructionist theory later demonstrated that the seemingly objective equivalence of a binary opposition is always already a hierarchy—that one need only rotate the binary opposition 180 degrees to see that one term is always inferior, and the other superior. The stockyards are evidently the inferior term, and the implied bullfight the superior term. I visually emphasize this relationship by graphically representing it on the blackboard, as follows:

(Implied) Bullfight

↓

World War I = Stockyards at Chicago

Once students actually see the diagram of the equivalent metaphorical relationship between World War I and the stockyards on the one hand, and the hierarchical metaphorical opposition between the stockyards and the implied bullfight on the other hand, they quickly recognize that a term is missing, since if the stockyards are the objective correlative for World War I, then the implied bullfight must also have an objective correlative, itself perhaps implied, which will serve as a superior term in relation to World War I.

At this point, I return the students' attention to the novel's title, noting that Robert Graves wrote a memoir describing his experiences in World War I entitled *Goodbye to All That,* published in 1929, as was *A Farewell to Arms.* I point out that the titles of Graves's memoir and Hemingway's novel are denotatively similar but connotatively quite different, and I ask them to describe this connotative difference. They are quick to point out that Graves's title has a brusque and informal quality, which they often translate as "Good Riddance," whereas Hemingway's title has a formal, stately, and even nostalgic quality, that it suggests the mourning of a loss. When I ask what "Arms" the title refers to, they quickly recognize Hemingway's pun. But if the elegiac "Farewell" refers appropriately to Frederic's loss of Catherine, I ask, does it not seem inappropriate to his rejection of World War I—indeed, his desertion, only a short while after he himself has shot a soldier under his command for desertion? What loss is Frederic here mourning?

At this point, I provide the students with some information about Hemingway's careful selection of titles for his novels, and I tell them about his source for this title, George Peele's 1590 poem "A Farewell to Arms" (detailed information about which is available in Bernard Oldsey's *Hemingway's Hidden Craft: The Writing of* A Farewell to Arms [10–34] and Michael Reynolds's *Hemingway's First War: The Making of* A Farewell to Arms). In this dramatic monologue, Sir Henry Lee describes his career as the queen's champion, wherein he has served her well in fighting at tournaments, and now asks that he be allowed to serve her as a poet because of his advancing age. I note that this knight has been successful in the martial arena governed by the rules of chivalry, and that he asks to turn now to the poetic arena governed by courtly love so that he may continue to serve her with honor as a courtly troubadour of sorts, if no longer as a chivalric knight. Noting the similarity in their names, I ask what characteristics Sir Henry and Lieutenant Henry share. Students are quick to point out that Frederic, like Sir Henry Lee, changes his identity from fighter to lover, and they are equally quick to point out that Frederic never really had a chance to fight honorably because the rules of chivalry were rendered irrelevant in World War I.

At this point, I tell the students that a manuscript version of the novel had included an exception to the "obscene" use of "abstract words such as glory, honor, courage, or hallow" (185)—"The only thing glorious were the cavalry riding with lances" (qtd. in Smith 34)—but that Hemingway had lined out this sentence in manuscript. I tell the students that cavalry with lances served in World War I but proved outmoded—even anachronistic—in the face of the new technologies adapted for military purposes. I then cite a passage from a 1932 letter that Hemingway wrote to Arnold Gingrich: "To Arms should clang more than the book deserves—that title could handle a book with more and better war in it" (*Selected Letters* 378). Noting Hemingway's reference in the letter to the "clang[ing]" sound of sword and shield absent from the novel, I ask the students why Hemingway chose to omit the sentence about the "glorious . . . cavalry riding with lances" from the famous passage. This question leads us to the absent objective correlative for the bullfight, which together exist in opposition to the related pair that we have already discovered, World War I and the stockyards at Chicago. The bullfight is reminiscent of the knightly tournament, where knights fighting with swords and shields on horseback become an iconic image. Both the bullfight and the knightly tournament are spectacles carried out in arenas, both are dependent on individual prowess, and both are governed by strict codes. Knightly combat, governed by the rules of chivalry, is the absent objective correlative for the absent bullfight, both existing in binary opposition to World War I and the stockyards, respectively. And just as the bullfight is the superior term to the inferior stockyards, so too is chivalric combat the superior term to the inferior World War I, a relationship emphasized visually by the completion of the diagram, as follows:

(Implied) Chivalric Combat = (Implied) Bullfight
$$\downarrow \qquad\qquad\qquad \downarrow$$
World War I = Stockyards at Chicago

Reminding students of Catherine's description of her fiancé's imagined and now resonant "sabre cut" and her assertion that instead "they blew him all to bits," I cite a passage from a letter that Hemingway wrote to his parents after his own wounding by a trench mortar: "When there is a direct hit your pals get spattered all over you. Spattered is literal. . . . Well I can now hold up my hand and say I've been shelled by high explosive, shrapnel and gas. Shot at by trench mortars, snipers and machine guns. And as an added attraction an aeroplane machine gunning the lines. I've never had a hand grenade thrown at me, but a rifle grenade struck rather close" (qtd. in Villard and Nagel 176). After reading this passage, I ask students to develop a list of the differences between chivalric combat and World War I. They quickly note such elements as the following: knights rode into battle on horseback, while the cavalry was ineffective in World War I; the sword gave way to the machine gun; battles largely gave way to trench warfare; the individual knight gave way to anonymous troops; individual prowess gave way to technology; individual valor gave way to the perceived meaninglessness of heroism ("Don't be a bloody hero," Frederic is told after his wounding [58]); a clear distinction between friend and foe gave way to mass confusion (Aymo, an Italian soldier under Frederic's command, is killed by friendly fire from the Italian rear guard during the retreat from Caporetto, and Frederic later escapes death at the hands of the Italian battle police only by desertion when he throws himself into the Tagliamento River). I suggest that the contrasts between chivalric combat and World War I may offer a way to understand Frederic Henry's ultimate disapproval of a war he went to willingly, resulting in his decision to make "a separate peace." Frederic may reject World War I because it is not chivalric combat—in effect, because it is not a bullfight but instead the stockyards at Chicago.

Here we return to one of the major questions about *A Farewell to Arms*. Is it an antiwar novel, a pacifist novel, as suggested by Hemingway's expressed concern that his novel would be scooped by Erich Maria Remarque's antiwar novel *All Quiet on the Western Front* (also published in 1929), and as represented in the editorial blurb included in the serialized edition published in *Scribner's Magazine*: "Such a picture of war as would discourage either victors or the conquered from that terrible solution of international troubles" (qtd. in Oldsey 7)? Or is it something else? Something perhaps peculiarly American (here abetted by America's late entry into a war not fought on American soil)? Is it related to that most American yearning, the desire to return to a perfect past—in this case not to the New Jerusalem of the Puritan colonists nor to the Eden of the Old Testament, but to a seemingly perfect era of war, an idealized warfare found only to a degree in Villehardouin and DeJoinville's historical *Chronicles of Crusaders* (a book that Hemingway was reading "while drafting and redrafting the closing pages of *A Farewell to Arms*," according to Michael Reynolds [*Reading* 26], and wherein are recorded, for example, the enormous number of deaths by dysentery during the Crusades)? Such idealized warfare is found fully developed, however, in the English and French romances whose characters notably included Sir Launcelot and King Arthur (whose legendary exploits Hemingway knew from having read Tennyson's *Idylls of the King* in high school) and Roland (the hero of *La Chanson de Roland,* the climax of which occurs at the pass of Roncevaux where Roland dies in a successful holding action against the Saracens that enables Charlemagne and his army to escape, a site on which a monastery is built and that Jake Barnes visits in Hemingway's 1926 novel *The Sun Also Rises,* and an event that Hemingway had discussed at length in 1924 with his World War I friend Eric "Chink" Dorman Smith [see Reynolds, *Reading* 93]). In *Hemingway's Reading, 1910–1940,* Michael Reynolds notes that Hemingway's "reading reveals one other warrior, little connected with Hemingway, whom we should have suspected long ago: the medieval knight" (26). In "Ernest Hemingway: Knighthood in Our Time," a chapter in my 1996 book *The Medievalist Impulse in American Literature: Twain, Adams, Fitzgerald, and Hemingway,* I provide a detailed exploration of how the codes of medieval chivalry and courtly love served as a particularly powerful model and contrast in Hemingway's modernist texts (Moreland 161–200).

The class discussion that I have described in this chapter is intended not so much to lead students to a certain conclusion about *A Farewell to Arms* as to develop a means by which they can learn to read the famous seven-eighths of Hemingway's fiction that remains under the surface, and to enable them to address the additional and increasingly sophisticated questions about the meaning and significance of this novel. Such questions for discussion include the following:

- If the novel criticizes World War I for being too technological and disorderly to meet the requirements of chivalric war, then what does that suggest about Hemingway's likely attitude toward later wars? Is there such a thing as a "good" war, and is that what Hemingway was looking for in his many later experiences of war? If so, was he looking for that "good" war in order to become a "good" man, and also to represent fictionally a "good" man?
- If chivalric combat is realized as a positive value and modern technological war is realized as a negative value in *A Farewell to Arms,* how does one deal with the historical fact that the first inevitably led to the second? That is, if the "progress" of war is to be reprehended, is progress itself suspect? Or is it only so in the particular realm of war?
- Does modern technological warfare obviate the possibility for male self-realization in its pressure-cooker environment? Is grace under this particular pressure still possible? Advisable?

- How does the increasing presence of women at war affect the conventional role of the male? Here I note that Hemingway's fiction addresses this modern phenomenon in multiple texts. In the back story of *The Sun Also Rises* (1926), Brett Ashley, a VAD, cared for Jake Barnes in an English hospital as he recovered from his devastating wound, a wound that "seemed like a hell of a joke" (27) received on "a joke front" (31). In *A Farewell to Arms* (1929), Catherine serves as a VAD at the British hospital in Gorizia near the front before relocating to the American hospital in Milan, where she cares for Frederic. In the Spanish civil war play *The Fifth Column* (1938), Dorothy Bridges is a war correspondent living at the Hotel Florida in Madrid, which is mere blocks from the front and is frequently shelled, and her character is based on war correspondent Martha Gellhorn, Hemingway's lover while he was writing the play and covering the war, and later his third wife. In the Spanish civil war novel *For Whom the Bell Tolls* (1940), Pilar, a woman on whom Robert Jordan depends while engaged in his assignment to blow a bridge, becomes the leader of the guerilla band fighting the Fascist nationalist troops. Does the increasing presence of women at war transform this heretofore male environment in ways that complicate male self-realization?
- Given the explicit binary opposition between the concrete and the abstract, about which Frederic speaks so passionately, is the abstract intrinsically inferior to the concrete? Or is that so only when the abstract values seem false to the historical circumstances? When, if ever, might the abstract term be superior to the concrete?

One of the brilliant aspects of *A Farewell to Arms* is that the major questions raised therein—questions increasingly relevant today, as our students inevitably realize—can be teased out of a single critical passage. And given Hemingway's identity as a modernist writer defined stylistically by his aesthetics of omission—his famous "iceberg theory"—a class exploration that takes not only his present but also his absent terms seriously and operates within their parameters not only acknowledges the effectiveness of his modernist technique but also acknowledges the abilities of students to address the purposeful absences in his work—a skill that they manifest by means of a class discussion of this sort. Moreover, such an exploration gives them appropriate confidence in their ability to address other sophisticated literary texts in a meaningful and subtle fashion.

The class discussion that I have described in these pages can be accomplished in its basic outline in a single session or two, though the larger questions I have posed would obviously require more time if they are not merely to be raised but explored in class (note that such questions might also be provided for small-group discussion and then class presentations, or they might be adapted for writing assignments). But before I end my teaching of A Farewell to Arms, I always return the students to the novel's title. Hemingway's pun draws an equivalence between the arms of love and the arms of war, an equivalence that he works hard to maintain in the final chapter of the novel: "Now Catherine would die. That was what you did. You died. You did not know what it was about. You never had time to learn. They threw you in and told you the rules and the first time they caught you off base they killed you. Or they killed you gratuitously like Aymo. Or gave you the syphilis like Rinaldi. But they killed you in the end. You could count on that. Stay around and they would kill you" (327). Here Frederic directly links Catherine's death in childbirth with Aymo's death in war—tragedies both, to be sure. But who is it that Frederic refers to as "they" in this passage? Is it the God to whom he so desperately prays for Catherine's survival? Or is it the powerful political and economic figures whose actions precipitated World War I? The first chapter of this retroactive narrative famously includes the striking metaphor wherein troops marching in the rain are likened to pregnant women: "Their rifles were wet and under their capes the two leather cartridge-boxes on the front of the belts, gray leather boxes heavy with the packs of clips of thin, long 6.5 mm. cartridges, bulged forward under the capes so that the men, passing on the road, marched as though they were six months gone with child" (4). Here again the linkage between death in war and death in childbirth is drawn, though the metaphor's impact can only be realized on a second or subsequent reading. The rain at the end of the first chapter that the soldiers march in on their way to the front is inevitably linked to the rain at the end of the last chapter that Frederic walks in after leaving the hospital where Catherine has died. But are death in childbirth and death in war indeed tragedies of the same order, existing on the same plane? Or do they exist on different planes? Is Catherine's death an ontological tragedy, a tragedy of being itself, while Aymo's death is a sociopolitical tragedy, a tragedy occasioned by the calculations and self-interested motives of various political and economic leaders? However brilliantly these two types of tragedy are merged aesthetically in Hemingway's novel, are they philosophically compatible?

Here it is useful to cite the last sentences of the first chapter: "At the start of the winter came the permanent rain and with the rain came the cholera. But it was checked and in the end only seven thousand died of it in the army" (4). Death by disease surely seems to be more closely linked to death by childbirth than to death by war, and it would thus seem to be another type of ontological tragedy. It is worth noting that in the final chapter Frederic includes Rinaldi's syphilis as another way that "they killed you in the end." But would the soldiers have contracted cholera if they had not been grouped so closely together under such difficult physical conditions, and would Rinaldi have been infected with syphilis if he had had other sexual outlets besides the military-sanctioned whorehouse? While death in childbirth and death in war seem to be philosophically distinguishable, the inclusion of death by disease in the context of war renders the distinction more problematic. Most provocatively of all, given the constancy of war in human history, is war perhaps part of the condition of being human—indeed, an ontological tragedy, a tragedy of *being?* Is war, like disease, an intrinsic part of the human condition? Now *that* is a question that will resonate for students far beyond the time allotted to the study of *A Farewell to Arms,* and even far beyond the context of a course in which Hemingway's novel is taught. And that is as it should be. That *A Farewell to Arms* elicits such important philosophical questions is yet one more reason why teachers should take the opportunity to teach this seminal novel in whatever contexts they deem appropriate.

# MODERNISM AND WORLD WAR I

# Teaching *A Farewell to Arms* from a Modernist Perspective

*Ellen Andrews Knodt*

How do we decide what to teach and when to teach it when we plan a modern American literature course? Often described in catalogs as "literature between the wars," Modern American Literature typically follows the chronology of publication of the works chosen; so, for example, *The Waste Land* (1922) or *The Great Gatsby* (1925) would precede *A Farewell to Arms* (1929). Because of its focus on World War I and because of its narrative point of view, *A Farewell to Arms* should be taught, I suggest, before the chronological position it usually occupies. First, some background on the course that affects my suggestion: the modern American literature course I teach at Penn State's Abington College is a 100-level course open to all students and carries a general education–humanities designation, which means that students can take it as one of the humanities requirements for any Penn State degree. While English majors also enroll in the course, the students in the class represent many majors. Most of my students have little background in this time period, their high school surveys not having emphasized the First World War's impact on literature or its importance in ushering in a modernist sensibility. Students know about the Roaring Twenties and Prohibition, but if they have heard the term "the Lost Generation," they have no idea why the generation may be considered lost.

Considering the lack of students' knowledge of World War I, it makes sense for students to read *Farewell* based not on the date of its publication but on the date of its setting in World War I Italy, before they read T. S. Eliot's poetry of despair and F. Scott Fitzgerald's postwar story of the American Roaring Twenties. Students need, I think, to understand the impact of the Great War in order to understand the poetry and novels that reflect the disillusionment and despair in postwar modernism. As one commentator remarks, "The twentieth century began on June 28, 1914. On that day Europe plunged into a vortex of metahistorical change called the Great War. What emerged four blood-soaked years later was a world utterly different from the one people had known for centuries. We would recognize it as the world we live in today. . . . Suspicion of authority, doubts about absolutes, irony and cynicism all defined modernity, in life and art" (Zakaria 91).

Another reason for placing *Farewell* before other modernist works is Hemingway's use of Frederic Henry as a retrospective narrator of his story. Students often do not catch on to the subtleties of Frederic as narrator and the difference the time of narration can make in interpreting the actions of a character in a novel. Students voice their confusion as they are reading the novel, claiming, "I can't get into it. It seems to move so slowly. I don't understand Frederic and Catherine's relationship." Leading students to see Frederic's depiction of himself through his telling of the story awakens their ability to read more actively. Their increased awareness of the importance of narrative perspective will also aid their reading when they encounter Eliot's multiple narrative voices in *The Waste Land* and Nick Carraway's complex retrospective narration of the events in *The Great Gatsby*, which he relates from others' accounts and takes part in himself. Studying *Farewell* before these other modernist works affords students a chance to understand World War I as a defining event that ushered in modernism, and experimentation in narrative stance as one hallmark of modernist style.

In her important essay on *A Farewell to Arms*, "Hemingway's Unknown Soldier: Catherine Barkley, the Critics, and the Great War," Sandra Whipple Spanier emphasizes that readers need to consider the context of World War I to understand and judge the characters in the novel, particularly, as she argues, Catherine Barkley. I agree with Spanier that the realities of World War I are often underappreciated by readers of *Farewell*, and that is particularly true of undergraduates, who often have no way to differentiate World War I from any other war. The horrors of the first "modern" war, with its intense shelling, use of poison gas, futile assaults from trenches across killing fields of no-man's-land, troop mutinies, and summary executions of soldiers by their own officers, are largely unknown to most of the students I teach. Most students think World War I was largely similar to what they have seen in films of World War II, a brutal war to be sure, but one in which armies and fronts moved rapidly and soldiers had a clear sense of the mission and what was at stake. One way to help students understand *Farewell* is to acquaint them with the conditions of the war and then lead them to see those conditions reflected in Hemingway's account in specific scenes with Frederic and the novel's other characters.

## Using Film as Background to *A Farewell to Arms*

Showing all or part of the film *Paths of Glory,* a Stanley Kubrick film starring Kirk Douglas, provides students with a vivid picture of World War I conditions and helps prepare them for discussion of the war in *Farewell.* In the first forty-five minutes or so of this film, the conditions of trench warfare and its effects on French troops are vividly depicted; even more importantly so, too, is the all-too-common practice during the Great War of generals disciplining their troops by random executions for "cowardice." Though the film focuses on the French, it will prepare students for a key scene in *Farewell* of executions by the Italian carabinieri of their own officers during the retreat from Caporetto. The film sparks discussion of the causes of World War I, the roles of the various nations fighting the war, the enormous toll in lives lost, and America's role during the conflict and afterward. I've found that students are eager for information on World War I after seeing the film and welcome what they might otherwise have dismissed as a history lecture, if it is presented as an introduction to the novel.

## Slowing Down the Reading

Typically, I like students to have read the novels we are analyzing before the first class discussion, but I have found a different approach works better with *A Farewell to Arms.* Reading the novel in smaller chunks and focusing students' attention on certain scenes seems to foster an understanding of both the impact of the war and Frederic Henry's development as narrator better than teaching the novel as a whole. The following analysis shows my suggestions for dividing the novel into sections for class discussion, focusing on these main concerns. Pre-reading questions for each section may be used as out-of-class assignments or in the first few minutes of class to foster discussion. Passing out index cards to students at the beginning of class and asking them to respond to the questions (or to put down their own questions) has proved to be a useful technique, as I have described elsewhere (Knodt, "Teaching" 105). There are, of course, many other worthy ways to approach the teaching of this great novel.

## CHAPTERS 1–9

> Pre-reading Questions: Who is telling the story? What do we know about the narrator's situation? Can you tell when the narrator is telling the story? What specific clues are there to the time of the telling? What do we find out about the war in these chapters? How have various male characters been affected by the war? What are their attitudes toward the war? How has Catherine been affected by the war? What is her attitude toward the war?

These questions focus students' attention on Frederic Henry as the narrator and on the nature of the war. As students begin the novel, they should be encouraged to notice Frederic Henry's first-person narration and his use of the past tense: "In the late summer of that year we lived in a house" (3). They also might notice early reflections on the war in the statement that "things went very badly" (4), and his observation of unsanitary conditions in the army causing disease and death: "At the start of the winter came the permanent rain and with the rain came the cholera. But it was checked and in the end only seven thousand died of it in the army" (4). Though interpretations differ (see Phelan), the narrator's "only" seems deliberately sarcastic, revealing his attitude. Time is truncated, and a whole year passes, summarized very quickly (5–6). The officers in the mess discuss girls and bait the priest but say little about the actual war.

But the focus on the priest intensifies, and a key passage reveals to the careful reader that Frederic Henry is being reflective in his narration, that is, that Frederic is telling this story after all the events have occurred—in hindsight, as it were. James Nagel calls the novel "a retrospective narrative told by Frederic Henry a decade after the action has taken place for the purpose of coming to terms emotionally with the events" (171). Frederic Henry says about the priest, "He had always known what I did not know and what, when I learned it, I was always able to forget. But I did not know that then, although I learned it later" (14). This enigmatic statement sends readers to clues in the rest of the novel for what the priest knew that Frederic Henry had to learn. It also signals that as Frederic recounts the events of the novel and his own part in these events, he knows what will happen. Those of us who have read the novel realize that Frederic often tells us things that do not always put him in the best light, and this realization raises a further question then: Why does Frederic Henry tell us the many unflattering details about himself that we learn in the course of his account? (See Phelan.) Students just reading these first chapters, however, need to be alerted to this passage and encouraged to be aware of how Frederic Henry presents himself as the novel continues.

We don't have to read very far before we encounter Frederic's unflattering realization that when he was on leave, "The whole thing [the ambulance unit] seemed to run better while I was away" (17). Shortly after that, he meets Catherine Barkley, the British VAD. Their relationship is inextricably woven into the context of war and Frederic's narrative. Students should recognize two main points revealed in the early conversations between Frederic and Catherine: first, that she suffers psychologically from the death of her fiancé at the Battle of the Somme; and second, that Frederic's reporting of their first encounter is "self-indicting in its selfishness" (Phelan 58).

Catherine tells Frederic that she was engaged for "eight years" (19) and that while she thought her fiancé might be wounded by a "sabre cut" (20), instead, "They blew him all to bits" (20). When Catherine pretends that Frederic is her dead fiancé—"Oh, darling, you have come back, haven't you" (30)—Frederic realizes that "she was probably a little crazy" (30). Catherine knows that she is emotionally close to the edge, regains her composure, and tells Frederic: "You don't have to pretend you love me. That's over for the evening" (31). For his part, Frederic, clearly "out of his depth with her" (Phelan 58), has told us that he lied when he said he loved her and further elaborates, "I knew I did not love Catherine Barkley nor had any idea of loving her. This was a game, like bridge, in which you said things instead of playing cards" (30).

As Spanier explains, Catherine understands the enormous cost of the war: Catherine's fiancé was killed "in the battle of the Somme, the British attack that began on July 1, 1916, and cost them 60,000 casualties on that day alone without gaining any ground whatever" ("Hemingway's Unknown Soldier" 83). Catherine tells Frederic, "People can't realize what France is like. If they did, it couldn't all go on. . . . We'll crack in France. They can't go on doing things like the Somme and not crack" (20). Frederic replies, "They won't crack here" (20), showing that he has not arrived at the same level of war weariness and skepticism that Catherine has. Later, Frederic naively reveals that "I knew I would not be killed. Not in this war. It did not have anything to do with me. It seemed no more dangerous to me myself than war in the movies" (37). Students should realize at this point that Frederic Henry is not Hemingway, that Hemingway, in Phelan's words, "distances" (64) himself from Frederic and portrays a character who has much to learn about war and love.

At the end of this section, Frederic Henry is badly wounded, and students will no doubt notice the irony of his earlier naive statements about war. They should also note the antiwar discussion that Frederic listens to among the ambulance mechanics (including an account of carabinieri and others executing their own men) just before the shelling that kills one and injures the others, including Frederic. His own statements still support the war: "I believe we should get the war over. . . . It would not finish it if one side stopped fighting. It would only be worse if we stopped fighting" (49). At this point students may well be curious about how closely Hemingway's experience parallels Frederic's. Michael Reynolds's excellent study *Hemingway's First War* makes it clear that while both author and character were wounded as members of an ambulance corps, the places, times, and conditions were different, and that Hemingway extensively researched military campaigns and interviewed many veterans in order to write this novel. Having driven a canteen unit to the front to serve the soldiers, the teenage Hemingway was wounded at Fossalta on July 8, 1918. Frederic Henry's service, however, came much earlier, culminating in the climactic events of the retreat from Caporetto in 1917.

## MORE ABOUT THE NOVEL'S POINT OF VIEW

Frederic Henry's retrospective narration can't be emphasized too strongly—it becomes a key to the way his character is interpreted. As is pointed out in this section, Frederic tells us unflattering things about his own conduct—that he lied to Catherine, for example. As the novel continues, he reveals behavior that calls into question his leadership, his judgment, and his ability to function under stress. Students tend to believe a first-person narrator without questioning his conduct, even if that means finding excuses for the character's behavior. So, for example, Frederic Henry's lies to Catherine become "boys will be boys" moments, and later when Frederic disappoints the priest by not visiting the priest's family while on leave as he had promised, readers can dismiss that as simply bad manners. But Hemingway subtly builds these transgressions into a larger picture that Frederic Henry reveals as he is telling this story after the fact. Why would a narrator tell so much that tarnishes his character? Interpretations vary, but I agree with what James Carothers has explained in conference discussions of *A Farewell to Arms:* that Frederic Henry is narrating a "confessional," an analysis of his conduct, for which he now feels guilty and from which he hopes to show he has learned. The importance of Frederic's obvious respect for the priest perhaps takes on greater significance if one follows this interpretation. These early chapters are too early a stage in the discussion of the novel to suggest this interpretation to students, but consistent attention to the narrative stance and what Frederic Henry is revealing to readers as he tells the story may point them toward understanding what Hemingway achieves by the use of this point of view.

## Chapters 10–20

Pre-reading Questions: How does Catherine and Frederic's relationship develop in these chapters? In what ways has it changed or not changed since they met? What discussion does Frederic have with the priest? Does this discussion explain what Frederic said on page 14 about the priest always knowing what he did not know? Are there any clues in this section as to what will happen later in the novel (foreshadowing)?

In this section, one class discussion could focus on Frederic's visit from the priest in the hospital. Since the comment by Frederic about the priest's knowledge early in the novel, readers should be alert to further encounters that might answer the riddle posed earlier. During their visit, the priest admits, "I hate the war," and says that Frederic does not yet understand: "Still even wounded you do not see it. I can tell" (70). They then have a conversation about loving God and loving in general, which also reveals the priest to be more knowledgeable than Frederic: "When you love you wish to do things for. You wish to sacrifice for. You wish to serve." Frederic answers, "I don't love." And the priest replies, "You will. I know you will" (72). Students should be encouraged to match that conversation with one that Catherine and Frederic have later when she asks him how many women he has "stayed with" (104). And though he is now claiming to love Catherine, he lies to her about his past relationships and even about whether he has told other women that he loved them. It is true that in this section Frederic says he wants to marry Catherine but still expresses ambivalence to himself and to us: "I suppose I enjoyed not being married, really" (115). As readers notice, Frederic has still not developed more admirable character traits, and as the narrator, he is still revealing all these faults to us, the readers. The question to pose to students is, why is he telling us these unflattering things about himself?

While discussion of the war is minimal in these chapters, there are still a few key passages. Frederic reads of the American entrance into World War I but realizes the problems of training men and getting them into combat. The toll of the war impresses him: "The Italians were using up an awful amount of men. I did not see how it could go on" (118), echoing both Catherine's and Passini's earlier remarks. But then he says resignedly, "Perhaps wars weren't won anymore. Maybe they went on forever. Maybe it was another Hundred Years' War" (118). Frederic still does not seem to know how he feels about the war. After the couple has listened to an Italian American hero brag about his potential promotion in the Italian army, Frederic asks Catherine if she wouldn't like him to have a higher rank. Catherine, with her practical nature and British reserve, dislikes the braggart and declares, "I only want you to have enough rank so that we're admitted to the better restaurants" (125).

## CHAPTERS 21–27

Pre-reading Questions: What crisis faces Catherine and Frederic? How do they each react? Have Frederic's attitudes toward Catherine or toward the war changed? When he goes back to the front, how does he say things have changed there? How have Rinaldi and the priest changed? Frederic and Gino talk about the war, and Frederic separates himself from Gino, the patriot, in a famous passage (184–85). Does this passage show a change in Frederic?

When Catherine tells him she is pregnant and asks him if he feels "trapped," Frederic admits, "You always feel trapped biologically" (139). He confesses to her and to us that he is not a brave man, which echoes his statement to Rinaldi earlier that he did nothing heroic when he was wounded: "I was blown up while we were eating cheese" (63). Though these statements seem similar to those he has made before, students should be encouraged to notice subtle changes in Frederic's attitudes: his realization that the hotel visit with Catherine was nothing like his earlier fantasy; his realization that paying someone to save a seat on the train was inappropriate; his changing relationship with Rinaldi, who asks, "What's the matter with you?" (167). The dialogue at the mess is a measure of the difference also. Rinaldi tries to bait the priest as before, but Frederic puts him off, eliciting a smile from the priest. Rinaldi responds, "There he is, gone over with the priest" (173). As Frederic and the priest talk after dinner about the possibility of the war ending, Frederic reveals something about his thought process and perhaps a clue to his changing attitude toward the war: "That's why I never think about these things. I never think and yet when I begin to talk I say the things I have found out in my mind without thinking" (179). This passage may prepare us for Frederic's famous passage beginning "I was always embarrassed by the words sacred, glorious, and sacrifice and the expression in vain" (184). The end of this section begins Frederic's taking part in the retreat from Caporetto, a key part of the novel and a key moment in the Italian conduct of World War I. John Keegan, the eminent World War I historian, explains the tragedy of Caporetto in his book *The First World War* and praises Hemingway's re-creation of the event: "Cadorna [the Italian general in charge of the eastern front] did his best to increase the number [of casualties], by a ruthless and characteristic institution of the summary execution of stragglers, an episode unforgettably described by Ernest Hemingway, an ambulance volunteer with the Italians, in *A Farewell to Arms;* he was not actually present but that does not detract from the veracity of his account, one of the greatest literary evocations of military disaster" (349).

## CHAPTERS 28–33

> Pre-reading Questions: Describe the conditions of the retreat. What passengers do the ambulances acquire? What does Frederic's dream show about his state of mind? What worries Frederic about being stalled in the column? What does he decide to do? What consequences result from his decision? Discuss the way you judge Frederic's shooting the sergeant. What connection, if any, do you see between this incident and Frederic's being held by the carabinieri at the Tagliamento bridge? How does Frederic view the war now? How does he escape?

This section of the novel is problematic for many readers. Michael Reynolds flatly tells us, "Frederic Henry is not a hero, and he realizes it" (*First War* 254). I have argued elsewhere that Frederic's account of the shooting of the sergeant clinches our impression of him as unheroic, and that Hemingway deliberately intends for us to see Frederic as a flawed human being overwhelmed by the war (Knodt, "Suddenly"). Shooting the sergeant, one can argue, is the most serious transgression Frederic reveals in his narrative. The incident often provokes lively discussion of the circumstances, and students often reach vastly different conclusions about the necessity of Frederic's act. But the question to the students remains, why does he reveal his weakness in his narration? The answer, I maintain, is that Hemingway wished to reveal the dreadful toll war takes on all human beings, and in his guilt-ridden retrospective narrator, readers see an otherwise typical man make corrupt and fatal decisions. Frederic is no better than the Italian officers who killed their own men at the Tagliamento bridge, and his decision to shoot at the sergeants is no more rational than the decision by others (also possibly Italian soldiers) to shoot Aymo or to hold Frederic for possible execution at the bridge. As Reynolds says, "Ultimately, Caporetto stood for the entire war experience, and that experience was defeat. . . . It was a defeat of the spirit epitomized in the French mutinies of 1917, the Russian October revolution of 1917, and the Italian disaster at Caporetto in 1917. . . . It is this concept of defeat which informs the action of *A Farewell to Arms*" (*First War* 282).

## CHAPTERS 34–41

Pre-reading Questions: Discuss Frederic's feelings about the war now that he has made a "separate peace" (243). How does his conversation with Count Greffi help us understand his thinking? Explain the plan of escape and Catherine's role in it. How has Frederic and Catherine's relationship developed in their Swiss exile? Discuss their relative roles and attitudes during the childbirth scenes. How has Frederic changed his life attitudes since the novel's beginning? Are we now able to understand why Frederic is telling us his story?

The final chapters of the novel show the working out of the idea of defeat of the spirit. Key passages show the war weariness and overall pessimism that have overtaken Frederic Henry. Even before he tells us of Catherine's tragic death in childbirth, Frederic reveals what he has learned: "If people bring so much courage to this world the world has to kill them to break them, so of course it kills them. The world breaks every one and afterward many are strong at the broken places. But those that will not break it kills. It kills the very good and the very gentle and the very brave impartially. If you are none of these you can be sure it will kill you too but there will be no special hurry" (249). Frederic has to learn to live with this spirit of defeat, and he gets some clues from his dialogue with Count Greffi. Catherine, too, helps him to understand how to live, even finding humor in their dangerous lake crossing to Switzerland. And, of course, she proves her bravery in her final moments: "I'm not a bit afraid. It's just a dirty trick" (331).

Perhaps we can now answer the question that we posed at the beginning, why is Frederic Henry telling us his story? Perhaps he wants readers to understand what he has learned: the power of love—in the priest's case, his love of God—in Frederic's case, Catherine's love. In Frederic Henry, Ernest Hemingway created a narrator who, like others of his generation, experiences the trauma of war and loss and emerges to tell readers the story so they may also learn to live in the modern age.

### APPENDIX: Syllabus for English 133: Modern American Literature to World War II

Course description: An examination of Cather, Eliot, Frost, Faulkner, Fitzgerald, Hemingway, Hurston, Wharton, Wright, and other writers representative of literature in the years between the world wars.

Required Texts:
Anderson, Sherwood. *Winesburg, Ohio*
Cather, Willa. *My Ántonia*
Eliot, T. S. *The Waste Land and Other Poems*
Faulkner, William. *The Sound and the Fury*
Fitzgerald, F. Scott. *The Great Gatsby*
Hemingway, Ernest. *A Farewell to Arms*
*101 Great American Poems*
O'Neill, Eugene. *Three Plays by Eugene O'Neill*
Wright, Richard. *Eight Men: Short Stories*

Syllabus:

| | |
|---|---|
| Weeks 1–2 | Introduction to Modern American Literature: The American Novel before World War I<br>    Cather: *My Ántonia* |
| Weeks 3–4 | Modernist Developments in the Short Story<br>    Anderson: *Winesburg, Ohio* |
| Weeks 5–7 | Modernist Elements in the American Novel: Understanding the Impact of World War I<br>    Hemingway: *A Farewell to Arms* |
| | Midterm |
| Weeks 8–9 | Modernist Poetry Reflects the Postwar Spirit<br>    Eliot: *The Waste Land and Other Poems* |
| Weeks 10–11 | Modernist Fiction Examines Postwar American Society<br>    Fitzgerald: *The Great Gatsby* |
| Week 12 | New Modern Voices: The Harlem Renaissance<br>    Selections from *101 Great American Poems* and Richard Wright's *Eight Men* |
| Week 13–14 | A Modern Voice from the South<br>    Faulkner: *The Sound and the Fury* |
| Week 15 | Developing Modern American Drama<br>    O'Neill<br>    Final Project Due<br>    Final Examination |

Term Project: The term project gives each student an opportunity to broaden his or her knowledge of literature, culture, history, or politics of the period 1915–40. Students may choose topics that require no sources other than the literary texts themselves or may choose to investigate topics that require secondary sources. A partial list of such topics follows the syllabus, but we will discuss additional topics in class.

Topic Suggestions Requiring No Secondary Sources:

1. Compare the portrayal of American life in *My Ántonia* and *Winesburg, Ohio*.
2. Discuss the idea of self-deception as it appears in any of the works we have read.
3. Discuss any two authors' sense of the past and its relative importance.
4. Read another work by one of the authors we have studied and identify a point of comparison between it and the work we discussed in class.
5. Read a work by another author from the period (e.g., Gertrude Stein, James T. Farrell, Sinclair Lewis, Edith Wharton, Theodore Dreiser, E. E. Cummings, Claude McKay, Zora Neale Hurston, Thomas Wolfe, John Dos Passos, John Steinbeck) and indicate its relationship to something we have read and to the development of modern American literature.

Topic Suggestions on Social, Historical, or Political Subjects:

1. Battles of World War I before American entry
2. Role of American ambulance drivers before American entry into World War I
3. American entry and impact on World War I
4. Postwar Europe
5. Isolationism and postwar American politics
6. Red scare
7. Ku Klux Klan and postwar racial conflict
8. Prohibition and rise of organized crime
9. Evangelism
10. National political scandals
11. Rise of youth culture
12. Popular music
13. Stock market boom and crash
14. Controversy over evolution: Scopes trial

# Teaching *A Farewell to Arms* at the U.S. Air Force Academy

*Jackson A. Niday II and James H. Meredith*

As with all great literature, what students take away from *A Farewell to Arms* depends to a large degree on what they bring to the text. English teachers who accept that statement as an axiom will most likely allow the following as a theorem: the more similar individual students in a classroom are in terms of their worldviews, the more likely it is that a class's reading of a work will fall short of broadening the intellectual horizons of its individual members. If the theorem holds, a class of military cadets presents one of the more formidable challenges a teacher can face when working with a book like *Farewell*. Though they are not cut from the same bolt (in spite of the fact they dress just alike), students at the U.S. Air Force Academy (USAFA) usually hold strong affinities for words like "patriotism," "honor," "nation," and "duty." Moreover, the most vocal students tend to hold views on human sexual relations that could be described as traditional or conservative. Upon encountering such characters as Frederic Henry and Catherine Barkley, many of these students balk. Whether explicitly or tacitly, they often ask the same question: Why should they devote time and energy to reflect on characters whose values may seem at such odds with their own?

Before we discuss how we teach *A Farewell to Arms* in a way that strives to answer that question, allow us to explain a little about how the Department of English and Fine Arts at USAFA handles its curriculum and add a bit to our description of cadets. As the newest military service academy on the block, we prize the development of new technology; thus, our curriculum favors engineering and the sciences over liberal arts (for example, even an English major is required to take seven engineering courses and receives a bachelor of science instead of the traditional bachelor of arts). Although the Air Force Academy is predominately and preeminently an engineering school, the academy does appreciate the value of the humanities and social sciences in the overall education of future U.S. Air Force officers. For example, we do allow an interested cadet to major in English or the humanities, and the core curriculum also requires all cadets to take three English courses: Freshman Composition, Introduction to Literature, and Advanced Composition and Public Speaking. English majors, of course, have a more extensive writing and literature curriculum. Moreover, since 1995, our best English majors have had the opportunity to hold summer research internships in the Hemingway Collection at the John F. Kennedy Presidential Library. In addition, over the years, the Air Force Academy has hosted international conferences and seminars on such literary figures as Joseph Heller, Stephen Crane, Ernest Hemingway, and Paul West, to name just a few.

While USAFA prides itself on offering cadets a core experience that is similar for all, the Department of English and Fine Arts allows instructors to exercise considerable discretion in selecting their texts. Thus, a cadet may have an instructor who chooses to teach *Farewell* in an English 211 course (an introduction to literature course taught at the sophomore level) or in an English 411 course (an advanced composition and speech class taught at the junior and senior levels). Because of the nature of our institution, both courses tend to have a focus on war, though not exclusively so. The students this curriculum serves have their own individual and collective identities. The mid–50 percent range on the verbal aptitude portion of the SAT for cadets is 590–670, with a mean score of 630. The student body consists of approximately 15 percent women and 85 percent men. The institution makes every effort to recruit students who are a cross-section of America and represent all the diversity that comprises the nation. And when we say many of our students balk at Frederic Henry, we are in no way suggesting that cadets are easily stereotyped. Like the individuals of any student body, cadets vary greatly in their reading experiences, as well as in their abilities to recognize and deal with the ambiguities with which good literature invites us to wrestle. Whether the proportion of any particular class who balks at the novel is 10 percent or 70 percent, our goal is to help them suspend judgment until they have had time to understand Frederic and Catherine as flawed characters, both holding their own mix of virtues and vices, so they can give them a fair hearing.

Toward that end, we structure our approach to the novel around three notions of distance over a period of seven classes of a forty-two-class semester. In the course of our assignments, we explore the novel in terms of geographical distance, chronological distance, and narrative distance. The exercises and discussions linked to the first two types of distance provide a necessary contextual foundation for a close engagement with the novel. Before getting to the novel itself, we devote one day to geographical distance and one day to chronological distance. We divide the class into study groups, assign each group a specific topic to research, and ask the groups to present their findings to the class in reports of approximately ten minutes each. The third notion of distance, narrative distance, provides a conceptual tool to help them read the text from a sharp critical perspective. We devote five days to class discussion of the novel's major issues and themes in terms of narrative distance. The ultimate goal is for the homework exercises and classroom discussions to help the students develop their own critical appreciation for how a novel so far removed from them in terms of distance and time can be so near to them in terms of human concerns.

## GEOGRAPHICAL DISTANCE

The first time we taught the novel, we thought geographical distance and chronological distance were clearly distinct concepts. However, our cadets quickly showed us that we needed to think through our concepts a little more thoroughly. They pointed out that geographical distance overlaps with chronological distance, since people measure distance more in terms of time than space. As transportation technology increases speed of travel, distance (measured in time) decreases. Considered in those terms, Italy was much farther from the United States at the time of World War I than it is in 2007. Responses like these are pleasing, to say the least. When students become this engaged in critical thinking so soon, we know we're off to a good start.

Having to grant them their point, we asked them to apply it. Our first group of cadets must research and report on the difference in travel times between the time in which they live and the time of which Hemingway wrote. How long did it take to travel to Italy from the United States in 1914? What would have been the most likely mode of travel in 1914? In 2007? Even when we press for sources or calculations, this report lasts five to six minutes at most. Still, it makes a good starting point for the cadets.

The next project requires the combined efforts of the remaining three groups. Its purpose is to help students get a handle on what geographical distance means in terms of cultural differences. Each group is required to research and "sell" the class a vacation package. The locations we will visit are Italy (second group), Austria (third group), and Switzerland (fourth group). They have generous latitude in assembling these vacation packages, but to get them moving in the right direction, we tell them we'll want to see some specific locations. In Germany, we'll want to see the Black Forest and the Harz Mountains. In Italy, we'll want to see Udine, Plava, Pordenone, and Milan. What will we see in Milan? What is the history of the city? What is it known for? What kinds of architecture will we see? What dates back to World War I? What dates back even further? In Switzerland, we'll want to visit Brissago, Montreux, and Lausanne. This report usually takes fifteen minutes. Our cadets have been quite resourceful in how they present these sales packages. Some have gone to travel agencies to get information. Others have made use of resources in our library, including Rogers's *Exploring Europe by Boat, Fodor's Europe,* and Monkhouse's *A Regional Geography of Western Europe.* Some have put together PowerPoint presentations using pictures from the Google image gallery. Others have used information from commercial travel guides to create tri-fold flyers.

This approach has been successful for years at USAFA. Archived lesson plans from the 1970s contain photocopied excerpts from Michael Reynolds's *Hemingway's First War: The Making of* A Farewell to Arms showing maps of the Italian front and, in particular, the war zones where Frederic Henry found himself. Reynolds's maps met the need of cadets (who have to study military history) to know exactly where they were as they explored Frederic Henry's war experience through literature—an issue that should not be forgotten at a military service academy.

## CHRONOLOGICAL DISTANCE

For students born after 1980, the year 1914 belongs to that age known as ancient history. They are removed from World War I not simply by four generations, but by advances in technology that have burgeoned largely within their own lifetimes. What was the world like more than ninety years ago? To help them get some measure of both the differences and similarities between that world and theirs, we send them to the library for a rummaging expedition to find sources from the World War I era that can make our reading of a World War I novel more enlightening. Such trips are limited by the library's holdings, but we prefer for them to make as much use as possible of any resources that date roughly to the time period of World War I rather than make exclusive use of other people's summaries of the period. We recommend that all four groups consult the *New York Times.* This is also a good opportunity for them to check *The Reader's Guide to Periodical Literature.*

The first group is given a fairly wide berth in terms of what they can fill their ten minutes with. The question they must answer is this: What was new in 1914? What were the hot items of the day? What did they look like? In what ways were they new? That is, what problems did they help solve, or in what ways did they add to quality of life? The resources we direct them to in our library include *Popular Mechanics;* the *Illustrated London News, N.Y. Edition;* the *New York Times Current History;* and *Survey;* and since we are at the Air Force Academy, we direct them to *Aviation* and *Aircraft* as well.

The next project builds a bridge between geographical distance and chronological distance. The second group must illustrate how the geopolitical landscape of Europe has changed between the time Hemingway wrote of in the novel and the day in which they read the novel. We have the students make poster-sized maps of the continent in 1918 and 1914—however, PowerPoint images have also worked well for this assignment. We recommend two atlases—Shepherd's *Historical Atlas* and Sellman's *An Outline Atlas of World History*—but several of the sources listed below also have good maps detailing the boundaries and battles of the war.

The third group must answer this complex question: What was the medical world like? What was the availability of contraception, and what was the Comstock Act? Our students never fail to express surprise over the nature of this law, the instances of opposition to it, and the late date of its repeal. A good recent source discussing such issues is Neil Heyman's *Daily Life During World War I.* Also, a number of Internet sites address the Comstock Act; these can be found by going again to Google.

And since we teach cadets, we always ask the fourth group for a report on how World War I started, who the players were, and what the status of weapons technology was. Since cadets have access to the libraries of military academies, researching the history of weapons development is a relatively easy task. Some of the sources we encourage them to consult are *History of World War I, The History of the First World War* (Leonard Wood et al.), *World War I: A Short History* (Lyons), *The Great War Illustrated* (Hammerton), *The Great War, 1914–1918* (Tucker), and *Harper's Pictorial Library of the World War* (Albert Bushnell Hart et al.). We recommend these sources for their useful maps; images from original sources; and approachable essays on weapons, battles, living conditions, and the like. (The *New York Times* also carries reports on weapons technology.)

## NARRATIVE DISTANCE

The exercises exploring geographical and chronological distance help cadets hone their research skills, create a vivid context for the story, and encounter Frederic and Catherine on terms perhaps more empathetic. When it comes to dealing with the novel itself, the most fruitful theoretical concept we've found to help students grapple with topics they find troublesome is narrative distance. Wayne Booth defines the term in *The Rhetoric of Fiction*. In short, all an author's choices are rhetorical. Through choices such as giving more or less detail, dwelling more or less on a specific item, and offering dialogue or summary, the narrator tells us what is important to him or her, and the author tells us what is important about the narrator's character. By establishing the distance that controls readers' perceptions, the storyteller controls the readers' encounter with the narrative.

To help cadets comprehend what is meant by narrative distance and what narrative distance does for storytelling, we begin where they are—in the land of film and movies. To lead into the areas to which cadets are most drawn in the novel, we ask for examples of how different directors have handled scenes dealing with violence, loyalty, and human intimacy and sexuality. The problem here is not finding examples, but selecting from among those students offer. With examples from the visual narratives, it is relatively easy to lead a discussion exploring how narrative distance as a film technique reveals insights into the tastes, values, and artistic achievements of the director and, if there is one, the narrating character. In one class, students contrasted the surrealistic and horrifically violent scenes from *RoboCop* with the more realistic but less graphic depictions of violence in *The Untouchables*. What we have found is that when we explore the notion of narrative distance in visual media, students grasp the concept more easily and are then more able to transfer that understanding to an application with written prose. We've had similar success with the ideas of loyalty and intimacy.

The next step to enable these young readers to apply narrative distance to prose is to help them make clear distinctions between author and narrator. For some students, a discussion of the two concepts may be review, but for many others the distinction is one they have managed to neglect, evade, or simply forget. All too often, when students encounter a narrator like Frederic in *A Farewell to Arms* or Howard W. Campbell in Kurt Vonnegut's *Mother Night*, the narrator and author become one. At one level, a student's failure to distinguish narrator from author leads to simple and sometimes humorous misreadings of the text. But even when students do understand that Frederic is not Hemingway (in spite of some biographical similarity), they still have a tendency to equate the two, slipping into the trap of thinking that Frederic speaks for Hemingway. In other words, we have found that even when students nod in agreement that Hemingway and Frederic are not the same person, they often fall back into making arguments suggesting that when Frederic says or does something, he reflects Hemingway's fundamental beliefs.

As we begin to apply the notion of distance to the novel, we tease out a more conscious awareness of Hemingway's framing device. We first ask, "Who wrote *A Farewell to Arms?*" Then, "Whose story is *A Farewell to Arms?*" This more ambiguous question most often evokes a more diverse response. For some, the story is obviously Frederic Henry's; for others, Ernest Hemingway's. To help students, we usually draw on a more blatant and familiar example: *The Scarlet Letter.* Hawthorne is the author of the novel. However, the book creates the image of a story within a story by presenting the tale of Hester Prynne as one found in a chest in a customhouse. Working from that more obvious example, students can more easily see Frederic Henry as having two roles with regard to this work: he is both character and narrator. What is the relationship between Hemingway and Henry? A few minutes' lecture on pertinent points from Hemingway's life follows. Yes, there are similarities between Hemingway and Henry, but Henry is not a pen name for Hemingway. If Henry is not Hemingway, who is he? How should readers think of the two in relation to one another and to themselves as readers of this story? In spite of the similarities between the two men, Henry is ultimately his own man, not in a literal sense but in a literary sense. Henry is a distinct personality, a man with a distinct set of values. Henry is the man through whose eyes Hemingway wants readers to view the events of the story. But he is not Hemingway.

As a useful addition to Booth's notion of narrative distance, his notion of *implied author* helps students maintain the perspective they need to keep narrator and author separate. Booth's notion of the implied author is fairly well-known to literature teachers. The emphasis on "implied" underscores the problems of discerning the intent of any flesh-and-blood author. The concept allows us to discuss values that are present in a work that may or may not accurately reflect the convictions of the flesh-and-blood author. While readers may not be able to pin down an author's intent, we can talk about the values expressed in a work as a whole by acknowledging that the implied author is the sum of his or her choices. Choices of perspective, tone, vividness, inclusions, omissions, and the like, point to a personality. Together, they give us a discernable impression of the author behind the story. In discussing narrative distance, Booth lists at least five ways in which it reveals important differences among implied authors, narrators, characters, and readers. For one, "the *narrator* may be more or less distant from the *implied author*" (156). For another, "the *narrator* may be more or less distant from the *characters* in the story he tells" (156). Third, "the *narrator* may be more or less distant from the *reader's* own norms" (156). Fourth, "the *implied author* may be more or less distant from the *reader*" (157). Fifth, "the *implied author* (carrying the reader with him) may be more or less distant from *other characters*" (157–58). We find it useful to prepare a handout with those distinctions (see appendix). Our goal in spending some time on this idea is to help those students who might balk at Frederic and Catherine recognize that the work as a whole may be making a different statement from what any particular part of it may seem to convey by itself.

Of all the relationships possible in the mix among implied authors, narrators, characters, and readers, Booth maintains that the most important to help readers gain a critical appreciation for a work is the distance "between the fallible or unreliable narrator and the implied author who carries the reader with him in judging the narrator" (158). We find we need to repeat this point several times in class discussion. For when reading *A Farewell to Arms*, we must distinguish among Frederic the character, Frederic the narrator, and Hemingway the author, and that is not always an easy distinction for young readers to make.

The best way to help students grasp these distinctions is, naturally, to call upon examples they're familiar with. Practically all our cadets are familiar with the works of Edgar Allan Poe and Arthur Conan Doyle. The stories of Sherlock Holmes offer a narrator distinctly removed from the story's author. Dr. Watson is no dullard, but neither is he the erratic savant that is Holmes, nor the methodic thinker that is Doyle. Poe, in way of contrast, blurs the distinction that Doyle maintains. When we encounter a narrator like that of "A Cask of Amontillado," we get a sense that there is far less distance between storyteller's voice as narrator and as actor, and we wonder about the author. Watson exists to tell Holmes's story. Montresor tells his own story. Some questions are worth pursuing in class. What is Watson's relationship to Holmes? From what you know or remember of the stories, is Watson a reliable narrator? That is, would he lie to us? Would he have accurate perceptions? What is Montresor's story? A confession? To whom? What kind of person is Montresor? How are his personality and values similar to or different from yours? Given who he is in terms of what he's done to Fortunato, might he be someone who would change the story to fit his perceived needs? The time devoted to these writers offers a basis for comparison and contrast with Frederic Henry. Frederic Henry the character is not Frederic Henry the narrator, and Frederic Henry the narrator is not Ernest Hemingway. We tell our students at the start of their reading to keep that fact in mind and to look for what separates the three.

### Hemingway and His Themes

Linked by the topic of loyalty, two themes take center stage with the cadets: Frederic's virtues and vices as a soldier of fortune, and the intimate relationship between Frederic and Catherine Barkley. But before getting to those themes in class discussion, we encourage the cadets to look very closely at the faceless narrator of chapter 1. What kind of man is he? There is little to go on. We have no evidence to reach solid conclusions about his character. But we can begin a study of him by making contrasts with other narrators. Unlike Melville's Ishmael, who announces himself at the start of *Moby-Dick,* this narrator has practically no presence in the opening of the novel. Which year? What house? What village? Which river? Which mountains? Asking these questions is only a start. The larger question is, why does this narrator begin his story this way? The flesh-and-blood author, Hemingway, could have begun the story differently. What does opening in this manner tell us about our faceless narrator? Responses are often varied. Sometimes students will hit upon the style as that of memoir; other times we raise the point. We ask them what is implied in memoir as a genre. In terms of narrative distance, one point should be obvious. Memoir necessarily implies a distance of time. The narrator recounting these events is removed from them by a number of years. We ask them to speculate as to how many years separate the narrator from the character. We also ask what time does to memory.

### Frederic as Soldier

For cadets who are taught to hold classical military virtues in the highest regard, Frederic Henry presents a prickly problem. He is an American in the Italian army holding the rank of lieutenant. We pose several questions: What does reading of such a character have to offer a cadet? What sense of dedication or loyalty to this mission could he have? His charge is to drive an ambulance, but he fails to complete his final mission. He then deserts to escape execution for a conviction of treason from a drumhead trial. The discussions of Frederic Henry as soldier focus on his purpose for being in Italy, his competence in performing his duties, and his commitment to the cause for which he volunteered.

A number of questions help the cadets focus on the significance of information that is conspicuous in its absence. What is Henry's purpose? Why is he in Italy? Why is he, as an American citizen, serving in the Italian army? In fiction, narrator silences can be just as telling as narrator or character declarations, even if a definitive conclusion evades us in the silence. The story raises the question of Henry's purpose early in a passage we have students consider in class discussion:

> "How do you do?" Miss Barkley said. "You're not an Italian, are you?"
> "Oh, no."
> Rinaldi was talking with the other nurse. They were laughing.

"What an odd thing—to be in the Italian army."

"It's not really the army. It's only the ambulance."

"It's very odd though. Why did you do it?"

"I don't know," I said. "There isn't always an explanation for everything."

"Oh, isn't there? I was brought up to think there was."

"That's awfully nice." (18)

True, there isn't always an explanation for everything, but for some things we expect explanations. When people have to make conscious choices and exert considerable effort in pursuit of a choice, we expect answers to, "Why did you do it?" The point of interest here is that the narrator is silent on the question.

What does that silence suggest? The question invites serious speculation from students. If the character offers no answer, does it mean he doesn't have an answer or that he is either reluctant or ashamed to state it explicitly? But what does it mean when the narrator offers no explanation? Ostensibly, the narrator has had time to gain a perspective the character could not have had. If he is silent on so pressing a question, are the explanations still missing? Or are they now unimportant?

Once cadets get a feel for the types of questions and insights that narrative distance invites them to consider, they find a number of other passages merit discussion. Two topics they've focused on when we've taught the book are competence and commitment. First, is Frederic Henry a competent officer? His failures in getting his ambulance entourage to Udine often elicit heated debate among cadets. We focus the discussion with questions such as these: Was the choice to break ranks in the retreat a prudent one for Frederic to make? Whether the cadets answer yes or no, we press them to give their reasons. Did Frederic have the authority to order the errant sergeants to cut brush to free the ambulance wheels from the ruts? Again, we press them for their reasons. Finally, did Frederic have the authority or justifiable reasons to shoot at the sergeants—and to authorize the killing of one? We ask them to look at the story in terms of tone and narrative distance. The incident is related dispassionately. Frederic gives the order. The sergeants refuse to obey. He repeats the order. They flee. He fires on them, hitting one. Bonello executes the wounded sergeant, following Frederic's detailed instructions on how to fire the pistol. The car won't budge. They give up. Then Frederic says, "Better throw the coat away" (206). Following that episode, this same man gives the two tagalong girls each a ten-lira note as he directs them to the nearest main highway.

We ask our cadets to ponder these questions. Is Frederic an officer meting out military justice? Or is he an opportunist whose poor decisions have led to frustration he is unable to manage, climaxing in a senseless murder? What can we make of the instructions to discard the coat? What kind of man orders an execution one moment and offers mercy the next? These questions move us to extend our discussion of Frederic as leader to Aymo's death and Bonello's desertion. To what degree may those two events be attributed to Frederic's leadership or lack of leadership?

A troubling related theme for the cadets weaves its way through the novel as the narrator returns to it repeatedly. That is, how committed is Frederic to the Italian cause? We have the cadets focus on four passages. The first passage is early in the novel, the one in which a relatively more idealistic Frederic debates with Gavuzzi, Manera, and Passini about what would be required to bring the war to an end. This debate raises some intriguing questions when considered in terms of narrative distance. The character Frederic argues with the others in his most idealistic frame of mind. When we get to the end of the novel, we know that the character's perspective on war, victory, love, and loss has changed radically. Therefore, we ask our cadets what Hemingway is up to here. Do the Italian mechanics offer the implied author's view of the war? Or are their opinions simply a foil for the young Frederic's naïveté?

Midway through the novel, Frederic has been wounded, and he has fallen in love. Now, as he anticipates a return to the front, Frederic shows a different attitude toward things martial. When Gino employs the high rhetoric of patriotism, Frederic the narrator offers us a glimpse inside Frederic the character's head: "Abstract words such as glory, honor, courage, or hallow were obscene beside the concrete names of villages, the numbers of roads, the names of rivers, the numbers of regiments and the dates. Gino was a patriot, so he said things that separated us sometimes, but he was also a fine boy" (185). We ask two questions here. First, what does this contempt for the abstract and esteem for the concrete suggest about the character? Second, why does patriotism bother Frederic, who is a volunteer?

The question of Frederic's commitment takes another turn in the dreamlike internal monologue we get when he's riding with the guns in the flatcar. We ask for a volunteer to read aloud the second, third, and fourth paragraphs of chapter 32. What is most notable in the passage? Most students can feel the difference in the narrator's state of mind that is reflected in the writing's style and tone, but often they have difficulty expressing the difference or knowing what to make of it. To help them grasp and express the significance of those differences, we ask a number of questions: Why does the story change to the second-person "you" here? What does the pronoun tell us when we think about it in terms of narrative distance? What does the shift from the first-person narrator to the second-person voice tell us about what is being said? What does the floorwalker analogy suggest about Frederic at this moment? Is it an apt analogy? These questions provoke active discussion. Obviously, the implied author is adjusting our view. For what purpose? We ask the cadets to consider the moment in Frederic's life and the topic on his mind. How do people experience such moments? How absurd is the situation? To help them see what's happening, we direct them to the passage where Frederic tells Catherine that he feels like a criminal because he's deserted. We assign a one-page thought piece for homework to invite preliminary assessments of Frederic as soldier. What we hope they get at this point is that Frederic is undergoing a profound transformation.

### Frederic Henry and Catherine Barkley

The relationship between Frederic and Catherine often troubles cadets. Here, narrative distance offers students a means to forestall a young reader's hasty condemnation. Our talk of forestalling hasty condemnation needs some explanation. The goal is not to persuade cadets to adopt an ethic they may deplore. The goal is to get them to open up to the text, to hear the story, and to consider Frederic and Catherine as real human beings—people with character flaws, irrational impulses, good intentions, and the capacity to love. In what follows, we outline how we guide class discussions.

Our first objective is to offer an extended introduction of Frederic Henry and Catherine Barkley. What do we make of Frederic's account of his first intimate encounters with Catherine? A number of passages reveal a complex tension among truth, simulation, and awareness among the author, the narrator, the characters, and the reader. Our narrator is nothing if not candid when it comes to telling us how Frederic the character regards Catherine. Beginning with Frederic the narrator's insight into Frederic the character's strategic reaction to Catherine's slap, we see a candor that is telling in itself. "'I'm so sorry,' she said." Assessing the moment, the narrator tells us that the character Frederic "felt [he] had a certain advantage" (26). And he was all too willing to make use of that advantage:

> "You did say you loved me, didn't you?" [Catherine asks.]
> "Yes," I lied. "I love you." (30)

The confession of the lie progresses to a more troubling picture of Frederic as character: "I turned to her so I could see her face when I kissed her and I saw that her eyes were shut. I kissed both her shut eyes. I thought she was probably a little crazy. It was all right if she was. I did not care if she was. I did not care what I was getting into. This was better than going every evening to the house for officers where the girls climbed all over you and put your cap on backward as a sign of affection between their trips upstairs with brother officers. I knew I did not love Catherine Barkley nor had any idea of loving her. This was a game" (30). A game, Frederic goes on to say, in which the stakes were not named and the uncertainty was okay.

Who is Frederic? A cad? A player? A guy in a war, acting like a guy in a war? Usually, students answer along such lines, and we encourage brief informal debate on the topic, but we always ask them to refrain from a final judgment until we have heard more of Frederic's story. But this passage offers more for critical readers to chew on. We help our students with a number of questions. Why does Frederic make this confession to his readers? More importantly, what does this confession do for the narrative? What difference would it make to the telling of the story had the narrator not told us that he lied to Catherine? We have our students read the passage, changing "I lied" to "I said." With that change, most readers get a feel for the delta separating the character Frederic from the narrator Frederic. The character Frederic has no reason to offer a confession. Only the narrator Frederic does. And in labeling the statement, he tells us something both of his vices and his virtues. Yes, he lied at the moment. But he recognizes the statement as a lie. We usually suggest to our students that the recognition of the character's lie is testimony to the narrator's veracity.

But Catherine is herself a character fraught with the complexities and contradictions revealed by a mask that simply won't stay in place. Is she duped by Frederic? She seems to be all too aware of the tacit motives and rules governing the interlude between herself and her would-be paramour:

> She looked down at the grass.
> "This is a rotten game we play, isn't it?"
> "What game?"
> "Don't be dull."
> "I'm not, on purpose."
> "You're a nice boy," she said. "And you play it as well as you know how. But it's a rotten game." (31)

We find class discussion of this passage helps young readers grasp the complexity of these characters and the narrator who tells their story. Throughout the novel, both characters make use of the word "crazy" to describe Catherine at times. How crazy is Catherine? What does the word mean in reference to her? There are a number of occasions when her behaviors or comments seem erratic or irrational. But the passage tells us that Catherine is not insane in any absolute sense of that word. Those times when she seems irrational may stem from having all too clear a comprehension of life's rotten games. Frederic the narrator reveals a woman who sees through all simulation. She knows Frederic's immediate motive and that his motive is only immediate. Yet, of her own volition, she embraces him in an intimate relationship.

The first step in the transformation of Frederic as cad to Frederic as lover comes after his injury on the battlefield. We have cadets examine the last half of chapter 14, where Frederic and Catherine are physically intimate for the first time. This passage, too, invites scrutiny in terms of narrative distance. We ask students to characterize the passage. For students in an introductory literature class, such a request can be quite challenging. Often they lack the vocabulary or reading experience to make an assessment of the passage. Again, we turn to their visual experience to get them started and ask, "If the book were made into a film, what MPAA rating would it get based on how this passage is presented?" This gets them thinking in terms of criteria with which they've become familiar through experience. As the discussion runs its course, we tell them that we characterize the feel of the passage as urgent but not graphic. That quality comes from what is conveyed without being specifically told. What does that tell us about the implied author? Can we distinguish between the implied author and the narrator here? The passion Frederic the character portrays suggests a person far too trapped in urgency to think in terms of good taste or virtue. But Frederic the narrator has had the advantage of time. Removed from the heat of the moment, he tells the story to admit to truth but not to descend into details of sordidness. What does that tell us of this narrator? Could this omission be a token of an enduring love?

The scene, however, is not a simple declaration of true love. In discussing the possibilities for physical intimacies in the future, we are made privy to this exchange and reflection when Catherine asks Frederic if he will be careful not to expose them:

> "You'll have to be. You're sweet. You do love me, don't you?"
> "Don't say that again. You don't know what that does to me."
> "I'll be careful then. I don't want to do anything more to you. I have to go now, darling, really."

We ask the cadets, "Why would the character Frederic refrain from answering Catherine's question?" The narrator, however, offers his own commentary, which is worth a second reading: "She went out. God knows I had not wanted to fall in love with her. I had not wanted to fall in love with any one. But God knows I had" (93).

With that introduction into the relationship between this man and woman, we organize the remainder of the class discussion around four topical categories examined under the lens of narrative distance. The categories are (1) the implied author's definition of love, (2) the narrator's depictions of intimacy, (3) the character's expressions of emotion, and (4) the final perspective achieved as distance between Frederic the character and Frederic the narrator collapses as we attain the ultimate perspective of the story's ending.

While they are certainly not the only ones to do so, two passages in particular impart a definition of love representing that of the implied author. We discuss them together here. In class, we discuss them as we encounter them in the novel. The first is in the last section of chapter 11. There, Frederic and the priest meander their way into a discussion of love. The priest distinguishes between passion and lust on one hand and love on the other. "When you love," says the priest, "you wish to do things for. You wish to sacrifice for. You wish to serve" (72). While the character Frederic shrugs off the comments, we have to ask why the author included them at all. Certainly they're not necessary to the plot. What purpose do they serve in the story? We don't offer an answer. But later we pick up the same theme with the conversation between Frederic and the count in chapter 35. Again, we ask what purpose this passage has for the story. Is it integral to the plot? Why is it included? For us, the answers come at the end of the chapter. As they conclude their game of billiards, the tone of the conversation shifts and becomes more religious. Acknowledging the effects of time, the count says to Frederic:

"Perhaps I have outlived my religious feeling."
"My own comes only at night." [replies Frederic.]
"Then too you are in love. Do not forget that is a religious feeling." (263)

These passages are not crucial to the plot. We ask the cadets to consider why they are included if they are not crucial. Once the passages are pointed out, cadets can usually distill the standard of love the implied author offers his readers.

With that definition of love established, we concentrate on two topics through the remainder of the novel. The first is the emotions expressed by the characters. The most prominent are curiosity, jealousy, shame, and fear. The passages we highlight include Catherine's curiosity about Frederic's prior relationships (105); Frederic's jealousy over Catherine's late lover (115); Catherine's shame in feeling "like a whore" (152); and Frederic's fear that surfaces first when Catherine comments the doctor thought her "narrow in the hips" (294), culminating in his anticipation of Catherine's death (320). The second is the weight of loss Frederic must bear once he learns to love.

Is intimacy in times of war heightened by the context of war? We pose the question to the class and ask if some notion of that exists in popular culture. Then we ensure that in the course of our discussions we give close attention to the role of the narrator in three of four passages. Those three passages are the narrator telling us that in their talk Frederic and Catherine "said to each other that we were married the first day she had come to the hospital" (114), the short stream-of-consciousness passage in chapter 28 (197), and the narrator's reminiscing in chapter 34 that they were never lonely and that "the things of the night cannot be explained in the day, because they do not then exist" (249). The fourth passage belongs to the characters, but it says so much about the intimacy the two share that we include it in spite of the difference in artistic rendering. That is the passage in chapter 38 where Catherine whimsically wishes she too had had gonorrhea, that she had stayed with all Frederic's girls so she could make fun of them, and that the two of them could cut their hair to look the same (299).

In the first three of the passages, we ask the cadets to comment on whose voice we hear. In addition, we refer to the narrator's confession of Frederic the character's lie as an indication of his own virtues. The questions we have them discuss concerning this topic are designed to get them to think more critically of our narrator and his ethos. Does Frederic and Catherine's saying they were married in the hospital make them married? Is this simply a rationalization? Or do they have a real commitment that transcends the institutions of state and church? Sometimes we follow up by asking them to consider common-law marriage. Focusing on who is speaking, we consider the next two passages along similar lines. In these passages, the gap between character and narrator narrows. Only the narrator can open up to us the thoughts of the character, but we are reading the thoughts of the character in these passages. In those thoughts we see Catherine, the woman Frederic longs for, hopes for, and cares for. Our question for these passages is this: What do they say about Frederic's commitment to Catherine? We as readers are seeing into the depths of the man's soul. What's there?

The fourth passage belongs to the characters and, as a choice of a writer, to the implied author. The passage seems particularly revealing of the intimacy shared between the characters. We ask cadets if it seems like realistic dialogue.

Is this an exchange that might take place in the most intimate moments of a couple who are in love? Then we ask if their expressions sound reasonable. Cadets have been quick to respond in their own terms that we've imposed conflicting standards. The talk of reasonable intimacy is not necessarily the talk of reasonable logic. We then ask what the dialogue reveals to us about the characters. How close are they? How close do they want to be?

The class ends as we take measure of Frederic's loss and his perspective on life from this experience. We have a cadet read aloud the paragraph in chapter 41 that begins, "I sat down on the chair in front of a table" (327). Then, we re-read the lines: "You died. You did not know what it was about. You never had time to learn"(327). At the end of the story, we see a man of bitter experience, a man who has his greatest adventures behind him, a man who has lost the one true love of his life. To help the cadets bring the novel to a close, we ask a number of guiding questions. Is he a bitter man, this narrator who has told us his story? Can we find a suitable single label for him? Is he a loser? Is he the deserving recipient of a just cosmic irony? Is he a victim of circumstance? Is he a tragic figure? Is he an antihero? What are our feelings about and for him as the story ends? To assess what the cadets have taken from this encounter, we assign a paper of five to seven pages in which they conduct a deep ethical analysis of one of the primary characters.

Strict discipline and compliance to regulations have always been a major component of overall instruction at the Air Force Academy, and the Hemingway code hero is a perfect literary role model for such behavior. Harkening back to the antiwar movement of the 1960s, and a questioning of the validity of military service itself, many English departments stopped teaching Hemingway altogether, largely because of a misperception of him as hawkish. The debate in the Air Force Academy's English department, however, unlike that in academia at large, wasn't about whether Hemingway should be taught, but which novel best demonstrated the virtues of the code hero, *The Sun Also Rises* or *A Farewell to Arms*. *Farewell* was selected, and it has been taught here for six decades.

The novel breathes life into what has become for too many cadets a threadbare phrase—the fog and friction of war. The novel compels students to grapple with war as a horror of human making, a thing that must be weighed against other things of human making, such as fear, courage, appetite, and love. As humans, we all are subject to failings and all are urged to pursue the higher virtues of our being. Both the failings and the virtues come at great price. With service comes the possibility of honor as well as the possibility of shame. With love comes the possibility of fulfillment as well as the possibility of ultimate loss. Moreover, one's end may be as much in the hands of fate as in the determination of the individual. We believe that if our cadets leave with a firm sense of the contingent in life, they are better prepared to serve their country.

## NOTE

We would like to thank Professor Donald Anderson for his editorial contributions.

## APPENDIX: Wayne Booth on Narrative Distance

For a complete discussion of these ideas, see Booth's *The Rhetoric of Fiction* (120–35, 154–59).

In *The Rhetoric of Fiction* Wayne Booth has offered some useful concepts to use when thinking about how the manner in which a story is told factors into our understanding of what is said, and the moral fiber (ethos) of the storyteller as well as the story's characters.

The first concept to be aware of is the notion of *implied author*. The reason we talk about an "implied" author is because it is practically impossible to say with any certainty what the intent of a flesh-and-blood author was. But we can note the choices an author makes in his or her art and draw inferences from those. Ask yourself, what is the image or the persona of the author who emerges from a story as you read it? Pay attention to what the author directs your attention to. What are you asked to see? In how much detail? What, if any, moral or philosophical problems are present in the scenes? Does the author impose an obvious narrator in the story? Or is the story related with the silence of a camera's eye?

The second concept to be aware of is that of *distance*. Distance is closely related to the idea of implied author, as it is one way we come to form an idea of who the implied author is through his or her choices in telling a story. Consider distance in this way. In Alfred Hitchcock's *Psycho,* we never actually see anyone stabbed. We see a knife raised, we hear music reach a strident chord, we see a shower drain filled with what is ostensibly blood—but we never witness a stabbing. Now compare that technique to the thriller/slasher films of today. The difference is not one of subject, but of distance.

In discussing narrative distance, Booth lists at least five ways in which it reveals important differences among implied authors, narrators, characters, and readers. For one, "the *narrator* may be more or less distant from the *implied author*" (156). For another, "the *narrator* may be more or less distant from the *characters* in the story he tells" (156). Third, "the *narrator* may be more or less distant from the *reader's* own norms" (156). Fourth, "the *implied author* may be more or less distant from the *reader*" (157). Fifth, "the *implied author* (carrying the reader with him) may be more or less distant from *other characters*" (157–58).

# A Conversation among Wars
## Teaching *A Farewell to Arms* as an American War Novel

*Jennifer Haytock*

STUDYING HEMINGWAY'S *A Farewell to Arms* among a variety of other war novels can help us define what a war novel is and how well Hemingway's novel both meets and creates that definition. Graduate students, and perhaps upper-division majors, have the luxury of studying such a narrow topic (although I have found that students don't find the topic narrow at all by the end of the semester) and thus are an appropriate group for this course of study. In this chapter, I base the methods and results of teaching *A Farewell to Arms* in a war literature course on my experience teaching a seminar on the American war novel for masters students at the University of Illinois at Springfield in the fall of 2003.[1] The course covers literature about four wars in which the United States participated, and *A Farewell to Arms* is part of a three-novel unit on U.S. engagement in World War I. The first two novels in the unit are Willa Cather's *One of Ours* (1922) and Thomas Boyd's *Through the Wheat* (1923), both of which illustrate how most soldiers and people on the home front understood the war. I present *A Farewell to Arms,* which appeared over a decade after the war ended, as a later reaction to the war and as part of the modernist movement that the war was instrumental in evoking, and thus also as a postwar novel.

Additional texts taught in the course in fall 2003 include Stepen Crane's *The Red Badge of Courage* and William Faulkner's *The Unvanquished* in the Civil War unit; James Jones's *The Thin Red Line,* Kurt Vonnegut's *Slaughterhouse-Five,* and Cynthia Ozick's *The Shawl* in the Word War II segment of the course; and finally, Michael Herr's *Dispatches,* Tim O'Brien's *The Things They Carried,* and Bobbie Ann Mason's *In Country,* all on Vietnam. The novels I selected include a mix of battle-front novels and home-front and postwar novels so that we may address some larger questions, such as what war means in United States society, how perceptions of war clash with the experience of war, and what it means to be a "war novel."

Other appropriate texts might be Charles Frazier's *Cold Mountain,* John Dos Passos's *Three Soldiers,* Edith Wharton's *A Son at the Front,* Leslie Marmon Silko's *Ceremony,* David Guterson's *Snow Falling on Cedars,* Joseph Heller's *Catch-22,* Tim O'Brien's *Going After Cacciato,* and Phillip Caputo's *A Rumor of War*—and I'm sure there are many others. (Of course, some of these texts are not novels: *Dispatches* is memoir and reportage, while *The Unvanquished, The Shawl,* and *The Things They Carried* are something in between novels and collections of short stories.) One problem with an American war novel class is the limited pool of texts by women and writers of color (hence the particular value of Silko's *Ceremony,* which also invokes the internal war between white Americans and American Indians), but most war texts refer, at least obliquely, to racial divisions in the United States. Civil War texts, of course, instigate conversations about slavery, and *The Unvanquished* discusses the African American experience as well as that of women left behind. World War I and II texts reveal the racism that permeated the military, for example in its insistence on segregation and its reservation of front-line positions for white men. Vietnam novels show an integrated military, with equal opportunities for being blown to pieces—thus the history of American wars is also a history of American race relations.

Assignments for the course include weekly writings on several discussion questions; students write about four pages a week for fourteen weeks, resulting in approximately fifty pages of writing (I lessen the load near the end of the semester, when students need to focus on writing their seminar essay). The discussion questions factor into the course in two ways: (1) I collect and grade students' answers, focusing my grading on their ideas. I ask them to write informally and not to worry too much about grammar. This process demands that they develop their own interpretations, preparing them for the process of writing their seminar essay. (2) Their written answers provide them with ideas to present to the class. Students are therefore thoroughly prepared to discuss the week's text, and if conversation should lag, I can call on a student to explain what he or she wrote. Students even started doing this themselves; occasionally someone would say, "I want to hear what so-and-so wrote on this question."

Other assignments for the course include a review of a critical book on a topic related to the course, a presentation of that book review to the class, and a seminar essay. The seminar essay actually consists of three parts: an annotated bibliography, to ensure that students start their research early, understand it, and can receive researched guidance if necessary; the seminar essay itself, an eighteen-to-twenty-page critical interpretation of one of the texts; and a presentation of their essays to the class. Most of a student's grade for the course comes from weekly writings, in-class participation, and the seminar essay.

## PREPARING FOR *A Farewell to Arms*

I began the unit on World War I by examining war posters and discussing the power of propaganda, especially in creating an ideology of gender. Maurice Rickards's *Posters of the First World War* is a classic text containing a variety of propaganda from most, if not all, of the participating nations in the war. Although we focused on American propaganda posters, I think it is useful for the students to see that similar strategies were used across nations. Walton Rawls's *Wake Up, America! World War I and the American Poster* concentrates exclusively on propaganda in the United States. It's also easy to find World War I posters on the Web (for example, at the Web site of the Georgetown University Special Collections at http://www.library.georgetown.edu/dept/speccoll/amposter.htm, to name only one), and if a classroom has a computer with a projection system, the instructor can present images from the Web, with the advantage that more posters can be seen in color. Some posters that lead to fruitful discussion are "Remember Belgium," which shows silhouettes of a German soldier dragging a young girl with streaming hair against a fiery background; "Destroy This Mad Brute," which has an image of a Germanic ape ascending the U.S. shore with the club of *kultur* in one hand and a woman in the other; "Gee! I wish I were a man," with a woman in sailor's uniform; and an untitled image of a woman and child drowning in a deep blue-green sea, a reference to the sinking of the *Lusitania*. These posters convey the public dehumanization of the Germans—their categorization as Huns and *Boches* and rapists of Belgium—and the attempt of the United States government to transform Americans into saviors of women and culture. Another illuminating poster shows a sailor plucking a newspaper from a civilian's hand, while the caption says: "The Navy needs you! Don't read American history—make it!" This poster lures young American men into believing that an individual can make a difference in war, an ideal that conflicts sharply with the experiences of soldiers such as William Hicks in *Through the Wheat* and Frederic Henry in *A Farewell to Arms* (but not Claude Wheeler in *One of Ours*). The clash of the ideal and the experience helps destroy these soldiers' illusions about the war.

Before reading *A Farewell to Arms*, students study two Civil War texts, Crane's *The Red Badge of Courage* and Faulkner's *The Unvanquished*, and two other World War I novels, Cather's *One of Ours* and Boyd's *Through the Wheat*. *One of Ours,* for which Cather won a Pulitzer Prize in 1923, traces the life of Claude Wheeler, a young man from a small town in Nebraska, through his attempts to find meaning and satisfaction in his life. His feelings of failure at the hands of his university, his family, farming, and his marriage all prepare him to join the military and to succeed as an officer, leading his men to victory though sacrificing himself in the process. *Through the Wheat* focuses only on front-line experience through the eyes of William Hicks, a soldier who quickly becomes disillusioned by the inanity of the war and who, though he remains committed to fighting, loses himself in the process. By the time students read *A Farewell to Arms,* they are familiar with how American culture created soldiers who were willing to subsume their identity in the military (Claude Wheeler) and who resented U.S. propaganda and ideology and suffered the numbing effects of technological warfare (William Hicks). We have already addressed some questions of authorship, since Crane, Faulkner, and Cather did not see war before writing about it—in contrast to Boyd, who was a World War I veteran. Cather's situation is even more complicated, of course, but by reading her work alongside that of male writers who hadn't seen war either, students see that noncombatant men and women were in much the same position. The students in my fall 2003 seminar concluded that they did not believe that a writer had to see war in order to be able to write about it, although they did find Cather's description of technological warfare to be far more sanitized and thus less realistic than Boyd's. They did, however, appreciate the backstory Cather gives to a World War I soldier; Claude's disenchantment with American capitalism, family structure, and enforced heterosexuality helped the students understand what happened to soldiers when they reached the front.

In the once-a-week seminar I taught in fall 2003, I usually required students to read a book per week, but we spent two class periods on *A Farewell to Arms.* Because it is the last book in the World War I unit, it makes sense to spread its discussion over two weeks. I asked the students to read two-thirds of the novel for the first class and to finish it for the second. For the second class I also asked them to read Freud's "Why War?" and excerpts from the chapter "The Structure of War: The Juxtaposition of Injured Bodies and Unanchored Issues" (62–65, 80–83, 86–91, 108–25) in Elaine Scarry's *The Body in Pain: The Making and Unmaking of the World.* In the second week we finish up lingering issues in the novel itself and then discuss all three World War I novels together. I add in the Freud and Scarry material at this time because students have read a significant number of war texts, have considered on their own some of the issues these pieces raise, and are ready to address broader issues of violence, the body, and civilization.

Because, like almost all students, graduate students have heard of Hemingway before they've read his work, I think it's important to spend some time differentiating between Hemingway's experience in the war and that of Frederic Henry. In the first class I lecture briefly about Hemingway's life and the writing of *A Farewell to Arms*. Michael Reynolds's *Hemingway's First War: The Making of* A Farewell to Arms and Henry Serrano Villard and James Nagel's *Hemingway in Love and War: The Lost Diary of Agnes von Kurowsky, Her Letters, and Correspondence of Ernest Hemingway* both document Hemingway's participation in World War I, his relationship with Agnes von Kurowsky, and the writing of *A Farewell to Arms*. Both books contain primary material such as letters, journal entries, and photographs, which make them interesting to pass around the class as we discuss the novel's background (x-rays of Hemingway's injury and the bullet behind his kneecap are particularly interesting). Students need to understand that Hemingway saw front-line fighting only briefly and did not become disillusioned with the war while in Italy. They also benefit from learning about Agnes's enjoyment of the war—that the war opened up the world for her perhaps more than it did for Hemingway. Reading aloud a few of her journal entries (for example, June 17, 1918; August 31 through early September 1918) reveals her cheery attitude toward her work and her experiences abroad. I also find it helpful, in measure, to show a few clips from the film based on Villard and Nagel's work, *In Love and War* (1996) with Sandra Bullock and Chris O'Donnell. To demonstrate the difference in maturity between Ernest and Agnes, I show the scene in which Agnes resists a doctor's intention to amputate and treats Ernest's leg herself (a five-minute segment approximately twenty-three minutes into the film); we see her inside knowledge and his bravado. Bullock's performance as Agnes is too subdued to capture the free spirit evident in her journals, I think, but the scene where she's working around the clock with the doctors at the front demonstrates to students that war is also women's work and that they could be just as dedicated to it as men. I also show the scene in which she's working at the front, Ernest finds her, and they meet at a brothel (approximately 1:09–1:15). Her decision to sleep with Ernest helps the students see how expectations for women's behavior change during war.

Reynolds's *Hemingway's First War* shows that Hemingway's novel, while not unrelated to his own experience, is more fiction than autobiography. Frederic Henry was in the war years longer than Hemingway; Frederic and Catherine both are disillusioned and war weary, as Hemingway and Agnes were not; and Hemingway researched his story, particularly the retreat from Caporetto, rather than experiencing it. Since we have already discussed Cather's writing of *One of Ours* based on her cousin's letters and interviews with other soldiers and Crane's use of photographs for research, students are able to compare writing methods.

To work around students' dismissive belief that Hemingway simply hated women, I refer to Jamie Barlowe's essay "Hemingway's Gender Training." This article helps explain Hemingway's complicated relationship to gender, a relationship that has often been viewed as misogynist but that Barlowe argues to be indicative of his greater interest in masculinity than in femininity. She explains the historical context of the women's movement, the degree to which the women in Hemingway's life were involved, and Hemingway's reaction to their participation.

Before discussing *A Farewell to Arms* in class, I ask students to write out answers to the following questions, the first four for the first week and the remainder for the second week:

1. Does Frederic Henry change through the course of the novel? Consider his attitude about the war, his relationship with Catherine, and his perceptions about himself. You may wish to refer to other "heroes" we have read about this semester.

2. An important part of *A Farewell to Arms* is Frederic's injury. What does this novel suggest about the relationship of injury to the war? How is bodily experience in general portrayed?

3. This war novel has a much more significant front-line female presence than any of the others we have read. What is Catherine's relationship to war? What is the war's relationship to her? How does bringing together war and a heterosexual relationship affect the meaning of war? Of a heterosexual relationship?

4. Consider the role of the priest or Rinaldi: how does his presence affect our understanding of the meaning of war?

5. How and where do idealism and reality clash? Consider, among other things, the divisions in the Italian army in attitudes toward the war, Frederic's rejection of words like "honor," and the Italian perspective versus the American perspective.

6. *A Farewell to Arms* may be considered *the* defining novel of World War I. Do you agree or disagree with that assessment? Explain your answer, as well as your criteria for evaluation.

7. Explain how Scarry's ideas about the purpose and/or activity of war help us understand one of the novels we have read.

8. Explain how Freud's ideas about the purpose and/or meaning of war help us understand one of the novels we have read (a different novel from above).

## THE NOVEL IN DISCUSSION

Although I lecture briefly about the novel, almost all class time is spent in discussion, during which I ask students to draw on their writings for the week. Each of the following sections explains how the above discussion questions can be used to stimulate and shape class conversation.

### Questions 1, 2, and 7: Frederic Henry and Injury

We discuss Frederic Henry in light of other literary soldiers who have experienced war and whether or not they change. I start the class by asking students how they responded to question 1. In the fall 2003 class, the student[2] who made the strongest case for Frederic changing looked at his attitude toward defeat: early in the novel Frederic argues with his men that "defeat is worse" than war (50), but later he reverses this opinion. After he's wounded, he tells the priest, "We are all gentler now because we are beaten. How would Our Lord have been if Peter had rescued him in the Garden?" (178) and that "I don't believe in defeat. Though it may be better" (179). We explore the implications of this last passage: Frederic's comment that defeat is better than war indicates the full horror of war but also offers the startling possibility that the Allies might not win and that therefore Europe might now be very different. Further, the hesitation in this sentence (not believing in defeat; "may be" better) reveals Frederic's increasing feeling that the war will never end—that, in fact, it cannot end. Finally, his lack of belief in defeat as a concept signifies how far his disillusionment has gone. What happens if a soldier fails to recognize the difference between winning and losing?

Many students, however, argue that Frederic does not change, so we look for moments in the text that signal his distance or indifference. They point out that he had entered the war casually ("'I was in Italy,' I said, 'and I spoke Italian'" [22]) and that he left it just as casually: "Anger was washed away in the river along with any obligation. . . . I was through. I wished them all the luck. There were the good ones, and the brave ones, and the calm ones and the sensible ones, and they deserved it. But it was not my show any more" (232). Many students see Frederic as selfish and as purposefully distancing himself from the war, especially through drinking. Students tended to compare Frederic with Crane's Henry Fleming, whom many of them had also seen as failing to move beyond a juvenile interest in his own honor. Frederic, they thought, seems unable to care about much beyond his own comfort. I ask the students to consider the implications of Frederic's lack of growth: How is it that such a devastating event as war can *not* change a person?

Frederic's experience in war involves his injury, so we talk about that event. In the first week of discussion, students have not yet read the Scarry selections, but they tend to bring up points that they will read about in more abstract terms for the following week. For example, Frederic's wounding demonstrates the impersonal technological aspects of World War I. Students noted the mundanity of being blown up while eating cheese as well as his later refusal to transform the event into something noble and heroic when discussing it with Rinaldi (63). They also pointed out the absurd necessity of the orderlies documenting Frederic's injury to protect him from later accusations of a self-inflicted wound. In the second class period, we discuss Scarry's arguments that war is injuring, that it is "the most unceasingly radical and rigorous form of work" (82), and that war is a contest. I find it important to emphasize the premise that injury is essential to war yet does not determine the winner. We also consider Scarry's points that the body becomes political and nationalized (111–12); that wounds themselves are a way of commemorating the war but do not reveal the winner (118); that war does not force the losing side to give in to the winner's demands but rather *appears to* force the losing side into doing so (120); and that the soldier, by agreeing to kill, "wrench[es] around his most fundamental sanctions about how within civilization (and this particular civilization, his country) another embodied person can be touched; he divests himself of civilization, decivilizes himself" (122).

The description of the actual moment of Frederic's injury (54) is also worth discussing. If students don't notice this themselves, it's worthwhile to point out that the shift in tone to a stream-of-consciousness narration suggests the intensity of the moment and a recognition that the body is the ultimate betrayer. The passage represents the modernist aspects of the novel, but it also connects the moment of Frederic's wound to the nights he spent with a prostitute (13), which are similarly relayed through Frederic's clouded senses and memory. Students then lead the conversation either to Catherine Barkley or to modernism.

### Questions 3 and 8: The Problem of Catherine Barkley

Unlike other war novels, A Farewell to Arms includes a romance that is central to the plot.[3] Most of the students in my fall 2003 course, I found, responded poorly to the Frederic-Catherine romance, finding Catherine herself insipid and overly submissive and the relationship to be hollow. Although I had anticipated this response, I had underestimated the degree of their disgust with Catherine and their refusal to believe in the love affair, so we spent more time than I had planned discussing the links in the novel between romance and war.

First, we talk about Catherine's relationship to the war, prompted by my asking the class what we know about her past: she has been a VAD since the beginning of the war,[4] her fiancé died at the Somme, and she has witnessed trench warfare and its effects on the body. Students tend to have greater sympathy for Catherine, I have found, when they understand that she is a real participant in the war. It may also be necessary to explain what Catherine's life could have been: students benefit from understanding the culture she comes from, a Victorian society that expects women to be submissive, stay in the home, marry, and sacrifice their personal needs for their families'. In that context, my students realize that Catherine's initial "craziness" is not so bizarre, and they see her as a true rebel, made so by the war—even more changed by the war than Frederic. Most students will have read *The Sun Also Rises* and will have higher expectations for Catherine, but when they realize Catherine, though written later, is a precursor to someone like Brett Ashley, she makes more sense.

Second, I ask the students to discuss parallels between Frederic's and Catherine's experiences, framing the question in terms of what jobs each must do: Frederic to lead, Catherine to nurse and then to bear a child. As a lieutenant in the Italian army, Frederic is in charge of his group of ambulance drivers. Students generally find, however, that he fails in this position: they point to his target practice with his pistol, his shooting of the mutinying soldier (whom he does hit but, as my students are quick to point out, does not kill), and his failure to get his ambulances back during the retreat. Many, if not all, of these failures are not Frederic's fault, but the key is for students to understand that that is precisely the point. The cards are stacked against him, and there is no possible way in this war for him to succeed.

Students point out that Catherine is a much better VAD than Frederic is an officer. She does nothing outstanding in the novel, but she works hard, and her patients seem to respect her. Certainly Frederic recovers, indicating to some degree the quality of her care. But students struggle with identifying her job, noting that it shifts in the middle of the novel: she becomes pregnant, and her job then becomes to deliver a child. I encourage students to explore the implications of the pairing of Frederic's job as soldier and Catherine's as child bearer. Just as Frederic fails as an officer, Catherine fails at childbearing. She tries to get rid of the baby, suggests that life would be better if the oar hit her in the stomach (many students were eager to discuss Catherine's possible attempts at abortion), and ultimately dies while delivering a stillborn child. Again, students see that her failure is not her fault; her body betrays her.[5] Both Frederic's failure to lead and Catherine's failure to deliver a child stem from circumstances beyond each character's control, and these individual failures become metaphors for soldiers' powerlessness in face of the technological power of World War I.

Finally, I ask students to consider broader connections between sex and death, using Freud's "Why War?" as a framework (this part of the conversation actually takes place the second week). In this essay Freud explains, among other things, his theories about the erotic instinct and the destructive instinct, arguing that the two are not easily separable: "It seems as though an instinct of the one sort can scarcely ever operate in isolation; it is always accompanied—or, as we say, alloyed—with an element from the other side, which modifies its aim or is, in some cases, what enables it to achieve that aim" (141). To prevent war, Freud argues, we must strengthen the Eros instinct: "Anything that encourages the growth of emotional ties between men must operate against war" (144). In *A Farewell to Arms,* students argue, it seems as though Freud's theory has some merit. With a loving relationship and a child on the way, Frederic walks away from war, and the Italian soldiers too want to put down their weapons and go home. This turns out not to be enough, however; not only does the enemy not want to walk away, but Catherine's death bleakly symbolizes the futility of holding on to love, perhaps even reviving the destructive instinct.

## Question 4: Rinaldi and the Priest

*A Farewell to Arms* is a useful text for demonstrating to students that the war novel genre expands beyond stories about front-line experience and that war affects not only soldiers but also many noncombatants. We discuss this issue earlier in the course, with *The Unvanquished,* in which the Civil War is seen primarily as affecting women and children and concludes with a picture of postwar life in the South. *One of Ours* and *Through the Wheat* are both stories of soldiers (although *One of Ours* gives a useful description of American life before the war and, through Claude's mother and one or two veterans in the last pages, hints at postwar disillusionment), but *A Farewell to Arms* presents very few front-line soldiers. Most of the characters are support staff: Frederic Henry, an ambulance driver; his men, who resist the war and its ideology; Catherine Barkley, a British VAD; Rinaldi, who is part of the medical staff; and the priest.

Students in the seminar were very interested in both Rinaldi and the priest. I had asked them to write about one or the other of these characters, but several students said they wished they had been asked to compare the two (and at least one student wrote about both of them anyway). In class, then, we combined our discussions of these two characters. Both Rinaldi and the priest are or become disillusioned with the war and with their society, and both fail to find satisfaction in their jobs. As a doctor, Rinaldi fixes his patients only to see them blown up later. The priest finds the soldiers too disillusioned to treat him with respect, and he resents their abuse: "In my country it is understood that a man may love God. It is not a dirty joke" (71). Several students noted that the two characters represented two poles or possibilities for Frederic Henry in responding to the war: the depraved indifference of Rinaldi or the sad help-lessness of the priest. Rinaldi also represents pleasures of the body in contrast to the priest's spirituality. Students disagreed on whether Frederic takes some-thing from both men or rejects them both.

Discussions of homosexuality, of course, came up in connection with both Rinaldi and the priest. Because Rinaldi is clearly engaging in heterosexual activity, students must address ambiguous sexuality, relations between men that are not necessarily sexual,[6] and sexual activity that may occur during war that would not occur during peacetime. Students found the priest to be more problematic than Rinaldi, for while Frederic appears to resist Rinaldi, the priest seems to evoke sexual feelings from Frederic. Students pointed to the conver-sation between the priest and Frederic after Frederic returns to the front, dur-ing which Frederic "stroked the blanket with [his] hand" (178). (The hints at homosexuality in A Farewell to Arms prepare students for the more graphic depictions of homosexuality in James Jones's The Thin Red Line.) I find that students get frustrated when they cannot come to a conclusion about whether or not homosexual activities take place or even whether homosexual feelings exist in the book, and I use this frustration as an important learning moment. What difference does it make in our understanding of the novel, I ask, whether Frederic and Rinaldi had sex? Or whether Frederic is attracted to the priest? We then play out scenarios of interpretation, which teaches students that such questions do not need to have one definitive answer; that multiple interpreta-tions can exist side by side; and further, that one interpretation can play off another, creating yet another reading of the novel.

### Questions 5 and 6: A Farewell to Arms *as a Modernist War Novel*

In response to whether A Farewell to Arms is *the* defining war novel, students generally agree that the question doesn't have to be answered (that is, why pick just one?), but it does open up the conversation about what is required of a war novel. We discuss whether different things are expected of a World War I novel (specific elements or events of the war, such as trench warfare and chemical at-tacks, both missing from A Farewell to Arms) and of an American war novel (several students had read All Quiet on the Western Front and would nominate it as a defining World War I novel). As the U.S. experience was different from that of other nations in World War I, we did feel that the American background was an important part of an American World War I novel. In A Farewell to Arms, stu-dents felt, this Americanness was demonstrated most in Frederic's half-hearted commitment to his military duty. As the British Catherine points out, "It's not deserting from the army. It's only the Italian army" (251).

Students extrapolated from our discussion of *The Unvanquished* (and also from their own knowledge of *The Sun Also Rises* and other 1920s disillusionment fiction) and pointed out that *A Farewell to Arms* is already a postwar book, one heralding the disenchantment of the 1920s. Since *A Farewell to Arms* was written in the 1920s and encompassed Hemingway's ten years of experience since the war, including his marriage to and divorce from Hadley Richardson and his marriage to Pauline Pfeiffer and her dangerous cesarean delivery, this reading is important. The literary movement of modernism was in full swing, and although we see aspects of modernism in the irony of *One of Ours* and in the futility and loss of sense in *Through the Wheat*, *A Farewell to Arms* is known as a modernist novel as much as it is as a war novel. Thus we discuss ways that categories of literature overlap—and can be confining if they are not allowed to overlap.

I feel it is important to discuss modernism in relation to *A Farewell to Arms* in an American war novel course for several reasons. An advantage of a war literature course is that students can track changes in American literature as responses to war: realism to the Civil War, modernism to World War I, postmodernism to World War II. This helps students understand that literature does not occur in a vacuum—that social, political, and cultural changes affect not only the content but also the form of literature. At the same time, literature helps readers understand their culture and the changes happening in it. Writers of war literature tend to be faced with the problem of conveying to their readers highly traumatic experiences that explode previously held ideas of reality, so those writers take on new forms and new language to relate a new understanding of the world. On a larger scale, however, I explain to my students that war alone does not change literature, and we discuss other events that affect literary practice. With *A Farewell to Arms*, we can focus on that decade between Hemingway's experience of war (and I remind them of our discussion of Hemingway's lack of war weariness at the time of World War I) and the writing of the novel, and I ask them what other social and political changes occurred in that time period. Students often identify significant events, including but not limited to the postwar economic boom, women's suffrage, and Prohibition, that created the disillusionment and rejection of established values that characterize modernism.

## *A Farewell to Arms* AND AFTER

After *A Farewell to Arms*, we move to Jones's *The Thin Red Line*, a novel that offers students a different approach to the war novel. Most war novels follow the bildungsroman structure, telling the story of the change of one man in war, but *The Thin Red Line* narrates the life of a company as it invades a Pacific island and faces its first combat. Students tend to be fascinated by the contrast; Jones's soldiers are so much a part of something bigger, even as they maintain, to some degree, their individuality, that Frederic Henry's unique position as an officer in a foreign army is thrown into sharp relief. At the same time students can still trace individual stories in *The Thin Red Line,* and we can tie both novels back to the pattern and issues established in Crane's *The Red Badge of Courage.* Hemingway responded to Crane by rejecting the notions of honor and courage that many readers find in Crane; and Jones, through Corporal Fife, also directly rewrites Henry Fleming's experience. *The Thin Red Line* helps shed light back on *A Farewell to Arms* as well, most particularly through the eroticization of combat that members of C-for-Charlie Company experience. For most of the soldiers, witnessing or participating in violence evokes sexual excitement and sexual guilt. Jones's explicit treatment of this reaction helps students reevaluate the romance embedded in or driving *A Farewell to Arms;* is Frederic's desire for Catherine, we wondered, really a channeling of his sexual response to war?

Some of the Vietnam literature also shows an evolution from Frederic Henry's disillusionment. Frederic rejects words like "glory" and "sacrifice" because "only the names of places had dignity" (185). In *Dispatches,* Michael Herr shifts meaning once more: "reading [the maps] was like trying to read the faces of the Vietnamese, and that was like trying to read the wind. We knew that the uses of most information were flexible, different pieces of ground told different stories to different people" (3). Names of places, although prominent in Vietnam literature, here are displaced in favor of people. Herr's memoir focuses not on events but on American soldiers, who often remain nameless but whose stories ring through and multiply in the text.

Near the end of the seminar, we came back to the definition of a war novel and discussed why "war novels" are so often "antiwar novels"—and yet war does not go away. In *Jarhead: A Marine's Chronicle of the Gulf War and Other Battles,* Anthony Swofford tells of his platoon renting Vietnam movies to get themselves in the mood for war: "Vietnam war films are all pro-war, no matter what the supposed message, what Kubrick or Coppola or Stone intended. . . . The magic brutality of the films celebrates the terrible and despicable beauty of [the marines'] fighting skills. Fight, rape, war, pillage, burn. Filmic images of death and carnage are pornography for the military man" (6–7).[7] Discussing Michael Herr's *Dispatches,* students were disturbed to note that the book does not dispel the glamour associated with war. At the time of this writing, the United States is engaged in the occupation and rebuilding of Afghanistan and Iraq and in the larger war on terror, and although we do not yet have much fiction about either Gulf War, I asked the class to speculate on what that fiction might be like. Students noted recent films such as *Black Hawk Down* and *Three Kings* as vehicles through which to understand the contemporary military, and we contemplated the changes not only in society but in literature that may be brought about by further technological changes in warfare and by women serving in increasing numbers and in combat roles.

## Notes

1. Many thanks to Kelly Alexander, Kandice Biggs, Joseph Carrier, Sarah Franklin, Jason Gallagher, Denise Howard, and Jeris Vascellero for participating in this seminar and teaching me about *A Farewell to Arms*.

2. Thanks to Sarah Franklin for this reading.

3. In "The Romance of Desire in Hemingway's Fiction," Linda Wagner-Martin, in fact, argues that "even the war scenes exist to prepare the reader, to reinforce the message of the conventional romance—that the deepest, the greatest, loves are doomed—to death" (61). Wagner-Martin's article gives useful background on Hemingway's understanding and use of romance and eroticism.

4. Jane Marcus's essay "Corpus/Corps/Corpse: Writing the Body at War" is helpful for explaining to students the cultural significance of the Voluntary Aid Detachment.

5. In "*A Farewell to Arms:* Doctors in the House of Love," Michael Reynolds argues that bad doctoring is one of the major obstacles in the novel.

6. Eve Kosofsky Sedgwick's *Between Men: English Literature and Male Homosocial Desire* might be a useful text to bring in; discussions of the homosocial would be highly relevant to a war novel course.

7. John Gregory Dunne's review of *Jarhead* in the *New York Review of Books* prompted me to include another war text in the course.

# GENDER ISSUES

# A Journey Shared
## *A Farewell to Arms* as Catherine Barkley's Story

*Amy Lerman*

"Don't worry, darling," Catherine said. "I'm not a bit afraid.
It's just a dirty trick."

IN THE last week of September 1929, *A Farewell to Arms* was published. By November, the novel resided at the top of best-seller rankings, and in 1930 it was added to the fiction section of the presidential library (Baker, *Life Story* 205, 209). While working on the novel, Ernest Hemingway had "begun to refer to his novel as '[his] long tale of transalpine fornication including the entire war in Italy and so to BED'" (Baker, *Life Story* 199), but critics saw it for more: Clifton Fadiman called it "the very apotheosis of a kind of modernism," Malcolm Cowley saw the title as symbolic of Hemingway's "farewell to a period, an attitude, and perhaps to a method also," and Allen Tate declared it "a masterpiece" (qtd. in Baker, *Life Story* 204, 205).

Over the years, I have taught *A Farewell to Arms* in a variety of literature courses, from first-year introductory courses, to Critical Reading and Writing about Literature (a class specifically designed for English majors), to Best Sellers in Literature, to Major American Authors and Survey of American Literature (a course taught at the junior-senior level). And each time I have selected the novel for a course, I have faced some type of opposition from my colleagues. Questions such as, "How can you teach a dead, white, male author in this day and age?" and, "Why choose a novel so debasing in its female characterizations?" and, "Don't you think the book is too sappy and sentimental to teach?" surface and resurface. Even I might admit that *Farewell* does not represent the most impressive selection from Hemingway's oeuvre, for it does indulge a bit heavily in melodrama, but its focus on characters of the same age as traditional college students, its traumatic love story, and its setting of war make it a timely text.

Moreover, I can counter with my stock answer, namely, that today Hemingway is frequently taught because he is considered essential to the canon of twentieth-century American literature. To the naysayers, too, I can also acknowledge that Hemingway often comes under attack for his seemingly politically incorrect dialogue as well as his stereotypical, demeaning female characterizations; many laymen (and women) readers and critics alike are hesitant to credit Hemingway for his sensitivity in the development and implementation of his fictional women. Claims, for example, that Catherine Barkley typifies "a one-dimensional pasteboard figure" (Lewis, *Farewell* 69) who suffers from "compulsive apologizing" (Fetterley 70) and "willingly abdicates from what little self she has to give herself over to his desires" (Comley and Scholes 39) cause many to dismiss her as too flat and ultimately a deficient representation of a woman.

Still, I feel confident in my defense of Catherine Barkley (and, given the opportunity, other Hemingway female characters) as a multifaceted, primary character in *A Farewell to Arms,* for the novel could not exist without her. While Frederic preoccupies himself with matters of war in the first half of the novel—his post, his friendships with Rinaldi and the priest, his injury, his desertion—he becomes increasingly consumed by his feelings for Catherine, particularly once he is able to rejoin his beloved. From his narrative perspective, amid an idyllic existence together, they function as one, incapable of being separated or alone, as Frederic's confession crystallizes: "I'm no good when you're not there. I haven't any life at all any more" (300). Frederic admits to both himself and to Catherine that she has a powerful hold on him, unaware, perhaps, of just how skillfully she guides and leads him for so much of their relationship. This is not to suggest that Catherine is manipulative; rather, her words, gestures, and actions resonate quite selflessly. In a non-didactic but natural, caring manner, she educates him about love and pending fatherhood, demonstrates (self-)confidence and contentment—"Then don't worry, darling. You were fine until now and now you're worrying" (155)—and embodies bravery and courage, traits Frederic hopes he emulates. Thus, if I can enlighten young readers' minds to the notion that at least one of Hemingway's female characters can be understood as sympathetic, independent, intelligent, brave, and highly motivated, a proposition many are resistant to accept at first, then I have provided my students, through their reading of *Farewell,* with a twofold experience, namely, a fine read paired with a critical interpretation that challenges stock ones of the novel.

Of course, my students, unknowingly, most of the time, pose the greater challenge and resistance to my book selection. And indeed, the novel swells with challenges, particularly for young adult contemporary readers. Why, for instance, does Hemingway, an *American* author, they like to remind me, sometimes refrain from translating the Italian? After Frederic is "blown up while . . . eating cheese" (63) and feels himself "rush bodily out of" himself (54), he describes his injured colleague's ramblings—"Dio te salve, Maria. Dio te salve, Maria"—and then himself shouts out twice for the "Porta feriti" so a stretcher can be brought for Passini (55). Many of my students are bilingual, and I remind all of them of our capacity to "code switch" and cater our tones and language to an intended audience. Thus, they come to realize how the Italian spoken reflects the realism and urgency of the scene: with powerful immediacy, Frederic provides firsthand blow-by-blow description as he calls for help, while he and his colleagues fight for their lives.

In addition, with Frederic Henry and Catherine Barkley, students wonder, "Why do they talk so funny?" She especially can annoy young new readers, as her conversation seems like a stream of non sequiturs: "You're such a silly boy. . . . But I'll look after you. Isn't it splendid, darling, that I don't have any morning-sickness?" (251). And with Hemingway's precise, graphic descriptions of evasion and elements of war, they inquire, "Why's there so much detail about all the scenery and blood and Frederic's going AWOL?" These questions signify the disinterest of so many who initially might well prefer a more readable romance or the timeliness of really cool special effects in a modern adaptation of war on film, such as *Pearl Harbor.*

And their reactions are understandable, at the very least, in a demographic sense. At flagship state universities in both the Midwest and the Southwest, my student audiences have consisted primarily of in-state, traditionally aged individuals; in other words, they are recent high school graduates for the most part. Likewise, my students at a Midwest community college literally surrounded by cornfields were of the same approximate age, but they were more diversified and could be divided into two groups: the local kids whose parents wanted them out of the house in between their jobs or, more commonly, farming responsibilities, and those from the city sixty miles away who attended this college because they could establish residency easily, enroll in their general education courses cheaply, and then matriculate to the state university six miles down the road. For these audiences, European travails seemed so far away, not so much exotic as remote from their immediate interests, responsibilities, and concerns.

Currently, my students at an urban university in Arizona often experience the same disassociation when they begin the novel. Because they are intimidated by the prose itself, I find that I get this excuse more and more lately: "I'm part of the TV generation, and my attention span is really short, so I really can't get into this book." As sympathetic as I am to their plight, I encourage—well, actually force, I suppose—them to push ahead, for Hemingway, like most good writers, requires active readership, and I assure them that their efforts will be rewarded in the end. As they focus on the development and changes of the two main characters, whose closeness to their own age, incidentally, they often overlook, students recognize the richness of the text, and they identify with the characters for whom they had little patience at first.

I understand why Hemingway's style, deliberately ambiguous and devoid of flowery diction, tests students' patience, but his characterizations seem even odder to them; they think Catherine completely weird. They are not alone. Among Hemingway's fictional women, Catherine Barkley has received a great deal of attention, since Frederic Henry's "wife" has been targeted continually as the most controversial or at least problematic character in the novel. Various readers and critics have alleged that Hemingway drew Catherine as deliberately vacuous and flat so that she can act as Frederic's minion and, in turn, can make him seem extra smart, brave, and competent.

What I say to my students—and in doing so, I am hoping that they might assess her with fresh, fair eyes—is that I am in agreement with those who identify Catherine Barkley as the character worthy of greatest consideration, but not because she lacks dimension or worth. As I see her, and as I point out to my classes, Catherine proves how her strength of character and will are repeatedly tested: the most extreme example of this strength surfaces as she finds herself forced to confront the imminent deaths of her baby and herself at the novel's end. As a Voluntary Aid Detachment (VAD) during the war, where many of her duties resemble those of a nurse, she has already faced the existential questions of how to live and how to die, for she witnesses death (among her patients and in general in a war-torn country) on a daily basis. In addition, prior to her relationship with Frederic Henry, she has lost a lover to battle: "a very nice boy [who] was going to marry [her] and he was killed in the Somme" (18). It seems that all these experiences have expedited her maturation into a full-fledged, urbane, and realistic adult, for "she has a fair idea of what it is all about, and it is her part to teach Frederic by example how to live in it" (Spanier, "Unknown Soldier" 76). Jamie Barlowe-Kayes concurs in "Re-reading Women: The Example of Catherine Barkley," where she credits certain critics for recognizing that "Hemingway created Barkley as an ideal character by arming her with the knowledge he personally privileged: awareness of the horrors of war—specifically its random malevolence in terms of individual deaths, the false sentimentality often associated with war heroes, and the general inadequacy of human responses to death" (31).

Certainly, contemporary students have many stresses to confront in their daily lives, including financial burdens, familial obligations, and jobs outside of school. Though theirs are different, maybe even more self-imposed distractions and anxieties, they can certainly identify with many of Catherine's and Frederic's concerns—related to love, health, life—throughout the novel. For example, they can sympathize with Catherine's predicament, especially since "Catherine is determined to forge a meaningful and orderly existence—if only temporarily—in a world in which all traditional notions of meaning and order have been shattered" (Spanier, "Unknown Soldier" 76). As if pregnancy (under the difficult condition of being unmarried to an enlisted man who has fled his post) is not enough, Catherine finds herself forced into a cesarean birth for their baby and suffers a great deal of pain. Still, she plays the constant nurse/caretaker to her husband, not treating him so much as a patient but coddling him as a child. Horrific contractions cause Catherine to beg for more hits of ether to numb her discomfort, though amazingly, she apologizes to Frederic for this behavior: "I'm not any good, darling. . . . I'm so sorry. I thought I would do it very easily" (317).

Her actions are selfless, for she repeatedly inquires about Frederic's condition, insisting that he "go out and get something to eat" (326) three times over the course of the labor. Moreover, as a VAD, she knows how dire her condition is after she has hemorrhaged so extensively. Out of concern for her lover, she pronounces that she does not fear death but only hates it (330) and prefers to focus more on Frederic's welfare than her own; she even goes so far as to inform him that should she not survive, she would like him to seek future lovers: "I want you to have girls" (331). As Sandra Whipple Spanier notes in "Catherine Barkley and the Hemingway Code: Ritual and Survival in *A Farewell to Arms*," "Catherine's ability to penetrate surfaces and to read the inevitabilities of the future underscores her stature as the wiser, more experienced of the pair, whose role it is to educate Frederic Henry" (139). Students often pipe up about how they would protect the one they love as Catherine does, yet they also comment on advances in medical care and how Catherine's condition might not be as dire in today's world. Most importantly, they respect Catherine for looking after her husband as well as their baby and herself.

Still, in a weird way, there's a strange backlash against what some students perceive as too much female-centered textual analysis; in recent years, both males and females in my classes have showed concern regarding male bashing. Rather than concentrate on possible misogynist strains, they are attuned to instances of misandry. Whether the advent of politically and religiously conservative male-centered organizations like the Promise Keepers or other cultural circumstances are the cause is unclear, but focusing solely on Catherine at the expense of Frederic provokes resistance from students who believe that sexism no longer exists; they prefer to express their opinions in defense of both sexes.

Thus, students are primed to consider Catherine as a woman embarked on a formative path of her own, so I encourage my students to read *Farewell* as Catherine Barkley's journey, preferably as hers alone or, at the very least, as hers as much as Frederic's. I ask them to think about several key episodes of the novel: when Frederic and Catherine first meet; when Frederic is sent off to Plava for the offensive and later injured; when Frederic reunites with Catherine while convalescing; when Frederic deserts his post; and finally, when Frederic, Catherine, and their unborn baby flee to demilitarized areas to live a blissful life. Because Frederic Henry serves as narrator, the initial tendency of the reader is to distinguish him as the potential protagonist of the novel. But, in actuality, could Hemingway have penned Catherine's story?

While I do not want students to discount Frederic's significance, as we do read his story of the front, his friendships, his desertion, and his love for Catherine, I want them equally to see how Catherine develops as a person. Because Frederic has a solipsistic tendency, at least at the start of the novel, to view circumstances and situations solely in terms of himself, his reporting of Catherine Barkley's story may be inadvertent (though Hemingway's is not). To claim we know less of Catherine is to ignore the subjectivity of first-person narration: "True, we know little about Catherine Barkley beyond what Frederic thinks about her and what Frederic reveals in dialogue, but what do we know of Frederic?" (Spanier, "Hemingway Code" 140). Thereupon, a discussion of (un)reliable narration surfaces among my students and myself, and typically, we accept that we learn a great deal about the type of woman she is and how she affects Frederic's immediate life as well as his future forever.

Thus, I try to get my students to consider the novel as Catherine's story of maturation at least as much as (if not more than) Frederic's. Amid extreme circumstances, the two seem to undergo a lifetime of experience: literally, Catherine's is a life-to-death experience. Hence, the case for the story as Catherine's seems viable.

Even fortified with this possibility, students want to read Catherine as exceedingly dependent on Frederic—comments like, "I don't take any interest in anything else any more. I'm so very happy married to you" (154) intimate her as needy. However, we contemplate too how her desire to share so much with him may well be a result of her growth. Having experienced love and extreme loss, she fully and freely gives herself to Frederic. In sharing herself with him, she invites him to grow with her—in matters of the heart, in particular. Perhaps her responses are even more revolutionary, as Nancy R. Comley and Robert Scholes attest: "We might . . . see Catherine not as erasing herself so much as assuming a role in a game of sex and love that allows her to transfer her affections to a man other than her dead fiancé" (37). Their initial romantic evening, which confuses students when they first read it—"Is she into him or not?" they wonder—demonstrates how she longs for the intimacy she once shared with her now-deceased lover. Catherine tells Frederic the sad story of her fiancé's death in battle and how they had enlisted together. She continues to walk with "a thin rattan stick like a toy riding-crop" (18), a final possession and remembrance of the boy she loved, and she questions Frederic about whether he, too, has loved another. He has not, but Catherine will soon expose him to this new world of emotions.

What I like to introduce to my students, too—since many of them are finding themselves during their college years—is her progressive struggle to reconcile her identity and sense of self with external ideas of what she should be. Besides her maturation with matters of the heart, Catherine grows into her womanhood. Therefore, Catherine Barkley's saga is one of contention, for the world seems to be at odds with her when her fiancé is killed, when Frederic gets injured, when she finds herself pregnant and then on the run, and finally, when she and her unborn baby must fight for their lives. She wants to keep growing, yet circumstances are against her, and Catherine herself is well aware of this "dirty trick" (331). She tells her beloved, "I'm going to die. . . . I hate it" (330). Her end is not her defeat, for her love and character will resonate with Frederic. Consequently, we discuss in class the brilliance of Hemingway's craft; essentially, he has used Catherine to advance Frederic's development and the plot of the novel, but he has also depicted a woman who has learned to love fully. Where she once was engaged for eight years, only to lose her fiancé, she now refrains from being so cautious in her romance with Frederic or in the adventures of their shared life. Experience has taught her what she wants, what she can have, and what she deserves, and she conducts herself with grace: when Frederic last sees her in the operating room, she winks at him, her "dear, brave sweet" (331).

Obviously, the opportunities for females are far broader and more varied today than they were during World War I, the setting of *A Farewell to Arms,* or even in 1929, when Hemingway published the novel; yet my students, female and male alike, still seem shocked by these truths. We talk about how Catherine, as a working woman of her era, might have been viewed as somewhat progressive even though her vocation clearly represented society's consent. What could be more appropriate than nursing, a profession that enabled women to exercise their maternal instincts, particularly upon wounded or sick men? In such an environment, she is forced to mature quickly, and she rises to the challenge both physically and emotionally. Catherine possesses physical stamina, treating the bloody wounds of young men, and "rowing in moderation" (275) while exhausted and well into her pregnancy as she and Frederic seek sanctuary in Switzerland. The fortitude of her character and her optimistic approach to her own and others' circumstances—cheering up the occasionally embittered Helen Ferguson, for instance—allow her to progress in this "growing-up novel" (Frye 78). In many ways, Catherine can be perceived by those around her as a highly traditional woman, a victim of both gender constraints and cultural preconceptions, but in truth, she graduates to the status of being a woman ahead of her time.

Still, approaching Catherine as so significant a character requires students to resist natural tendencies, for she is not the narrator of the novel, plus she is a male-created female character in a focal role: this is tricky. As readers, we learn about Catherine and her development more through inference (on Frederic's part) than through explicit dialogue, actions, or voice. Of course, Frederic's mood colors his descriptions, too, and while he is first wooing her, he makes her out to be unstable and a bit of a tease. He reflects on the first time that he tries to kiss her: "I leaned forward in the dark to kiss her and there was a sharp stinging flash. She had slapped my face hard" (26). Only minutes later, when Catherine feels bad that she has hurt Frederic, she allows him to kiss her again, after which she tearfully asks him if he will treat her well. His dismissive thoughts—"What the hell, I thought. I stroked her hair and patted her shoulder. She was crying" (27)—paint him as the cool, capable man. Because one moment she seems confident and the next she seems desperately codependent, students initially want to write her off as crazy and emotional. But she proves very much in control of her mind and her circumstance, as Sandra Whipple Spanier notes: "Catherine is playing at love not for diversion but survival. Hers is a sophisticated game, over his head, and Frederic does not understand the stakes" as she does ("Hemingway Code" 135). Ultimately, as the story progresses and Frederic and Catherine become more involved and dependent on each other, Catherine garners more respect from her lover and, therefore, her readers. In truth, Frederic has provided her story, which recounts what a thorough worker, devoted "wife," and brave young woman she really is.

So as a class, we explore how Catherine Barkley, through her love of Frederic Henry, essentially enables him to become an actualized man. As I suggest that she personifies patience, grace, humility, courage, and domesticity to a great extent, I resort to James W. Tuttleton and his article "'Combat in the Erogenous Zone': Women in the American Novel between the Two World Wars." He lends credence to the idea that Catherine embodies Hemingway's favorite type of woman: Hemingway "had the greatest sympathy with the prevailing stereotype of the 'womanly woman,' the woman with an old-fashioned sense of her role as life-giving, nourishing, life-sustaining presence ministering to her husband or family" (292). I ask my students to consider this perspective of Catherine, while they might also recognize how she satisfies Frederic's less provincial preferences, too, in the way that she breaks rules (as a VAD) by providing Frederic with contraband vermouth, sleeps with him (a patient) in the hospital "when they were all asleep and she was sure they would not call" (114), and becomes pregnant out of wedlock.

Again, we talk about the two lead characters' significance, and it has been my experience that following the aforementioned discussions, students are more apt to consider if not accept Catherine's journey. While it is true that Frederic does evolve into a more mature and loving man as the novel progresses—arguably, Catherine is responsible for a great portion of his conversion—Catherine's own development is rarely acknowledged. We examine particular episodes and passages to reach this view. Early on in their relationship, for instance, Frederic demonstrates self-serving adolescent behavior as he attempts to show his readers how suave he can be with the ladies. In sweet-talking Catherine Barkley, he reveals in all his bravado, "I knew I did not love Catherine Barkley nor had any idea of loving her" (30). Students always get a good chuckle out of this comment—the noncommittal dating scene is alive and well in the twenty-first century—and they too understand his motivation. He is interested in her sexually, of course, and "in those days, a declaration of love was the minimum prerequisite for sexual intercourse between well-bred people. Knowing this, Frederic plays the love card to win a trick for his desire" (Comley and Scholes 36). While he might be successful in winning her affection, of course—and female students really love to point this out—the joke later turns out to be on him, for he ultimately behaves as if he is more consumed with Catherine than she with him. For example, early on, Frederic thinks to himself, "Well, I knew I would not be killed. Not in this war. It did not have anything to do with me" (37). The line proves ironically prophetic, for the war, metaphorically—and arguably, literally, as well—destroys Catherine and their baby and thereby "detonates" his existence. When students reflect on Catherine, they determine that she possesses an understanding of the dangers and realities of battle (since she views so many of its victims) that might even surpass Frederic's (who may be more caught up in the romance) and therefore bestows upon him a St. Anthony's medal for protection as he heads toward the fighting. Whereas she has grown to comprehend and appreciate the experiences and situations around her, Frederic is slower on the uptake.

We go to a later scene, too, in which he returns to the front for the second time, well after he and Catherine have professed their mutual love, and Frederic can no longer function as the smooth, strong-willed, somewhat careless young man he once was. His thoughts go constantly to Catherine, especially as he flees his post for Milan—and her: "I was not made to think. I was made to eat. My God, yes. Eat and drink and sleep with Catherine. To-night maybe. No that was impossible. But to-morrow night, and a good meal and sheets and never going away again except together" (233). As Comley and Scholes aptly note in *Hemingway's Genders: Rereading the Hemingway Text,* "In *A Farewell to Arms,* Frederic Henry's childish status is reiterated throughout. . . . [In] his return to the more adult world of the war, . . . his desire is always to return to the waiting Catherine, the faithful and loving mother-mistress" (39). If I ask students to focus on Frederic as the needier one in the relationship, they very astutely recognize that even though he meets with some success—once again, his maturation, however great or small, deserves affirmation—counter to Catherine's progression throughout the novel, he may well undergo a form of regression. Where he was initially confident and unflinching in his masculine wiles and military acumen—it is key to remember, I insist to my students, that he has been an ambulance driver while in service, and his valorous behavior has been a result of being in the wrong place at the wrong time—he seemingly becomes more dependent on Catherine and less in control of himself and his life.

From this discussion, I move to Philip Young's notion of the "code hero," and I indicate that we might want to consider that, as first proposed by Sandra Whipple Spanier in 1987, Catherine may well be the code hero of the novel—a notion complementary to the idea of the novel as Catherine's journey. Catherine is a character whom Frederic tries to emulate—according to Young, the code hero is just such a type—for she seems to harbor a sensibility of life and the world that Frederic progressively attempts to adopt. I do not want my students to become concerned with literary jargon, nor do I want them to feel compelled to fit characters into particular molds. Rather, I introduce the notion of Catherine's possible "code heroic" status because it can add credence to the idea that her story reflects a lifetime of aging in only a few short, frenetic years.

Again, my intention is not to disqualify Frederic's worth or importance to the novel with my students. I want them to consider alternate interpretations, for I am a woman defending Hemingway (and I am not alone, though my company is limited), and my hope stems from a desire for them to give the author credit for his dimensional crafting of Catherine. Thus, I try to incorporate and emphasize this way of thinking in a variety of assignments with my students. Sometimes these assignments are out-of-class essays:

- The bildungsroman is typically associated with a man's apprenticeship or journey from adolescence to adulthood. Yet a case could be made for Catherine Barkley's moral and psychological education as fulfilling characteristics of this type of novel. Defend or refute this idea.
- Assuming you admire Hemingway's characterization of Catherine Barkley in *A Farewell to Arms,* refute the following anti-Hemingway sentiment: "Hemingway's women are weak, dull, and uncomplicated people lacking intellect, sensitivity, and feeling. In fact, they function only to enhance the images and presentation of their male counterparts." In the course of your defense, please be sure to touch on the issue of Catherine's journey, as we have discussed in class.

Other times, I give short-essay test questions on the same subject:

- Can Catherine Barkley of Ernest Hemingway's *A Farewell to Arms* be read as innocent? She tells Frederic that she feels like a "whore" and is often hesitant to break the rules with him. Determine whether or not Catherine Barkley epitomizes innocence in the novel. In doing so, indicate how this possibility fits into our discussion of the novel as the story of Catherine's maturation.
- Catherine Barkley lives during a time of gender-based double standards. On occasion, she acknowledges the differences and/or ironies that exist between men and women of her time. Indicate what some of the prevailing inconsistencies are and then explain how she deals with and confronts her respective society/situations. Is her awareness an aspect of her growth, and does it provide more evidence of her story as one of progress, at least to some extent?

Depending on the class, too, I like my students to do short informal response papers. Two questions that generate more thought toward Catherine's (primary?) role in the novel are, "How would the novel be different if it were told from Catherine's, rather than Frederic's, point of view? Would it be better, worse, or the same?" and, "Many read *A Farewell to Arms* as Frederic's bildungsroman. But do any other characters in the novel also go on journeys? If so, which ones?" We always discuss the material after in-class writings, and as we approach the notion of theme, students often deduce, going from the broad to the particular, that a central idea of the novel is that life is a journey of experiences.

As a final note, I would caution against overusing biographical criticism when teaching *A Farewell to Arms* or virtually any of Hemingway's fiction.

Hemingway's use of real-life experiences for the basis of his fiction has become a topic of fascination for many, including me, and the parallels between his own war experiences and those described in the novel merit introduction and some discussion. After all, Hemingway made no secret of the fact that *A Farewell to Arms* was significantly based on his experiences in World War I as a nineteen-year-old Red Cross ambulance driver injured on the front, hundreds of pieces of shrapnel embedded in his feet and legs (Lynn 81–83). His budding relationship with nurse Agnes von Kurowsky, seven years his senior, and his early departure from overseas are other well-known stories. Still, for years, critics have debated the extent of the relationship between Hemingway and Agnes—no one seems certain if it was even consummated, for instance—and soon after his return to the States, Agnes wrote that she would marry an Italian doctor. According to most biographers, Hemingway was distraught and angered by her rejection. His sentimentality must have gotten the best of him, as he chose to portray elements of her in his future writings, most notably in *Farewell*.

No doubt, the connections one can see between the biography and the fiction are fascinating and significant, but they should not be overinterpreted or primarily emphasized. Agnes did not realize that her Dear John letter might lead to her fictional death, in the guise of Catherine Barkley, years later. Of course, his portrayal, I have argued, is more complimentary than mean-spirited. Nevertheless, the tendency to seek traces of biography seems great, especially with an author as public as Hemingway, and should be monitored. For me, that often proves the biggest obstacle in teaching any of his fiction.

The scholarly classroom exercise that yields rewarding conversations and thoughtful writing assignments embraces *A Farewell to Arms* as Catherine's story. In *The Resisting Reader,* Judith Fetterley avers an absolute: "Catherine has always made the critics uneasy" (66). Superficially, she seems so flaky and strange, and it seems that Frederic's only attraction to her would be physical or the result of a Florence Nightingale syndrome. But critical readers will find that Catherine actually is quite bright and in excellent control—in fact, in greater control than her lover—of both her life and her romantic relationship. As Frederic thinks about the nature of war and its victims, he comes to this conclusion: "If people bring so much courage to this world the world has to kill them to break them, so of course it kills them. The world breaks every one and afterward many are strong at the broken places. But those that will not break it kills. It kills the very good and the very gentle and the very brave impartially" (249). Although he himself is perhaps oblivious, Frederic has just described the true nature of Catherine, who possesses all these traits; hopefully, our students will end the novel understanding and appreciating this courageous woman's journey, as well.

## APPENDIX: English 200 Assignment

For this paper, you will be incorporating research. The purpose of the assignment is to enable you to understand better the respective poem(s) or novel (Ernest Hemingway's *A Farewell to Arms*) of your focus via secondary sources. This research, then, is meant to augment your own ideas; outside information is not of primary focus as much as your analysis of the literature is. In other words, please do not let your research overwhelm your writing and the points you make.

This paper will be your longer assignment for the semester (approximately six to eight pages in length), and, of course, should be typed or word processed. Please use three to six scholarly sources only. And as a reminder, I will expect each paper to include a cogent thesis statement; logical organization; effective diction and syntax; decent control of grammar, punctuation, and spelling; and a descriptive title.

I've provided you with some sample topics below, which you are welcome to use. Most importantly, they should be a means to generate thought, as I'm sure you'll come up with far more original ideas than I have. I am delighted to help, so if you have any questions or want feedback, clarifications, or advice, do see me.

1. Robert Frost was poet laureate of the United States and the author of an inaugural poem for President John F. Kennedy. Why was his poetry, so steeped in images of recollection and nature, so admired? Incorporate your findings into an analysis of "After Apple Picking."

2. Robert Browning sets "My Last Duchess" and (presumably) "Porphyria's Lover" in Italy. Investigate what kind of time he spent there himself and why that locale might have intrigued him and inspired his poetry.

3. E. E. Cummings was known for his mastery of linguistic foregrounding in his poetry. Research this technique and then apply it to an explication of his poems, including "r-p-o-p-h-e-s-s-a-g-r."

4. William Carlos Williams is associated with the poetic school of imagism. Research his ideas and this movement's philosophy and draw on your findings to analyze "The Red Wheelbarrow" and/or "This Is Just to Say."

5. T. S. Eliot's *The Waste Land* is seen by many as the quintessential example of modernism. However, "The Love Song of J. Alfred Prufrock" also demonstrates many characteristics of the movement. Research the topic of modernism, and incorporate your findings into an analysis of Eliot's poem.

6. Many view Sylvia Plath as a confessional poet, and the poem "Metaphors" might serve as evidence. Explore Plath's life and perhaps admission that her poems reflected herself and her life experiences, and determine how "Metaphors" corresponds to this claim.

7. Billy Collins served as poet laureate of the United States for two years. How does a poet attain such a position? What does the role entail? What criteria are considered when such a representative is selected? In researching these questions, see what you can learn of Collins as well, and, through analysis of "Schoolsville," indicate if you think he was deserving of such an honor.

8. Much Hemingway scholarship addresses the notion of the "code hero" and the "Hemingway hero," two personae coined by critic Philip Young that exist in most Hemingway texts. Research who/what these characters are as well as the nature of the relationship between the two, and apply your research to a discussion of *A Farewell to Arms*.

9. Hemingway was a very public figure, and *A Farewell to Arms* is at least somewhat based on his experience as an ambulance driver during World War I. Via biographical sources, learn what you can about Hemingway's actual wartime experience, and see if you can provide parallels between that and episodes in the novel.

10. Having endured war and injury, Frederic Henry has some residual haunting of experiences past. Does he suffer perhaps from post-traumatic stress disorder? Research the syndrome and then see if you can make a case for his showing any signs of previous trauma.

11. Catherine Barkley works as a VAD during World War I, a vocation many other brave women adopted. Investigate what life was like for the VAD. See how accurate Hemingway's descriptions of Catherine's circumstances are as you examine the reality against the fiction. (You may also address the Florence Nightingale syndrome, where the patient falls in love with his nurse/caretaker.)

12. At the end of the novel, Catherine must undergo a cesarean section. Has that procedure evolved over time? In other words, is it any safer now than it would have been during the time of the novel? See what you can learn about the operation then versus now. Has Hemingway provided a plausible scene and description?

13. For years, Hemingway has been touted as a sexist and/or misogynist. Indeed, he had many conflicted feelings about the women in his life. Investigate, via biographical materials, his feelings and comments about and reactions to women—to whom he was related and/or at-

tracted—and determine if such labels are apt. Of course, you'll want to tie your own findings into a discussion of the novel.

14. Hemingway has been praised for his authentic descriptions of battle, particularly relating to World War I, in the novel. Much has been written about the war; thus, you might want to do some historical research (look at locales, etc., in the text) to see if any of the battles or conflicts in the book (or similar ones) are described in nonfiction sources. Has Hemingway taken any liberties, perhaps?

15. Choose your own topic (please see me for approval).

# My Problems in Teaching *A Farewell to Arms*

*Peter L. Hays*

Teaching *A Farewell to Arms* always gives me problems. For some reason, the novel always leaves me more dissatisfied than does *The Sun Also Rises* or *For Whom the Bell Tolls*. Unlike the main characters in those novels, the protagonist of *A Farewell to Arms,* Frederic Henry, seems less well defined. For that reason I never choose to teach *A Farewell to Arms* in my American novel course or in a twentieth-century survey course; for those I pick *The Sun Also Rises*.

I teach at the University of California, Davis, one of the nine general University of California campuses, where by charter we take the top 12.5 percent of the state's students. Our campus is heavily science oriented, and our students are bright, although not well read—not even the English majors—and not very good writers. Thus, I teach *A Farewell to Arms* only in Hemingway courses, either small senior (or graduate) seminars limited to fifteen students, or large upper-division lecture classes of about seventy students. (In what follows, I'm describing what I do in the large classes; the seminars are usually student run, with only my occasional intervention.) In the lecture course, I have one half-time teaching assistant, usually a creative writing graduate student who has read little Hemingway but is quite willing to read more, to help me grade papers. Frequently fewer than half my students are English majors, even though the course is an elective that fulfills no requirements for nonmajors. For English majors, it is one of many courses that fulfill a modern period requirement. The last time I taught the course, 42 percent of my students were English majors;

the rest ranged from American studies, psychology, and political science to animal science and electrical engineering majors; these included three foreign students in Davis for the year.

In these Hemingway courses, before coming to *A Farewell to Arms,* my students have seen a biographical movie about Hemingway (*Hemingway: Grace under Pressure,* written and narrated by Anthony Burgess) and read the short stories of *In Our Time,* including "A Very Short Story," and *The Sun Also Rises* (see appendix). Because they have read nothing the first day, introducing Hemingway through a fifty-five-minute film is a good way to provide biographical information on the author as well as images for today's visually oriented students. As a result, they know of Hemingway's brief service in Italy in World War I, of his romance with Agnes von Kurowsky, of his antiromanticism, his "iceberg" technique, and something of his style. Burgess even includes film clips from the 1933 movie of *A Farewell to Arms* with Gary Cooper and Helen Hayes, as well as the scene from Twentieth Century Fox's *Hemingway's Adventures of a Young Man* in which Nick Adams is inducted into the Italian Ambulance Corps.

Before we discuss *A Farewell to Arms,* I very briefly discuss "A Very Short Story," pointing out how the first edition named Milan as the setting and "Ag" as the nurse before Hemingway changed it to make it less autobiographical; then I point out the cynicism of that story in order to contrast it to the romance of *A Farewell to Arms.* Moving on to the novel, I pass out maps copied from Michael S. Reynolds's *Hemingway's First War* that identify where Hemingway served and was wounded—in the more central part of northern Italy—and where Frederic Henry served, on the eastern front, adjoining what is now Slovenia (4). I also give my students Reynolds's detailed map of Frederic's battle area (90), so they can locate Gorizia, the Bainsizza Plateau, Caporetto, and Udine (although few of them are as compulsive about placing characters geographically as I am). Then I closely read the first chapter, stressing the sense of domesticity of the "we lived" and subsequent descriptions; I point out the contrast between mountain and plain, echoing Carlos Baker's argument in *Hemingway: The Writer as Artist* (94–116), and preparing them for the symbolic weight of the Abruzzi and the mountains of Switzerland over the decadent plain; I stress the ominous nature of the rain; and I conclude with the image of the soldiers pregnant with death, their capes bulging over their cartridge cases, before the final ironic statement of how few died of cholera.

The writing is excellent. As with his best short stories, Hemingway packs a great deal into his words. But then we meet Frederic in person, back from his leave, and I begin to have problems. I can believe that Jake is a newsman and that Robert Jordan could teach Spanish, but I cannot believe that Frederic Henry ever studied architecture: he never says anything about any building's shape, size, or structure, except for the barn he hides in later in the novel; he never mentions building materials, stresses, or engineering principles. And I don't know if Catherine is English or Scots. The novel has her as both (English: 21; Scots: 115, 126). But those points are minor. Most importantly, I also don't know how to take Frederic Henry. Is he the hero of the novel, or the object of Hemingway's satire? But I try not to let my personal feelings intrude, and I teach the novel as straight as I can.

In chapter 3, after a brief indirect introduction, we meet Frederic after his very long leave, just back from a whirlwind tour of Italian whorehouses. He returns from leave expecting the ambulance corps to have ceased functioning because of his absence and is disappointed that that did not happen (16–17). His conduct on meeting Catherine Barkley is that of a sexual predator; he behaves more like Jim Gilmore of "Up in Michigan" than such sympathetic characters as Nick Adams or Jake Barnes. He's considerably immature throughout most of the novel, a point underscored by almost everyone he meets calling him "boy" (e.g., 31, 87, 99, 104) or in Rinaldi's case, "little puppy" (27) or "baby" (e.g., 40, 41, 170, 171). And at one point Catherine tells him to get out of the rain (158), as a mother would a child. While I do try to conceal my prejudices, I do point out to the class how curious it is that Hemingway should constantly infantilize his protagonist, but I also point out how much carnality occupies Fred Henry (Hemingway does shorten the name to "Fred" on page 123) and how much he is in need of greater spirituality, a point also conveyed by the novel's priest (72).

My students are not enthralled by Frederic's behavior, although the males, at least, can identify. Catherine, however, poses a problem. Coming to her from Brett Ashley, and having heard of the independent Agnes von Kurowsky, my female students are divided. We never know why Catherine decides to attach herself to Frederic. Is it because, after the loss she has suffered of her fiancé in France, Frederic is the first decent-looking English-speaking bachelor she has met? Many of the students agree with the critics who find her complacent and identity effacing, a sexual toy for Fred Henry. Others see a mentally distressed woman seeking someone to cling to, a self-prescribed love object. Does she fall in love at first sight with a soldier? It hardly seems likely to have occurred that rapidly, since she says, on their third meeting, on the occasion of their first kiss, "Because we're going to have a strange life" (27). I've always interpreted that remark and her open-mouth kiss as her statement of commitment to him. We discuss in class her motives, her instability, and her needs (Frederic's are obvious). Does she recognize his immaturity and consider him pliable, easily manipulated? And does she thus choose for herself a boy toy, an object of emotional security for herself? And does she keep him by making herself sexually available to him, as he so obviously desires? (Unlike her fiancé, Frederic is someone who does come back to her.) In my most recent class, several female students said that Catherine is manipulative in letting Frederic think that he is making love to her. That is, she allows him to think that he is seducing her, that he is the dominant figure in the relationship. Yet Hemingway gives her the whip hand, her dead fiancé's riding crop, actually a British's officer's symbol of authority, a swagger stick. The stick is plainly phallic; she wields it, and when she and Frederic first make love, because he is flat on his back with a wounded leg, she assumes the superior position.

I point out in my lectures that Catherine tries to control their social interactions, keeping them in a private world of two, away as much as possible from others. And as a class we discuss that as well: Is it healthy for two lovers to seek almost total isolation? Are their statements that they have no identity apart from each other (115, 299, 300) romantic or desperate and damaging? It's Frederic Henry's account, but does Hemingway imply approval for the nature of the relationship or not? We discuss this against the backdrop of Robert Penn Warren's essay on the novel, in which he discusses "the religion of love" in *A Farewell to Arms,* which I summarize orally for the class. Because of the size of my classes, most of the time I lecture, but I always leave time at the end of each class for questions and discussion (see appendix for a list of my discussion topics). Since World War I and the retreat from Caporetto are distant historical markers at best for my twenty-first-century students, romance and psychology constitute our most vital topics. Beyond the surface details of Frederic's recuperation, return to the front, retreat, and escape into the Tagliamento, the themes that occupy most of our discussion are the nature of the lovers' relationship and the extent to which Frederic develops morally and spiritually, since Catherine seems kind, competent, and brave throughout.

We see continuing evidence of Frederic's immaturity mount. He enlisted because he was in Italy, although he expresses little enthusiasm for the Italian war effort or desire to define himself through war (18, 22). In fact he's marvelously free of deep thoughts. Whereas Jake discusses, beyond his own plight, moral philosophy, religion, literature, the aesthetics of bullfighting, and ethnography, Fred Henry, besides his desire for drink and Catherine, speaks only of tactics and war, briefly of religion with the priest and Count Greffi, and little of anything else. He knows Rubens, Titian, and Mantegna; recites Marvell and "Oh Western Wind"; and calls Othello a "nigger" (257) but does not know who penned, "The coward dies a thousand deaths, the brave but one" (139–40) and has read Barbusse and H. G. Wells presumably because their books were in the hospital, where Frederic had little else to do.

He cares for men under his command, but as an officer, he's mediocre. Hemingway consistently undercuts Frederic as successful soldier. He's assigned to transport ambulances and medical supplies and fails, getting them stuck in the mud in an empty field. The humanitarian who stops to help someone with a rupture tries to kill two fellow Italian soldiers because they won't help Frederic push his stuck ambulance, foreshadowing other Italian soldiers shooting at him. And his two sequences of action in the novel—diving into the Tagliamento River and rowing the length of Lago Maggiore—come in his desertion from the army (even though Catherine excuses it by saying, "It's only the Italian army" [251], to which he owes no loyalty). That is to say, he's not heroic—he "was blown up while . . . eating cheese" (63)—and as a military officer, he's barely competent. While Jake and Robert make choices that help us define them, Frederic, after he has met and decided to seduce Catherine, follows orders and largely avoids making character-defining decisions, except for taking his ambulances along unknown country roads, shooting at the two sergeants, and doing what is necessary to escape. Except for his sexuality, he's vague, and my students struggle with him. They ask if they're supposed to like him or admire him but find it difficult to do so. Few have had military experience, so they have nothing in common with him on that score. For most, he is simply a man on the make.

When Frederic is about to leave Catherine pregnant and go back to the front, he asks her whether she has a father and how she will manage her pregnancy (154–55). How could a man living with a woman, as he essentially does, not notice that her periods had ceased two months before? Why, in those three months (137), did he never ask her about her family? What do he and his lover talk about those nights when they are together? We never know. Most importantly, and extremely indicative of his solipsism, why, after learning of her pregnancy, did he ask how she—not they—would deal with it? At Stresa, he asks Catherine, the nurse's aid, how they should escape the military police (251), when he knows that Switzerland is just down the lake and he has asked Simmons about being interned there (241). Why the question? Does he want her confirmation of his military genius? Or is he insecure? His idea of an occupation is growing a beard (298), or is that another instance of Catherine's having fun at his expense? At one point in the novel Frederic tells us that, going to Stresa, dressed as a civilian in Simmons's clothes, he feels as if he's a masquerader (243). He is several times a counterfeit or masquerader: as an American in the Italian army, as Catherine's dead lover who has come back to her in the night, as a civilian, as a boxer with a beard, as Catherine's husband, and as a doctor in a gown. Is he also in disguise as the novel's hero, really an antihero instead?

Frederic does not help Catherine in planning how she will cope with her pregnancy at the hospital; she takes responsibility for herself and makes her own plans. (She also researches whether their child will be legitimate if and when she marries Frederic.) As to the idyll in Switzerland, Frederic says he wants to ski, but we never see him doing so. For over three months he and Catherine take such walks as her pregnancy allows, drink wine, eat chocolate bars, and play several different games of cards. We're never told that they read anything beside the newspapers, or that they have any long discussions as to where they might live or what they might do; they seem to tell each other very little about their pasts, and what little Catherine reveals makes Frederic jealous. They make love, but even Hemingway's alter ego cannot do so every waking hour of every day and night. Some students see their stay above Montreux (where Hemingway stayed with Hadley) as a belated honeymoon. Others feel that it is a very quickly told account—the three months pass in twenty pages with little detail—of being trapped in a cabin in winter with another person, something to endure. Again, we do not know what they talk about, other than whether to buy candy bars with nuts or without, or that foxes sleep with their tails curled around them. Could their three months in Switzerland have been that empty, or does narrator Frederic not remember what should have been the most idyllic period of their brief life together? Their motto seems to have been "Let's not think about anything" (252).

As I have said, romance and psychology are what interest my students, not accounts of World War I, as I know from both class discussion and from the topics they choose to answer on tests. I do not ask objective questions on my exams—dates, character identification, plot outlines—things easily looked up in *Cliffs Notes* or online. My exams are composed entirely of essay questions. I ask students to choose one topic from several, usually four, similar to the study questions in the appendix. The questions are comparative in nature between several texts, both to encourage students to see connections of their own, but also to discourage them from lifting papers that discuss single texts off the Internet. The exams are open book because I insist that the students support their interpretations with quotations from the texts under discussion. Students might be asked to discuss *A Farewell to Arms* and *For Whom the Bell Tolls* in terms of the families the main characters form or try to join; bravery as Hemingway presents it in "The Undefeated," *A Farewell to Arms*, "The Short Happy Life of Francis Macomber," and *For Whom the Bell Tolls*; self-definition of Catherine and Maria; how they see Hemingway expressing his philosophy of life through these works; and how they, as students of the twenty-first century, can identify with characters of the third and fourth decades of the previous century.

Often in class discussion, my students want to know more about the relationship of Hemingway to Agnes von Kurowsky, or, for those who have seen the film *In Love and War,* starring Chris O'Donnell and Sandra Bullock, the accuracy of this account of the Hemingway–von Kurowsky romance. I tell them about Agnes's Dear John letter to Ernest, refer them to "A Very Short Story," and tell those interested in learning more to read Agnes's diary, reprinted in Henry Villard and James Nagel's *Hemingway in Love and War.* But I also tell them that biography is largely irrelevant to understanding the novel. Hemingway was still attending Oak Park High School during the retreat from Caporetto. His account of it is made up, based on his own experience and his reading, including a history of the ambulance service by British historian G. M. Trevelyan, director of the First Ambulance unit of the British Red Cross, which was stationed in Schio as Hemingway was. The stay in Switzerland, where Hemingway never went with Agnes, is probably based on vacations he took there with Hadley. *A Farewell to Arms* is a novel, I tell my students; it's fiction, regardless of elements of autobiography. And it's as fiction that we must interpret it. And it's the interpretation I find difficult.

Hemingway considered *The Sentimental Education,* the title of Gustave Flaubert's novel, where he got the spelling of Frederic without a *k,* as a title for *A Farewell to Arms* (Oldsey 19, 25), and certainly we do see Frederic's education in feeling for another, but that development is incomplete, and the novel ends abruptly. Although Frederic tells us on his return to his company after convalescence how quiet the mess is, how many are missing—the implication being that many have been killed in his absence—he voices no sympathy for his dead comrades. Nor does he feel any grief over the death of his son, only anger that the birth led to Catherine's death. Although he narrates the novel some years after the events (Nagel 171–72), we simply do not know how Catherine has changed Frederic. Is he less solipsistic? Is he more solicitous of the feelings of others? The evidence is to the contrary. The novel illustrates, as Hemingway would later say in *Death in the Afternoon,* that any love story, continued long enough, ends in tragedy. Here, long enough is ten months.

My students also voice confusion about the novel's aims. Some have become more emotionally involved than others, hoping for Frederic and Catherine's success, crying at her death. Few, however, like or identify with Frederic, seeing little to admire in him, and they share my frustration with the novel. Perhaps their and my dissatisfaction comes ultimately from the novel's extreme pessimism. The good do die young: Passini, Aymo, Catherine, and her son. Count Greffi says that love is a religious feeling, but Frederic's religious object dies in the novel. Is the novel his testament to her, his belated awareness of her qualities and her love? We are given repeated examples that war is absurd—no lines of defense for a retreat, Italians shooting fellow Italians while the Germans bicycle into Italy across undefended bridges—yet the war continues. We are initially given hope that love is an escape from the madness of war, yet love dies, and nothing seems to be there to take its place. The novel most definitely reveals Hemingway's pessimistic view of the world, his sense that love does not provide adequate, long-lasting shelter from life's woes.

*A Farewell to Arms* could be a drawn-out plea for pity by the narrator. That would make the narrator much less than stoic and distance him from typical Hemingway protagonists, which seems unlikely. Or the novel could be a satirical portrait of a narcissistic American. If so, then it fails, for very few have read it that way, or we need to drastically change the way we read the novel. If it is Frederic's tribute to his lost love Catherine and what she meant to him, then it also fails, since many critics have seen Catherine as complacent beyond belief; Millicent Bell calls her an inflated rubber doll of a woman available for Frederic's sexual fantasies (114), while a 2003 *Hemingway Review* article says that she "continues to efface herself in favor of Frederic's desires" (Hewson 56). If it's a tragedy pointing out that life is futile, destroying those we love and thus, ultimately, ourselves—catching us off base and killing us—then it's weakened by having an ignoble protagonist, one with whom it's frequently difficult to identify.

My students and I feel sorry for Jake but are hopeful that he's learned to separate himself from Brett. We mourn Robert Jordan and pity Maria but are glad that Jordan learned to love before his death and that he died for something he believed in. We sympathize with Catherine and grieve over her death. We should be glad that Frederic's learned to love, but the novel leaves me, at least, and many of my students feeling dissatisfied. Some enjoy it as a sad love story, marvelously told. But for others, there is confusion. Although the story is told retrospectively, we don't know how Frederic lives or feels. He implies that he has not found anyone to replace Catherine (249), and we do have the book to indicate his feelings, but how has Catherine changed him? Does he see his early immaturity, or does he only report what he did and what he and others said? I admit that *The Sun Also Rises* is also told retrospectively—we do not know what Jake has done after his epiphany with Brett in Madrid—yet that ending bothers me not at all. In *The Sun Also Rises,* the struggle for self-definition is the subject, and at the end, Jake has reached a plateau. Since I'm unsure of how to take Frederic, his silence about the years since Catherine's death is no help.

At the end I'm left with only Fred Henry, and I don't much like him.

## APPENDIX: Syllabus for English 177

Approximate Syllabus (based on 90-minute classes):

Day 1   Introduction and film
Day 2   *In Our Time* numbered interchapters, "Indian Camp," "Doctor and the Doctor's Wife," "The Battler," "On the Quai at Smyrna"
Day 3   "Up in Michigan," "Soldier's Home," "Big Two-Hearted River," "Out of Season"
Day 4   "The Killers," "The Undefeated," "Hills Like White Elephants," *The Sun Also Rises*
Day 5   *The Sun Also Rises*
Day 6   *The Sun Also Rises*
Day 7   *The Sun Also Rises* and review
Day 8   First midterm
Day 9   "A Very Short Story," *A Farewell to Arms*
Day 10  *A Farewell to Arms*
Day 11  *A Farewell to Arms*
Day 12  *A Farewell to Arms,* "In Another Country," "A Clean, Well-Lighted Place," "Day's Wait," "Now I Lay Me"
Day 13  "The Short Happy Life of Francis Macomber," "The Snows of Kilimanjaro," "Fathers and Sons," *For Whom the Bell Tolls*
Day 14  *For Whom the Bell Tolls*
Day 15  *For Whom the Bell Tolls*
Day 16  *For Whom the Bell Tolls* and review
Day 17  Second midterm
Day 18  *The Old Man and the Sea*
Day 19  *A Moveable Feast*
Day 20  Final review

## STUDY QUESTIONS

1. In the works we've read, how successfully has Hemingway presented women? Are they fully drawn, believable human beings (at least as fully realized as his males)?

2. In Hemingway's early stories, Nick and other alter egos are initiated into pain and an awareness of death and life's many problems. In the works we've read so far, is initiation still occurring, and if so, are characters still being initiated to the same awarenesses or to different ones?

3. Discuss Hemingway's varied uses of wounding and/or impotence. Do the works we've read since *The Sun Also Rises* use this theme as Hemingway did in *The Sun Also Rises?* Does it now seem belabored?

4. In the short stories and novels we have read so far, Hemingway seems to suggest that any endeavor of love or marriage is doomed to fail—either because it will end due to tragic circumstance or because intense love will burn itself out into anger or tedious habit. Something always seems to be preventing Hemingway's characters from experiencing ideal or enduring connections. By depicting love this way, is Hemingway saying love is futile? Or do his works suggest that despite love's fallibility, it is nevertheless essential in the quest for self-definition and happiness? Choose one short story and a novel, and discuss the possibilities for, and purpose of, love in Hemingway's worldview. Develop your essay using clear examples of both married and unmarried couples (friendship included) as presented in the works you have chosen.

5. We have talked in class about Hemingway's concern for the dignity of his characters; in fact, a title he considered for *The Old Man and the Sea* was "The Dignity of Man," but Hemingway rejected that title as too pompous. Yet the ants burning at the end of the log in *A Farewell to Arms* are clearly meant as human analogs, as is the dog nosing in the garbage can, and the title of one of Hemingway's short story collections, published in 1933, is *Winner Take Nothing.* How do you reconcile Hemingway's preoccupation with losers and inevitable loss with his concern for dignity?

6. A classic work of literature reflects its own time and also speaks to subsequent ages, though each future generation might interpret a work differently. What is there in Hemingway for a modern audience; specifically, beyond entertaining stories, what themes relevant to you did you find in Hemingway's works?

7. In Hemingway's Nobel Prize acceptance speech, he said: "For a true writer each book should be a new beginning where he tries again for something beyond attainment. He should always try for something that has never been done or that others have tried and failed." Based on the works we have read for this class, did Hemingway follow his own prescription?

# "The Things She Said . . . Wouldn't Amount to Very Much"
## Teaching Gender Relationships in *A Farewell to Arms*

*Thomas Strychacz*

IN A moment of amused candor, one of my students told me that the "only two things people talk about in lit classes are sex and death." No doubt she overstated her case. But her comment does point to one reason for *A Farewell to Arms*' enduring status in the classroom. It has sex. The "light over the head of the bed shone on her hair and on her neck and shoulders," relates Frederic Henry. "I went over and kissed her and held her hand with the brush and her head sunk back on the pillow. I kissed her neck and shoulders" (258–59). It has plenty of death: Catherine Barkley, her baby, Passini, and the sergeant Frederic has to shoot, not to mention "only seven thousand" (4) dead of the cholera while the novel is still in its infancy. Moreover, as the title famously implies, sex and death are everywhere entwined. A farewell to the killing fields leads Frederic to Catherine's arms—and thence to the killing field of the hospital, where Frederic thinks, morbidly, "And this was the price you paid for sleeping together. This was the end of the trap. This was what people got for loving each other" (320).

Why then is *A Farewell to Arms* such a difficult novel to teach? Of the three full-length Hemingway works I rotate into my regularly scheduled course in modern American fiction (the other two are *In Our Time* and *The Sun Also Rises*), this novel, I find, typically causes the most puzzlement, resistance, and sometimes animosity on the part of my students. It is not because of any lack of academic preparation. Modern American Fiction at Mills College is an upper-division course, often with a fair sprinkling of MA and MFA students. And these students come to the novel having read the first novel on the syllabus, Willa Cather's *The Professor's House* (1925), which serves as a good intro-duction to early twentieth-century cultural contexts—confusion, dislocation, communication breakdown, shifting gender roles—and also to the difficulties of minimalist writing, in which, as Hemingway said famously, seven-eighths of the interpretive iceberg remain hidden.[1] Moreover, students have already had a foretaste of Frederic Henry in the cool tones of Cather's professor (not to mention in the professor's cool attitude to women).

As we begin *A Farewell to Arms,* however, I am aware that my students' discomfort can be understood most readily in terms of gender politics. Mills is all women at the undergraduate level, and my students tend to be acutely (though not dogmatically) aware of problems in reading works written by men. Though few of my students know of Judith Fetterley's groundbreaking work *The Resisting Reader,* which focuses on *Farewell's* perceived misogyny in order to delineate strategies of feminist resistance, the shape of their reading experience often does run roughly parallel to hers. They feel distinctly uneasy about its depiction of war, which they agree Hemingway does well, but which seems to function as a testing ground for men, not women. And they seem particularly suspicious of the narrator, Frederic Henry, with his monochromatic emotional range and (what appears to my students) his stilted, even asinine, relationship to Catherine. Many of my students are alert to the consequence, which is that Frederic's voice chokes off Catherine's. As one of my students wrote: "I had to trust the man's representation of the woman—you always got an impression of her that was mediated by him. . . . [Frederic's] point of view was so narrow that hers couldn't be imagined with any depth. If you did a content analysis of the things she said it wouldn't amount to very much."[2]

Critics, in point of fact, have rarely viewed Frederic Henry as a thoroughgo-ing hero—he is too "emotionally disabled" (Broer and Holland 42), too cynical and bleak—though it would be fair to say that most interpretations have seen him undergoing some kind of "initiatory and learning experience" (Lewis, *On Love* 39) that takes him from callow youth to a man who has "learned to love" (Benson 112) while becoming wise in the destructive ways of the world. James F. Light writes of an early "naïveté that Lt. Henry must—and does—lose" (170). Only the more recent scholarly reevaluations of Frederic Henry see him throughout as "self-indulgent or self-pitying" (Way 165), "immature, indeed babyish" (Svoboda 162), and a character obsessed with masquerade (Messent 60). In that respect, though my students are more ready than many Hemingway scholars to couch their responses in terms of gender politics, their hesitancies do reflect a pattern of discomfort with Frederic that has slowly been growing even among readers who are not disposed to accept Fetterley's accusations of a hate-filled misogyny.

The irony is that my students take for granted that their discomfort implies narrative failure rather than success. Several key assumptions, I believe, guide their thinking. Most important, as many students admitted when asked to write about their preconceived notions of Hemingway, was the assumption of his "notorious machismo." (One student wrote more colorfully of her friends "making gagging noises when his name was mentioned.") My students felt that, despite their misgivings about Frederic Henry, Hemingway must consider him noble, or noble in defeat; that his relationship with Catherine bears the sanction of Hemingway's views on relationships between men and women; and that the novel's narrative voice conveys and stands behind deeply "masculinist" perspectives on the issue of gender.

My general approach to these issues is to complicate my students' appraisals of Frederic Henry and his relationship to Catherine, and thereby of the narrative voice he governs, and thereby of the ways this novel speaks to issues of masculinity and gender. But I do so by emphasizing gender roles rather than simply presenting a new approach to the character of Frederic Henry. It is an important emphasis, and I cite by way of elucidation the comments of a student who had attended classes on Hemingway at another institution, only to discover that the "male-female relationships among characters seemed poisonous. . . . I didn't want to identify with those women," said this student, "seen always from the outside, from a male perspective, within the context of a troubled relationship, and did not want to identify with the male characters with respect to their relationship with women." Students had discussed "various characters and their relationships," but "without considering Hemingway's overall approach to female characters." For me, the really interesting insight here concerns the pressure to *identify*, which I find typical of approaches that seek to appraise character: after all, the more complicated students judge a particular character to be, the more likely they will feel impelled to recognize his or her "humanness" and thus to discover points of affinity and likeness. The goal is a noble one. But it is especially problematic in *Farewell* if Catherine, seen "always from the outside, from a male perspective," will never "amount to very much" for female students like this one. The endeavor to recognize the complexities of Frederic Henry may very well have the unhappy effect of inviting students to recognize the "humanness" of Frederic over against the character he dominates.

What made all the difference in my course, this student claimed, was my "allowing our attention to settle on male-female relationships and the unhappy pattern Hemingway kept weaving between men and women." My student was recognizing, I think, the effort I make to pose character within structural relations of power, so that information about (say) Frederic testifies not only to the "who" of character but to the "what" of the cultural roles that encompass both Frederic and Catherine. As we shall see, I tend to organize my thinking about those roles around the novel's concern with masquerade, with the goal, again, of allowing Frederic the masquerader to inform a larger discussion of gender masks and masquerades. But my student had still another idea in mind—one I can hardly claim responsibility for—when she spoke of my course "allowing" a new kind of attention. She continued: "I believe the fact that Mills is a mostly women college had the greatest impact on my classroom experience. . . . I felt less inhibited about . . . dwelling for a while on an aspect of Hemingway's work that some would consider a 'women's issue.' I knew I would not hear any sighs of impatience, rustlings of patriarchal guilt, or tongue clicks of irritation."

It is the kind of statement one frequently hears at Mills. I do not propose to argue here for its truth or for the general value of the all-female classroom. (Being male, I have no idea what that might be like.) I quote it here at length to suggest that many women's experiences of a devalued Catherine Barkley might be matched and reinforced by a classroom experience in which they feel that *they* do not amount to very much, either because they are faced with a novel of largely male experience, narrated by a man, in which "women's issues" seem secondary, or because they are responding to an institutionalized structure that grants more authority to male voices. Indeed, I think it possible to argue that my students' tendency to identify with a devalued Catherine is a *consequence* of devalued classroom experiences: perhaps they read Catherine as a metaphor for their own life in higher education. But it is imperative to recognize that, as the student I quote above insists, the inverse also holds true. A revalued educational experience that allowed her and her classmates to dwell on a "women's issue" made it possible for the novel to unfold in all kinds of rich, provocative, and fulfilling ways. To me, my student's statement is a good answer to the kind of concerns Judith Fetterley poses about reading Hemingway. It argues that the novel does not have to be construed within a misogynist structure of male experience. It argues that the novel responds handsomely to a classroom that gives particular emphasis to opening up a space in which a number of gender issues can be debated and negotiated, and in which readers can be critical without simply being critical of the novel. And it argues that for many students *A Farewell to Arms* might be most interesting when taught most against the grain—as a "women's issue."[3]

Since much of the material I use in addressing such matters occurs near the end of the novel, I generally structure my first class on Hemingway differently in order to give students a chance to finish the whole book. We cover biographical details and a brief history of World War I, branching out to include Frederic's famous remarks about his horror at debased words such as "glorious," "sacrifice," and "in vain" (184), and we look at the ironies of the opening chapter. (Here, I still find indispensable Walter Ong's magisterial account of how Hemingway controls narrative distance and audience response in the first sentences of the novel.) Then we embark on a reading of the very early stages of the lovers' relationship, to which my students seem quite attuned—perhaps an odd response, given that it is then, as Frederic confesses, a charade. After being slapped while trying to steal a kiss, Frederic thinks, "I was angry and yet certain, seeing it all ahead like the moves in a chess game" (26). A little later: "This was a game, like bridge, in which you said things instead of playing cards. Like bridge you had to pretend you were playing for money or playing for some stakes" (30–31). This cynical sex play resonates with my students, who are savvy about the shallowness of young love, particularly when it is a case of men "coming on" to women, and who are disposed to respect Frederic's honesty. And most students are willing to admit that the conditions of war and the death of Catherine's fiancé might compel precisely this kind of precipitous, brutal beginning.

But this is prior to one of the crucial turning points of the novel, which occurs when Catherine first walks in after Frederic's wounding: "When I saw her I was in love with her. Everything turned over inside of me" (91). It is the moment that puts paid to the earlier charades and sets up Frederic's maturation and the final tragedies. It also sets up what I have always found to be a problem for my students: they seem completely unimpressed by Hemingway's representation of the lovers' intimacy. So at the beginning of the second class on *Farewell*, I like to open up the topic not of sex (and in fact the sentences I quoted in my first paragraph might be the only erotic moment in the novel) but of *love*. Almost any snippet of dialogue from the Swiss idyll can be used to pinpoint students' discomfort. Here is one: "Oh, you're so sweet. And maybe I'd look lovely, darling, and be so thin and exciting to you and you'll fall in love with me all over again" (305). Can anyone utter, "Oh, you're so sweet" out loud without cringing slightly at having to eavesdrop on and repeat love talk this coy, or without wanting, as so many have done, to parody it? "This dialogue is silly," wrote one of my students, adding forgivingly, "but that is expected from two young people in love." Other passages, however, are worse. I like to refresh their memories of this one: "I want what you want. There isn't any me any more. Just what you want," says Catherine, to which Frederic replies, predictably, "You sweet" (106).

Equally predictable are the responses from my students. "I thought the lessons contained within were damaging to the young female psyche," wrote one student with reference to this scene, noting that it contains a common representation of "male demand and female concession." In one way or another, that comment echoes through my classroom, whether couched in terms of "typically sexist" or "male fantasy" or "this is love?" or even that well-worn refrain of the half-hearted defender, "What can you expect from the time period?" It is a useful pedagogical moment because it allows my students to define so many issues of male power and female concession so uncompromisingly. What does Frederic want? He wants Catherine, body and soul; and he wants her to want it. And she does: she wants to yield her entire self. This is "sweet." It sounds vaguely romantic. Even the most romantic of my students, however, have to admit that yielding oneself seems rather ominous when, "There isn't any me any more." Some of my students, as they nod vigorously in agreement with what their classmates are saying, appear to be thinking that after five minutes of this discussion they have already discovered the novel's heart of misogyny.

I take this as my starting point for inquiring more deeply into this destructive-seeming relationship. In particular, I want to open a debate about two areas I have always found intensely problematic. The first is that, while Frederic and Catherine fall readily into conventional gender roles, they use those roles in an attempt to exercise power over each other. Those roles therefore inspire, and sometimes disguise, a good deal of anger and frustration. The second is that these roles always seem to be under negotiation. Catherine and Frederic keep changing; they seem to have no truly stable character at all. That is why I want to move ultimately from a discussion of gender roles to the novel's concern with masquerade. Multiple gender roles imply that these characters keep putting on different masks; and the fact of multiplying masks implies that there may be no conception of stable identity to underpin "Frederic" and "Catherine." This helps to explain what an emphasis on gender roles can achieve. Simply arguing that Frederic is not a very good man will never, for my students, erase the structure of power that allows his voice to dominate Catherine's. The issue I find Hemingway exploring is not who Frederic is, but how he and Catherine invent themselves. And the conditions under which they do so necessarily involve an inquiry into questions of power.

I begin this discussion with a close reading of a conversation from book 5 (299–300), starting where Catherine inquires, "Darling, why don't you let your hair grow?" and ending with, "I got out the chess-board and arranged the pieces. It was still snowing hard outside." Sketching in a rudimentary context ("Let's look at one more lovers' scene before we move on") and inviting students to focus on a general question ("What does this scene reveal about their relationship?"), I ask two students to perform the long conversation. Here is a short section:

"I wouldn't let you cut yours."

"It would be fun. I'm tired of it. It's an awful nuisance in the bed at night."

"I like it."

"Wouldn't you like it short?"

"I might. I like it the way it is."

"It might be nice short. Then we'd both be alike. Oh, darling, I want you so much I want to be you too."

"You are. We're the same one." (299)

The scene is enough like the "I want what you want" conversation to make plain that it deals with similar issues. But my question, "What does this scene reveal about their relationship?" usually elicits some observations about how Catherine has come to life: the tenor of "I want you so much I want to be you" is much more aggressive than "I want what you want," and it is Catherine who lays out the procedures of hair trimming and hair growing designed to make them look "alike" and be the "same one" (299).

I then focus the discussion on the topic of hair. The question, "Why is Catherine so concerned about changing hairstyles?" pays immediate dividends, especially when supplemented with another question about students' changing hairstyles. It is not that Catherine's suggestions sound so radical to female students familiar with cropped hair, colored hair, or no hair. But it is an exemplary women's issue. All my students are experts in the relationship between hair and power: they know it intellectually, because they have learned that hair has always been a traditional signifier of womanhood; they know it politically, because they have chosen to transform their hair to make a statement, or to keep their hair long to make a statement. And they know it through the familial politics of outrage ("What have you done to your hair!"). Out of the many, many hair stories my students share arises a new respect for Catherine, who wants to look like Frederic, who is "tired" of her long hair, who wants quite aggressively to craft Frederic too by having him grow his hair longer, and who wants to get categories of gender, as she says, "all mixed up." (Students who have read The Garden of Eden can speak to its much more overt fascination with issues of androgyny and confused gender boundaries, described in part through hair play.)

But Frederic plays a role in this too, and I try to build on an emerging kernel of interpretive doubt about Catherine by asking my students to reflect on the pattern of Frederic's responses to her. I repeat a few out loud for emphasis: "It's long enough now," "I wouldn't let you cut yours," "I like it the way it is." Frederic, it soon becomes evident, tries to resist every one of Catherine's suggestions—and fails. She even ignores his imperative, "I wouldn't let you cut yours." How, I ask my students, can we explain this? Varied responses are certainly possible. I have had students propose that Hemingway is trying to implement a newly mature relationship for the couple. Others, more skeptical, have suggested that Hemingway has simply reinvented Catherine as an omnivorous bitch: first she wanted to give up her entire self; now she wants to possess Frederic utterly and be him too. Others (and this is the approach I favor) see that beneath the rhetoric of "darling" and "sweet" there is a power struggle going on. Catherine's "why don't you let your hair grow?" evokes a series of varied resistances on Frederic's part—he questions, temporizes, refuses, deflects—and in each case Catherine returns to the assault, culminating in that statement, "I want you so much I want to be you too," which is the result of, and caps, a verbal struggle for ascendancy. When I ask my students to think again about Frederic's response within this developing power game—why does he *insist,* "We're the same one"?—it becomes clear that the tenderness of his comment might mask something else entirely. It can be read as an ironic gesture of conciliation, which I translate roughly as, "Yes, yes, I get the message, we're the closest couple in the universe, so just shut up about growing my hair and let's talk about something else."

I always rephrase Frederic's remark in some vernacular form—shut up, get off my back, enough already, yes dear, whatever you say dear, all right all right!—because these phrases, and the structure of male-female relationships they imply, iterated endlessly in private lives and popular culture, are so familiar to all my students. This moment, I think, is a turning point in our discussions. If the language of love masks a structure of power, students suddenly see that they may have been too quick to condemn Hemingway for trying to "do love" and failing. Best of all, my students find that they are extremely knowledgeable about these kinds of power transactions and, once encouraged to think about the lovers' relationship in these terms, very good at elucidating numerous hidden contexts. Why does Frederic say, "I haven't any life at all any more"? Because he is obediently responding to Catherine's "Why, darling, I don't live at all when I'm not with you," which clearly comes with a rider attached: "I've given up my all. What about you—dear?" Frederic, however, forgets to add, "When I'm not with you," turning his agreement into a surreptitious account of the life he has lost, not gained. Why does Frederic not answer Catherine's "We'll have it together, won't we?"? It is a moment of foreshadowing, to be sure. But since Frederic does not know at this point that she will die, there are much more mundane ways of accounting for his lack of response: "(Sigh.) Haven't I already said 'I won't ever go away'? This is getting so tiresome. Do we have to go through this again?" Why does the scene end with a chess game? Because the chess game of love ("I was . . . seeing it all ahead like the moves in a chess game" [26]), which was supposed to have ended when "Everything turned over inside" Frederic and he was "in love with" Catherine, still seems to be going on. The whole scene we have been analyzing, in fact, can be read as a chess game of gambit, counterattack, and checkmate—actually, Frederic's refusal to "mate"—using words, emotions, and even body parts as the pieces.

This seems a good point in class discussion to pause and take stock of some interpretive options. By and large, my students come to this scene comfortable with conventional readings of the novel: it is a tragic love story in which a man is tested in war and love, and a woman—well, a woman learns what befalls women in Hemingway's world. There is no gainsaying the logic of this reading, and I try to give it full credence in summarizing the interpretive distance we have covered. But our conversation about the chess scene has allowed a new and convincing possibility: that Hemingway interprets human relationships not in a "silly" mode of "darling" and "sweet" but in terms of power relationships. It is a novel in which Catherine wants to give herself up body and soul and then possess Frederic body and soul, while refashioning their bodies; a novel in which Frederic says he is in love but refuses to answer when Catherine inquires whether they will have a fine life together; a novel in which the rhetoric of love implies manipulation and struggles for power; a novel in which Catherine and Frederic have been involved all along in a "game" of chess.

In the spirit of troubling the issue of gender relationships, however, I point out that there are some problems with accepting this scene as the *only* key to Frederic and Catherine's relationship. Scenes before and after this one seem to depict a more light-hearted version of their Swiss idyll: Frederic bursts out with, "Oh, darling, I love you so" (293) after watching Catherine at the hairdresser's and later makes the straightforward-sounding comment, "We had a fine life. . . . We were very happy" (306). And it is still difficult to reconcile the Catherine of the changing hairstyles with the "sweet" who professed, "There isn't any me any more," or Frederic the game player with Frederic the lover, who perhaps mutates back to game player. So I feel that there is still one more important set of questions to address the very unpredictability of the characters. Why, I ask, are they so changeable? Several answers are usually forthcoming. Some consider the war to blame. Catherine is a "mild lunatic," one of my students wrote, but "when the reader considers the chaos around her, her actions and words are not absurd, what is absurd is war, period." This student neatly covers a range of possibilities: the war has made Catherine mildly mad, but she is nowhere near as mad as the war. Perhaps this begins to explain her shift in temperament in Switzerland:

away from the war, pregnant, her dead fiancé fading into memory, Catherine can relax into what she was before (which seems to be for many students, unfortunately, a bona fide Hemingway bitch). This justification, however, does not explain why my students were able to read this scene as such a common cultural drama: trapped male and hen-pecking wife; protestations of love underpinned by a deeper structure of frustration. It would seem that Hemingway is at least very much alive to a gender war so deeply ingrained into our culture that students of today comprehend it virtually as a fact of life.

The preceding discussion of how changing hairstyles get gender roles "all mixed up" allows the class to pursue a different option: that gender, and indeed a character's entire identity, might be no more than a mask, put on for a while and then replaced with another in a different situation.[4] I move here quickly toward examples of *masquerades* in the novel, either by reinforcing something a student has just said ("Can anyone think of other characters playing fake roles, or masquerades, in the novel?") or by bringing up the issue myself as a way of extending Catherine's fascination with body sculpting.[5] There are many instances early in the novel. It is not merely that Frederic plays fast and loose with Catherine, and that Catherine, aware of the "rotten game" (31) they play, feeds her "lover" the right lines ("You did say you loved me, didn't you?"). The entire opening phase of the war is "bloody theatrical" (28): Rinaldi carries a "holster stuffed with toilet paper" (29), Frederic feels the "ridiculousness" (29) of carrying a pistol, and at one point Frederic pretends that he and Catherine would go off to a hotel where, "Maybe she would pretend that I was her boy that was killed" (37). Even the "many victories" (5) turn out to be hollow.

It is of course true that the early masquerades have a way of turning deadly serious. The "picturesque front" (20) explodes; flirtation becomes love, becomes death. Pistols lose their ridiculousness when Frederic shoots a deserter during the retreat from Caporetto. Frederic's uniform, which he derides early in the novel, nearly gets him shot at the bridge over the Tagliamento—a scene that leads him to the second critical recognition of the novel, when he realizes that the war "was not my show any more" (232). And as Catherine struggles for life under her gas mask, one has to be aware that the stakes of the lovers' game of chess are now very high indeed. Nonetheless, all interpretations of the novel that have Frederic and Catherine abandoning masquerade for a less illusive and more mature relationship must contend with the fact that masquerades continue to thrive during their Swiss idyll, and beyond. Catherine and Frederic masquerade as a married couple; they get across the border into Switzerland by pretending to be tourists; Frederic gets rid of his uniform, at which point he thinks, "In civilian clothes I felt a masquerader" (243); at the hospital, he looks in the mirror and sees "myself looking like a fake doctor with a beard" (319). Catherine dies under a mask (of anesthesia), and her death forces Frederic to compose the cold, tough mask of fortitude that has him saying, famously, "I do not want to talk about it" (332).

In order to explore this issue at greater length, I turn the class's attention to the paragraph that begins chapter 34. I sketch in not only the first sentence, "In civilian clothes I felt a masquerader," but the consequences of his masquerade: "There were some aviators in the compartment who did not think much of me. They avoided looking at me and were very scornful of a civilian my age" (243). What exactly, I ask, is the masquerade to which Frederic refers? The first step is easy. Someone is bound to say that, obviously, Frederic has been in a soldier's uniform so long that he feels strange in civvies; it is a feeling everyone who has dressed for a very formal event recognizes. I respond just as quickly. A masquerade suggests that one has a real identity and a masked identity; a fake identity masks the true one. So what is Frederic really—a civilian or a soldier?

Normally I avoid either/or questions because they attract one-word answers and thus place the teacher behind the eight ball. In this case I find that the question works because it dramatizes some key problems in reading Hemingway's masquerades. For, as we talk, students begin to realize that the question cannot be resolved—or that it can be resolved in a number of ways. Frederic seems to feel that he is really a soldier and is masquerading as a civilian. But he has just said he was putting off the "show" of the military. Moreover, the aviators recognize him (and scorn him) as a civilian. So, we might say, he really is a civilian. But what if the aviators saw through his masquerade and realized that he was a deserter? Then, all of a sudden, Frederic would be a soldier again—until the moment the firing squad pulled the trigger. So, we might say, he really is a soldier—until the moment he reaches Switzerland, at which point he can really be the civilian he masqueraded as in Italy. So is he really a soldier in Italy and really a civilian in Switzerland? If true, however, that distinction eludes the aviators; he is just as much a civilian to them as he is to the doctor in Switzerland. It quickly becomes clear that the question, "Is Frederic a civilian or a soldier?" supports contradictory assessments impartially; none of the answers settles the issue. The question is a riddle about the nature of masquerades, which invites a bit of reflection ("It seems that we keep reaching different conclusions about when and how Frederic is in masquerade") and a further question: "Why is that?"

The implications of this question for reading Hemingway are enormous, but posing it now offers students the advantage of being able to reflect, less abstractly, on the classroom discussion that has just ended. My main goal is to open up a general discussion about different modes of creating identity, centered on the rich topic of what it means to live in masquerade. In the next few paragraphs I summarize what I have found to be the most likely responses to my query. I recall here only the material pertaining to *Farewell,* though one of the reasons I like this topic is that it is open ended, and questions that invite students to reflect on the role of masquerade in their own lives—When have you observed others masquerading? Why do people do it? What about your-self?—can elicit a rich context for a discussion of Hemingway's characters.

One reason we might reach different conclusions about Frederic's masquer-ades, which students seem to be very familiar with, is that interpretation is a pluralist enterprise: texts possess multiple meanings, and readers bring mul-tiple perspectives. We are always reaching different conclusions about literary texts! I cannot gainsay the general validity of these ideas—and would not want to when we are reading Hemingway, a topic upon which my students begin by sharing a remarkable unanimity of opinion. But I remind students who pur-sue this route that the previous discussion could be characterized more aptly as several individuals each confidently mustering evidence for their quite dif-ferent perspectives. Students generally approach the question, "Is Frederic a soldier or a civilian?" as a problem to be *resolved* rather than as a confusion to be *recognized.* In part, I believe this is because we—and here I mean everyone, not just students—tend to think in terms of real and fake selves. We think in terms of a coherent self who sometimes chooses to wear a mask, and each de-scription of masquerade consequently marks out an original and prior self. So Catherine is changeable, but this could mean she is the kind of woman who manipulates different contexts of power—she offers Frederic her all when the point is to "catch" him but bosses him around when, being pregnant, she knows he is "caught." In that case, we recognize Catherine as a coherent individual who stage-manages her various appearances, and it is thus logical to call her (say) a "mild lunatic" or "bitch," because one is trying to grasp the character-istic that motivates and governs all her behaviors.

Or does Catherine's changeability imply that shifting contexts of power af-ford human beings different identities—so that Catherine *is* that person who offers herself up and then, much later, is that person who derives authority from her pregnancy and civilian "marriage"? In the latter case, one recognizes many Catherines. "Catherine" is constructed anew by changing circumstances. So, in the hairstyle-changing scene, Catherine certainly plays the role of possessive wife well enough to drive Frederic to frustration—but that does not mean she was pretending earlier when she offered to give up all to her lover. If the roles we inhabit are all we know as human beings, then it makes no sense to distin-guish a true self from a fake performance: all selves would be performances, and we would be forever mistaking the performance for the "real." Frederic too would be no more than the sum of his masks. He would be a soldier at times (as when, in Switzerland, he keeps harking back to the war), and at times a civilian. What if being in love with Catherine amid the erotic energies of the hairdressing scene does not preclude, some other time, a frustrated Frederic and devouring wife? Indeed, we might only suppose there to be a single solid Frederic or Catherine because we can readily identify their masquerades and thus presume that there must be a "real" self that generates them. This sum-of-masks theory implies a decentered or sliding construction of self and is one way of explaining why Catherine and Frederic are so bound up with masks at the end of the novel. They have never been out of them.

Another way of construing the issue of masked identities, which I find still more conducive, is to view them as wholly contextual. On the train to Stresa, Frederic knows himself to be a deserting soldier (as do the Italian authorities); the aviators know him as a contemptible civilian. Had they penetrated Frederic's disguise, they would certainly have read him as a soldier; but such might not be true of Mr. and Mrs. Guttingen or the Swiss doctor, who would surely be disposed (had they known) to view him as a civilian who had once been a soldier. In this sense, identities are not indeterminate: each interpreter of Frederic is positive he or she knows who and what he is. But identities must be contingent and contextual: the determination of whether Frederic is a soldier and/or a civilian (or something else entirely) depends on who is making the judgment and the circumstances under which the judgment is made. To me, this seems a natural consequence of the soldier/civilian debate because, as I say to my class, it describes so well the tenor of the discussion just concluded. Perhaps, like the aviators, we have fallen into the trap of reading one of Frederic's masks and proceeding to construe his entire personality by way of it.

In the classroom, this discussion of the meaning of masks in *Farewell* can proceed differently. Students are quite capable of answering my soldier-or-civilian question with, "It depends," in which case we address the issue of contingent identities sooner. But all paths lead back to a reconsideration of gender. From the standpoint of the novel's fascination with masquerade, it no longer seems so obvious to my students that Frederic is a misogynist, or indeed that he is any one thing at all. Nor does it seem so obvious that Catherine's character must be constrained by (say) her propensity for giving herself up body and soul to her lover. This is one major benefit of thinking in terms of masquerade: it means that readers cannot move tranquilly from any one scene or characteristic to a determination of the whole self, though it may indeed draw attention to our tendency to do so.

Perhaps more importantly, the principle of masquerade can be used to place emphasis on the socially constructed nature of the roles that men and women inhabit. In one sense, my students have always been aware that the novel grants them insight into gender roles. They instantly recognize the significance of hair for women and the general cultural validity of Catherine's "There isn't any me any more"—that sense that the female self does not "amount to very much." Yet, to begin with, that insight into gender roles is quite specifically imagined to be *theirs* as feminists or as twenty-first-century women; it is what they bring to a misogynist work and what allows them to contend with it. The key to their confidence, I think, is a way of reading character: "There isn't any me" determines the essence of Catherine; Catherine determines the essence of her author. Masquerade confuses this seemingly logical sequence. The notion that identities can be switched, transformed, and "all mixed up"; the notion that Catherine can play one stereotypical role, and then another, and yet another; the notion that "There isn't any me" might speak more to a single masquerade than to her essential being; the notion that changing hairstyles might signify growing and trimming gender roles—all these possibilities suggest ways in which the *novel* might be considered responsible for provoking reflection on the ways men and women in our society fashion identities and keep fashioning them. These are the kinds of "women's issues" my students are familiar with. It is to me a profoundly satisfying moment when students realize that Hemingway, Hemingway of all writers, might have been familiar with them too.

## Notes

I would like to thank all my students at Mills for their tremendous help, particularly those who have contributed comments to this essay: Melissa White; Constance Wiggins; Lyn Woodward; Melanie Smith; and Judith Rathbone, who contributed the quotation in my title.

1. A typical modern American fiction course begins with Cather and Hemingway and then turns immediately to William Faulkner's *As I Lay Dying* for a different approach to experimental style. I continue with Ralph Ellison's *Invisible Man,* Toni Morrison's *Song of Solomon,* Maxine Hong Kingston's *Tripmaster Monkey,* Louise Erdrich's *Love Medicine,* and Sandra Cisneros's *Woman Hollering Creek.* I aspire here to as much diversity in the course as possible. But I also choose works that will advance the twin themes I propose with Hemingway and Cather: the function of experimental writing strategies and the question of changing gender roles.

2. All quotations are taken verbatim from actual pieces of student writing. In this course I usually assign two long papers, each to be handed in as a draft and then rewritten with my

comments in mind. I also sometimes teach a special topics course on two modernist minimalists, Hemingway and Cather, and in that course I assign writing journals. I find it useful to begin a long course of study of Hemingway by having students write informally about him in order to establish a basis for talking about shared preconceptions. The comments printed here are taken from these pieces, from journal entries, and in a couple of cases from e-mail conversations.

3. See Jamie Barlowe-Kayes's "Re-reading Women: The Example of Catherine Barkley" for a fine interpretation of how "feminist critical and theoretical re-readings of Hemingway's female characters expose cultural codes and attitudes about women which continue to haunt and limit their lives" (35).

4. See Marilyn Elkins's "The Fashion of *Machismo*" for a very interesting essay detailing Hemingway's interest in clothing, style, hair, and their relationship to machismo.

5. Peter Messent, in *Modern Novelists: Ernest Hemingway,* first drew my attention to this topic.

# PEDAGOGICAL APPROACHES

# Teaching *A Farewell to Arms* through Discussion
## Harkness Strategies for a Student-Centered Classroom

*Mark P. Ott*

As a novel of passionate love and jarring violence, *A Farewell to Arms* still has the essential ingredients to capture the imagination of today's high school students. For many, it is their first introduction to Hemingway; they have heard the name, and they want to know what the fuss is all about. Hemingway is a brand name in their minds, associated in some foggy way with things tough, cool, cynical, and self-destructive. Like reading Shakespeare, reading Hemingway becomes a badge of intellectualism in a high school environment; it is something students want to do for reasons they are reluctant to articulate. Yet once they are dropped into the rainy, war-torn landscape of Italy during World War I and the dramatic misfortunes of Frederic and Catherine, students quickly come to another realization: *A Farewell to Arms* is a great novel.

Although curricula vary, most teachers agree that *A Farewell to Arms* is a novel best taught in either the sophomore or junior year. The novel has a complexity that draws readers of this age quickly into the text, as Hemingway's language hints at mysteries and understated emotions. The first instinct of high school students is to read for meaning. What makes the novel so teachable are the accessible themes, easily recognizable imagery, memorable characters, and engaging, exciting plot lines. Again and again, students want to know, what does Hemingway mean? Helping students to clarify and explore the meaning of the novel through student-led discussion is the essence of a Harkness class, a pedagogy that empowers and transforms the way students understand literature.

### INTRODUCTION TO THE HARKNESS PEDAGOGY AND THE READING JOURNAL AS A DISCUSSION FACILITATOR

The Harkness pedagogy originated at Phillips Exeter Academy in 1929 and since then has been increasingly refined as an egalitarian discussion-based method in which the teacher is a facilitator, rather than an authority, and the students have primary ownership of the learning.[1] As a teacher, I have found this method extraordinarily rewarding, as it turns over the novel to the students, and they, in turn, control the content of the discussion and avenues of exploration. Ideally for a Harkness class, students sit facing each other at one large seminar table (or tables), rather than in rows of desks. Ideally, too, there is no open space in the configuration, so that the continuous tabletop symbolically links the students in the discussion, compelling them to work together. The instructor is seated with them, rather than addressing them from a chalkboard or podium. Notably, this is a student-led, text-centered approach that works best for classes of twenty students or fewer. The pedagogy expects that students are prepared for class and have their own copies of the novel, which they are then required to mark and note.

Truly surrendering the class to the students requires a leap of faith on the part of the teacher. Naturally, there is a concern that students will not stay focused on the discussion and will daydream. Another fear is that students will lose sight of important elements of the novel and focus on minutiae. Yet entrusted students have a strong instinct for what is essential, and if they are given freedom within a well-understood framework of expectations, they rise to the occasion. That said, I always make certain that students know how I will be evaluating their participation. The expectations are that there will be no interrupting and no side conversations; one student speaks at a time, and no one whispers while someone else is speaking. They need to learn how to be attentive listeners and look at the person who is talking. There is no doodling allowed, and everyone's book must be open. The chalkboard or whiteboard remains untouched, as students must listen and respond, concentrating on the discussion with their classmates.

Trained to instruct, teachers are often reluctant to surrender the classroom stage to the students. Yet to learn about literature, students must have the freedom to explore what they know by talking about it with their nonevaluating peers. Once the teacher jumps in, students stop exploring their own ideas and begin pursuing the "right" answer. Thus teachers must be extremely self-conscious about their authority in the classroom. In a Harkness classroom, their role is to question without hinting at an answer. They need to resist the impulse to pronounce their own interpretations or to display the depth of their learning or their cleverness. With any book I teach, I tell the students that I have never read it before; it is their job to tell me what it is about.

In secondary schools, discussion is often confused with debate, especially in literature classes. Accustomed to quiet classrooms of students taking notes, teachers often welcome the sparks that come from impassioned students trying to verbally persuade each other that they are right and the other is wrong. Students, too, seem to thrill to the contest of wits. Yet a debate polarizes a class and relegates the majority of students to the role of spectators, implicitly telling them that their ideas do not matter, that the class is open only to aggressive, verbal students. Therefore the energy of argumentation needs to be promptly redirected by the teacher into a cooperative inquiry.

It is crucial that a teacher give the students a chance to warm up before discussion. In my classroom, students use reading journals to chart their own journeys through the novel; for each class and reading assignment, they prepare text-citing entries on significant images (i.e., rain, light, darkness, etc.), themes (i.e., love, religion, irony, sexuality, patriotism), a character, or their personal response to the reading (did they like/dislike what they read?).[2] Journal entries are required to be (at a minimum) a page in length, with at least three citations to the text circled. (Students are discouraged from using the Internet for research or biographical material until after they have finished reading the novel.) If a class meets four times a week, the students prepare journal entries for two of those classes. On other days, shorter exercises suffice.

Generally, I give the first five to ten minutes of each class to exercises that get the students grounded in the text and prepared to think and respond. It is important, too, that the students use this time silently reading, writing, and thinking, so distractions should be kept to a minimum. On days that they have journal assignments, I have them pass their journals to the student to their right, and that student, in turn, reads the journal entry, commenting on ideas in the margin and, at the conclusion, writing a two- to three-sentence response, perhaps agreeing with the ideas explored or encouraging his or her classmate to view the topic differently. I have the students write their name at the end of their reply so that when I grade the journals, I can give them credit for their responses. While students are quietly reading and writing, I walk around the classroom, checking to see if everyone has done the assignment. Maintaining a climate of accountability is crucial to the success of a Harkness classroom, as unprepared students are either silent, contributing nothing to the conversation, or else bluffing their way on unsubstantiated ideas. Every other class, I make it a point to check students' copies of the text to see if they are underlining and

taking notes as they read, stressing that active reading is part of their assignment. When I encounter unprepared students, I do not upbraid them, but I
have them sign a piece of paper on a clipboard, with their name, the problem,
and the date. When it is time to assign the student a grade, I then have a record
of their class preparation, or lack thereof. And the clipboard quickly affects the
climate of the class; students simply do not want to sign it and therefore come
prepared. I also do not hesitate to assign seats to students. It is self-evident that
if they are allowed to sit next to a friend, students find it much easier to start
side conversations that distract from the larger classroom discussion.

Journal entries are not essential for every class. Instead, I might have students
write down the numbers of five pages they would like to discuss in their journal,
while also jotting down a sentence about what is interesting on those pages. Occasionally, I have the students create a paragraph about the most interesting thing
in the previous night's reading. Other times, I have them create two questions
rooted in the text about the reading; for this assignment they are prohibited to
use the words "meaning," "symbolize," "significance," and "represent." (When I
allowed those words, too often students would write lazy questions such as, "What
does the rain on page 185 represent?") Good questions, I tell them, are usually
two to three sentences long. The students exchange journals and answer each
other's questions. Other times, I have the students make a list of pages we need to
discuss, putting the page numbers on the left-hand side of the page, and a comment on the passage opposite it. After the warm-up exercises, I use a variety of
approaches to get them started. Often I have students read a passage from their
journal or select the most interesting passage in the previous night's reading. As
the conversation progresses, students and the teacher can refer to the warm-up
work in the journals, using it for fuel or to jump-start the conversation in a slug-
gish moment; the teacher can ask the students, "Did anyone have anything else
in their journal they would like to discuss?"

Thus a Harkness classroom focuses on building the students' literature skills
rather than on assessing their mastery of content. For each class, four students
are assigned roles: (1) topic chooser (who sets the agenda for the discussion),
(2) topic resolver (who makes certain that a topic is resolved as much as possible before the class moves on), (3) comment responder (who makes sure that
each significant remark is responded to, and recognized, in discussion), and (4)
involver (who solicits comments from quieter students to make sure all voices
are heard).[3] By designating responsibilities to the students—on which they can
then be evaluated—the teacher shifts the focus of the class to the students, making it known that the success of the class hinges on their participation. In their
reading, they must notice important details and interpret them plausibly. They

must be able to connect related passages and to articulate broader insights. In discussion, they need to ask questions about the text and address them with their classmates. They need to listen actively and respond to their peers. When they present ideas, they must support them with specific passages. Ultimately, they need to offer thoughtful, well-supported interpretations of a text.

How do teachers cultivate this range of skills in their students? By carefully crafting the questions they present to the class, and by withdrawing whenever possible from the discussion. To give students a voice in class, the teacher must be willing to give them silence and time so that their voices can fill that space. An interrogative mode puts the focus on the teacher, not the students, and it cuts them off. As a teacher, I begin every class by asking: "Where do we want to begin today?" Students then have to confront the text and their ideas, and generally several students quickly initiate the conversation by sharing what is on their minds. Another approach is to ask, "Does anyone have a favorite passage from the text they would like to discuss?" If the responses are muted, I follow up with, "What is the most important thing that happened in today's reading?" Often the natural entry point for discussion of *A Farewell to Arms* is obvious: meeting Catherine, Frederic's wounding, the reunion with Catherine, the dive into the river, and crossing the Lago Maggiore to Switzerland are all natural centerpieces for the beginnings of a conversation. Having the students read a page or two aloud drops them back into the text, and once a reading is concluded, I ask, "What do you notice about this scene?" As the conversation begins to move of its own momentum, the teacher's role becomes to clarify and synthesize the student responses. A typical teacher comment would be, "What pages is that on?" Another approach would be to ask, "Where do you see that in Hemingway's language? Can you take us there?" The teacher must force the students not only to return to the text, but to hear their own comments; otherwise the conversation spins in all directions. And so repeatedly I ask, "Where do you see that? Can you be more specific?" Since the students have actively been marking their books and tracking their ideas in their journals, it should be easy for them to respond. If students begin to get off topic, I recenter them by saying, "I have lost track. Why are we discussing this?" At another divergence I might ask, "Is this idea important? Why isn't it important?" After a moment of reflection, someone can usually articulate why a topic does or does not matter.

Always, there is the issue of silent students. Shyness, cynicism, lack of preparation, and an intimidating atmosphere can all conspire to keep some students quiet in discussion. I tell all my students that I am not grading them on their personalities; outgoing, talkative students do not necessarily get higher grades than quiet ones. Yet if they choose to be silent, they still must be attentive listeners and undisruptive. If they want an above-average grade, they must compensate for their silence by doing exceptionally thorough and thoughtful work in their journals. But when invited to contribute, most students avail themselves of the opportunity. In order to draw out students, I often ask, "You look like you were ready to say something?"

Before the topic shifts, I always try to ask if anyone wants to add a comment before we move on. I then ask the involver if there are students who have not had a chance to speak, and I ask those students directly if they have anything to share. For a Harkness class to succeed, it is more important that students feel they are valued and can speak if they wish than for everyone to contribute every day.

## BEGINNING THE NOVEL: SPOTLIGHTING HEMINGWAY'S INTRODUCTORY LANGUAGE

The opening chapter of the novel provides students with an introduction not only to Hemingway's beautiful language but also to its difficulty. The rhythms of the novel's first paragraph ("In the late summer of the fall of that year . . .") strike the students as demanding and original. Sentences seem unusually long, and they must concentrate hard to grasp their meaning even as the narrative begins to move forward. Chapter 1 is only four paragraphs and two pages long, yet there are enough images packed into the language for us to explore for a full class period. Thus, even though I assign the first five chapters (through page 21), we do not cover them. Instead, lingering on the first two pages sets the framework for subsequent classes, providing students with a road map for the novel.

What do the students need to see? The stylistic marvels of Hemingway's first pages often are missed by high school students, yet spotlighting them early is crucial. I begin by having the students read the first two pages aloud. When they are finished, I have them take a few minutes to underline and highlight the images and words that strike them as either notable or unusual. Then I have them turn their attention to the first paragraph again, and I ask them to circle all the words that are repeated. Their list will include "river" (two), "dust" (three), "leaves" (four), and "white" (two). The river, of course, introduces the image of water that will run throughout the novel, and it is crucial that students recognize that it is pure and untainted at this point, running swiftly over the rocks. The dust causes the leaves to fall early, which signals to the reader that the cycles of nature have been disrupted by the war. Students may also note the connection between "clear" and "blue," as well as the use of "falling" and "fell" and "rising" and "raised." Focusing on the movement in the paragraph helps them begin to see Hemingway's complex architecture: the river water is clear and swiftly moving; the troops move, stirring the breeze; the dust rises; and the leaves fall. The interconnectedness of these elements is easy for students to recognize once it is highlighted for them, and it forces them to begin to see the richer implications of the narrative.

Beyond the first paragraph, students need to recognize Hemingway's deliberate language. The plain, still fertile and rich with crops, is juxtaposed against the mountains, which are barren. That relationship needs to be pointed out alongside the importance of the nights, the summer lightning, and the feeling of a storm coming. Relationships in the language that are quickly apparent to trained readers and teachers who have taught the novel for years should be pointed out, but the students at this point will be struggling to orient themselves in Hemingway's Italy.

Consequently, I adjust my expectations for the discussion to make sure they are aligned with the abilities of my students. The complexities of Hemingway's form of modernism will be a mystery to them, and I do not expect their conversation to be that of a graduate seminar on the Lost Generation. Once the nuanced language of the first pages is opened up to the students, it is important that they then have a very clear signal that the conversation is theirs. If they want to talk about rain, I let them talk about rain. If they want to talk about color imagery, I encourage their exploration. The point is not whether they find a resolution or answer to their inquiry; rather, it is crucial that they find their own voices, talking to each other about the novel as they explore it for the first time.

What will the first student discussion resemble? To the teacher's initial discouragement, the comments will be disjointed and unrelated; aggressive students will seek to push their ideas, while quieter students will withdraw into a shell. Thus it is crucial that the teacher assign the roles of chooser, resolver, responder, and involver to students who represent a broad range of abilities. I have found that making my best, least shy student the involver enhances rather than thwarts the conversation, and assigning the role of topic chooser to an earnest, hard-working student—not a star, but not a slacker—sets the right tone. That way, class will be centered on topics that all students can access. It can be difficult for the teacher to be patient with a class that seems to be going nowhere, but patience pays off. Students need several classes to become comfortable with each other and to appreciate their independence from the teacher. To be sure that students feel freedom in the discussion, I make it a point to give them—in a fifty-five-minute class—at least ten minutes when I will not interrupt, interject, or clarify what they are discussing.

Once they have journeyed through the first nine chapters, to Frederic's wounding, general patterns for the discussions will have emerged. I have found that students are first character driven, and they will try to begin understanding the novel through the characters they like or dislike. By chapter 9, students may not be especially impressed with Frederic; his frequent drinking may cause students to disrespect him. His purposelessness frustrates them; until he is wounded, he is unremarkable. And Catherine's character is baffling; often they find her "weird." Rinaldi and the priest are very much secondary characters to them, and their importance only emerges later. But they quickly notice the importance of the imagery of the natural world—especially the stream—and how it reflects the events of the war. I make certain, however, that they do a close reading of the wounding, noting the implications of the language and how it signals a rebirth for Frederic. As chapter 9 ends with Frederic soaked in blood, it only takes a moment for students to recognize this as a baptism into the real war, one that Frederic once felt "did not have anything to do with me" (37).

By the middle of the novel, in books 3 and 4, discussions sharpen considerably. Students recognize now that the rain imagery foreshadows something. They look back at page 4 and ask, "What is cholera?" They find it odd that Frederic and Catherine do not get married, and the references to Catherine's hair are mysterious to them. When the pregnancy is announced, students feel the tension in the scene. I make sure that they explore the implications of the line, "You always feel trapped biologically" (139). Frederic's drinking, to them, seems alcoholic. But they notice how he has changed as he returns to the war, how he seems oddly more committed to the cause and eager to be a hero. The reunion scene with Rinaldi causes real consternation; students want to know if Rinaldi is homosexual. They ask, "Why is Rinaldi jealous?" I let them draw their own conclusions. When Frederic shoots the sergeant, they note the change in his character and also the disintegration of order in the war. I select a student to read aloud the famous scene where Frederic states, "I was always embarrassed by the words sacred, glorious, and sacrifice and the expression in vain" (184). We toil over every sentence, and I press the students to make sense of the passage; they note the evolution in Frederic's thoughts on the war. When Frederic leaps into the river to escape the war, I encourage the students to connect that scene to the baptism in blood that occurred earlier. Religion, at this point, is a theme the students will want to explore. The scenes in Milan and Stresa reinforce the changes in Frederic; he is now a civilian, in love with

Catherine. Students wonder—because she is drinking alcohol and not showing outward signs of her pregnancy—if Catherine has been lying to Frederic about the baby. The dialogue with Count Greffi catches their attention; references to religion keep occurring, and I take the students back to the beginning of the novel, when Frederic states of the priest: "He had always known what I did not know and what, when I learned it, I was always able to forget" (14). As they cross into Switzerland, students want to talk about the role of the wind and the rain; they now have "cheerful" rain. They notice the religious joking at the end of chapter 37, and we talk about the meaning of the word "sacrilegious."

Suddenly, the final pages are looming, and students want to finish the novel quickly. Switzerland, the students quickly notice, is a different landscape, far from the war. Frederic is always drinking alcohol, and this seems, to them, to reveal his inner turmoil. Maybe he does not want the baby. Maybe he does not love Catherine. The arrival of the baby is imminent, and the students begin to note signs that all is not well. Catherine is drinking beer, and they are still not married. The word "crazy" is appearing with much greater frequency in the text, and some students declare Catherine to be completely unbalanced. They notice the snow comes in January, but they wonder what a "false spring" is. And as the tension of Catherine's labor begins to build, I make sure that we dwell on the "log on top of the fire," and why Frederic does not take the opportunity to be "a messiah" and save the burning ants (327–28). I make a point of telling the students to carve out time away from friends, cell phones, TV, and other distractions so that they can savor the final pages. I stress to them that they do not want to spoil the ending by rushing through it.

## RESOLUTIONS: WHAT IS THE MEANING OF THE ENDING?

As the students proceed through the novel, even in the midst of their disagreements, they begin to speak with one interpretative voice. They begin to see how the novel works, how Hemingway's realism becomes so compelling that they take it as their own. Arriving at the final pages, with Catherine's death imminent, they struggle to understand Hemingway's vision of the world. Is there only more death waiting for Frederic as he walks back to the hotel in the rain? Is he going to commit suicide? Because Frederic's sorrow becomes their own, students often respond angrily to the darkness and pessimism of the final pages; they want to resist the idea that Hemingway's world is their world. The resolution—so masterfully unified and satisfying—delivers a truth that is inconsistent with the happy endings they have been conditioned to expect.

Yet Hemingway's message is delivered in a language that sounds like the students' own; they hear it and it echoes. They see, finally, the heroism in Frederic's conduct as he struggles to be equal to his corrupted ideals. It is a struggle that students endure every day, brushing up against the coldness of the adult world while living in a morally treacherous universe of teenagers. The Harkness pedagogy allows for secondary school students to experience the novel as sensitive, honest readers, and through that they begin to recognize the values and morality that transform stories into literature. In the words of legendary Phillips Exeter Academy teacher Harvard Knowles, "In giving us stories that root us in our own experiences, Hemingway shows us not only who we are but also forces us to consider what we may become. What greater teacher could we possibly want for our young?"

## Notes

1. For a general overview of Harkness pedagogy, see the articles by Heath, Rindfleisch, Ruenzel, and Terry. "The Amazing Harkness Philosophy" at the Phillips Exeter Academy Web site (http://www.exeter.edu/admissions/147_harkness.aspx) also provides a thoughtful summary.

2. The best resource I have found for using student journals in the classroom is the time-tested *Inside Out: Developmental Strategies for Teaching Writing* by Dan Kirby, Tom Liner, and Ruth Vinz. See chapter 5, pages 57–71.

3. The Harkness pedagogy used at Phillips Exeter Academy and elsewhere does not utilize these roles; they are a modification that I have made in order to make it more effective in my classroom. As the entire curriculum of Phillips Exeter is taught through Harkness pedagogy, the students there do not need formalized roles; I believe that assigning roles to students would enhance the success of the pedagogy everywhere else.

# A Multimedia Approach to Teaching *A Farewell to Arms*

*David Scoma*

In my classes, I tend to find that the students can be grouped into three categories when it comes to reading interest. There are the ones who will voraciously devour whatever written word you put in front of them. This tends to be the smallest portion of the class. Next, there are the students who will occasionally pick up a book or a magazine to read, but only as a last resort—say, if they are stuck in a dentist's office or on a long flight. The majority of my class tends to fit into this category. And finally, there are the men and women scattered throughout the classroom who could not care less for literature and would be more than happy if they never had to read a printed word ever again, thank you very much. They would rather spend their free time with television and video games, along with any other sort of amusements not directly associated with reading. They are the ones who complain when you speak of plot points and character development. They are the ones who audibly sigh when you assign fifty pages of reading for homework. And the irony is that those television-drenched pupils are the ones who have more tucked up in their minds when it comes to short story structure, character development, and denouement than most of the other students in the room—even the good readers. They just do not know it yet. They have not made the connection between stories as told in written form on the page and stories the way they are used to seeing them—sometimes sixty or seventy hours' worth each week—on television.

Television. As educators, we are so used to thinking of it as the enemy that we very often forget how easily it can become our ally as well. I am not necessarily speaking of the fine educational and instructive programs that abound on

PBS, as well as the dozens of cable channels now available to every subscriber. I am talking about the films that play and replay on HBO. I am talking about the terrible made-for-TV movies filling up time between the sitcoms and the news. I am even talking about the sitcoms themselves. And believe it or not, I think there is even something redemptive to be found in soap operas—perhaps it is no accident that their creators wish them to be called "daytime dramas."

Before you roll your eyes, please keep something in mind. To some of us these television programs are crude and at times unthinkable tools to use in expanding the mind. Yet these are the very sources that many students return to in their leisure time again and again. Each of those sources contains, in no matter how rudimentary a form, the building blocks for narrative storytelling—in a compact, visual format. Students' familiarity with television can become a way to draw an otherwise intellectually inactive student into reading. Perhaps it can even be a catalyst for bringing a mediocre reader to a fuller appreciation of literature.

Although students have changed a great deal in the last generation, in some ways they are exactly the same as the collection of young folks trying to get something out of the images from *Islands in the Stream* on the screen before us that I remember from my own high school English class. If you tell a group of students that they are going to watch part of a video—be it five minutes or fifteen—they start to brighten up. They actually start looking for the details and genuinely try to explore the nuances you ask them to search for. They jump into class discussions with fresh insights to accompany those that they developed from reading the material. Most importantly, though, they realize that watching something unfold before their eyes on a screen need not always be a waste of time. That is what so many of them have grown up being told—that all they could ever expect from television was garbage.

On the contrary, if used properly, television and film can actually be the impetus for students to find out that learning may be far more fun and involving than they ever would have admitted. And by tying visual experiences directly into their assignments in particular, video can then act as a bridge for those who are not in love with reading at the start of a semester. In this way, such students may then have the opportunity to appreciate how rewarding the study of good literature can actually become.

This way of approaching lessons and activities requires an open mind and the creative outlook that so many teachers already possess more than it needs any kind of specific media training. Though I earned a degree in communication and have a background in film studies and theory, I discovered early on as an undergraduate that what I truly wanted to do was become a college professor. Having taken a heavy concentration of video, film, and visual media courses, it was easy to see how much more engaged the students became—especially those from other disciplines who were taking our classes as electives—when media was selectively and skillfully applied to lectures. At that time, my minor was in education. Years later, after having gone through interdisciplinary graduate course work at both the masters and doctoral levels—in which media studies and English were given equal billing—combining the two fields when possible became second nature.

However, it was in practice more than in the classes I took that I saw how effective such an approach could be. For several years I was an educational media specialist at two brand-new multimillion-dollar facilities. I had to order every single book, video, and computer program and build the media centers from scratch. Then those resources had to be used in an effective way that could draw in children ages four through twelve and foster their learning. That was truly a boot camp for learning the balance between bringing in an appropriate amount of media to augment a lesson without risking oversaturation and maintaining continuity with the written word. It also showed me that, even at such a young age, children are remarkably open to putting numerous learning styles into play with various media options.

I got the chance to further the implementation of these types of strategies on a deeper level when I began working with high school students and in private college settings. Though of course the means and the programs differed significantly from those at the younger age levels, a great deal of the balance and the diversity of scope when it came to planning activities remained intact. In the last few years, I have used media in courses involving history, English, literature, and small-group communication. My students range in age from just out of high school to recently retired. The bulk of my students tend to be right in the middle of that range. I consistently have one section a semester filled with students returning to full-time course work while maintaining their careers. They are a joy to teach and bring a fervor and attention to these exercises that catch some of their younger classmates on fire. Though not all my students have anywhere close to that drive, I have been fortunate in that they have been, for the most part, moderately prepared and modestly interested in the subject material when they enter my classroom. The techniques, exercises, and suggestions that follow have successfully been put into play with juniors and seniors from both my literature and twentieth-century world history courses.

## A MEDIA OVERVIEW

As I have taught the novel *A Farewell to Arms* successfully in both literature classes and history courses, I plan to use the films themselves as the unifying factor in approaching this topic. Rather than saying, "This strategy worked well when it came to the literature students, but not so well in the history classes," instead I will be approaching the novel, and especially ideas for encouraging student discussions of the text, through three motion pictures in particular. Two of these films were created with the novel *A Farewell to Arms* as their direct inspiration. The third is the romantic biopic *In Love and War.* This feature sought to re-create the early period in Hemingway's life that became the basis for the World War I action of the novel, and during which his relationship with real-life Red Cross nurse Agnes von Kurowsky took place. Ironically, I find portions of this melodrama easier to use when discussing *Farewell* with a class than I do either of the films based directly on the book. Finally, I will also deal with the use of film and electronic sources as a medium for teaching or introducing various concepts concerning literature in a visual way.

When it comes to the question of screening such films in connection with a reading, I am usually asked which I prefer—to show the entire film, or certain portions alone. Do you screen before, during, or after the reading? The reading is, of course, the most important and influential portion of the lesson. The novel *A Farewell to Arms* is the primary focus—even if it is being used in a history class, as in that context it is being studied as a work of art produced from a distinct wartime experience. My approach is a combination of before and after—showing scenes early in the reading and then shortly after they have finished the book. On one hand, I do not want to color the reading of the students or unduly influence the vision of the characters and settings that develop in their mind's eye. Yet on the other hand, I have found introducing various short clips of distinct, important scenes from all the films at the mid- to late point of their reading useful. It has helped to spark some of the more compelling and thoughtful discussions of the book between teacher and students. Doing so at a point in time when the students then get to return to the text—invigorated, and on the lookout for new insights—sets the stage for a wonderful and triumphant discussion period following the entire reading.

I tend to divide those final talks into two sections—the first takes place directly after the reading assignment is completed. Of course, the class by then has spoken about the book—in sections—a number of times already. It is after the initial sessions that I begin introducing short clips from the movies as counterpoints to their reading. The selection itself depends on the scenes and circumstances I find that the students are bringing up in class. This leaves a great deal of freedom for the instructor to pick and choose from the films, as well as from the scenes and circumstances the pupils themselves seem to be cleaving to—some of which change from course to course depending on each group's temperament.

Following the book wrap-up, I then pick one of the films to show in its entirety, and we end the screening with one last discussion. This final talk tends to be the most animated and lively of them all, as the students themselves—now personally invested in *Farewell,* having spent hours reading and dissecting the text—get to see changes to characters, situations, and even settings in the filmed versions. Students get upset. They become angry and indignant when they realize their favorite scenes, or the themes and circumstances they felt were key to the plot, have been left on the cutting room floor—if they were ever shot at all!

All this emotion and energy turns into wonderful fodder for furthering the groundwork of the key discussion points I try to emphasize all along: What makes the novel work? What scenes, images, or circumstances work to weaken the overall story (this often becomes apparent to students when they see what has been removed from the same story in the motion picture format)? And what, if anything, comes across more strongly in the film than it did in the novel?

Certainly, most of these areas can be addressed in a number of ways without showing part or all of a film. Yet I have found that the incorporation of visual means, in even the most limited and guided of circumstances, has worked to enrich the debates I have with students about the book. It has also worked to enhance the depth and assurance of their responses to such a degree—both to me and to each other—that I can hardly imagine not putting them into play. Due to the nature of the story and the number of resources available to enhance such instruction, *A Farewell to Arms* is an ideal novel for the teacher who wishes to delve into the realm of visually assisted lessons.

## A Farewell to Arms, *1932 and 1957*

The two film versions of *Farewell* differ as much from each other in many areas as they do from the novel that inspired both productions in the first place. A simple comparison between the divergent paths each movie takes in dramatizing the speech Catherine makes to Frederic about her slain fiancé would suffice in demonstrating this point. At first, the screenwriters' taking of such liberties with Hemingway's text may seem to make it impossible to use the films effectively in teaching the book. However, I believe that various aspects of each film can easily be integrated into successful lessons and discussions surrounding Hemingway's novel.

Let me begin by saying that I have not always found the showing of either film in its entirety to a classroom full of students to be successful. A number of pupils tend to be turned off immediately by the acting styles. In addition, while they seem to prefer the Technicolor of the 1957 version over the black and white of the 1932 film, it is by a slim margin at best. The modern student, who has typically been inundated with the use of black-and-white film stock in music videos, is no stranger to the format. However, most music videos tend to compile a mixture of styles, forms, and, most importantly, editing frequencies in the course of the three-minute mini-movie. In showing the 1932 version of *Farewell,* you will be asking students to sit through an eighty-minute black-and-white feature film. They will be watching a story that, while familiar from the reading, is being presented in an antiquated acting style. In addition, the motion picture will be unfolding at a pace that, to most of them, will feel like something only slightly more speedy than the onset of the ice age. For a number of students, this is understandably a bit much. Media should be used in order to encourage students to delve further into the original text, not to send them running away from the story filled with boredom or contempt.

My advice is to consider that sometimes the best approach is to implement a few key scenes or segments in your lectures on the novel. Regardless of the makeup of an entire body of students, there will hopefully almost always be a handful of top-drawer individuals in each class. These particular people will not only appreciate seeing each version of the film but might benefit greatly from such viewings. I would recommend lending those students the various versions to watch on their own time near the conclusion of the assignment—so as not to give the other students an impression of favoritism. To be honest, after watching only a couple of scenes from either film as a class, the majority of your students probably will not be interested in taking the videos home in the first place. However, for those who demonstrate curiosity, there are a number of factors in each film from which they will benefit—that is, of course, with a little guidance and then perhaps some debriefing following their viewing.

The 1932 production, starring Gary Cooper and Helen Hayes, is available on DVD from a variety of studios, including Delta, VidTape, Genus Entertainment, KRB, and Image Entertainment, and on VHS in a collection entitled Video Film Classics, which also features movies such as *All Quiet on the Western Front.* The 1957 production, starring Rock Hudson and Jennifer Jones, was released on DVD by Twentieth Century Fox Home Entertainment in 2005 and in a remastered version by A2ZCDS the same year. (*The Ernest Hemingway Film Collection,* a five-disc boxed set issued by Twentieth Century Fox in 2007, includes the film, as well.) Twentieth Century Fox Home Entertainment also released a VHS version in 1998 under its Studio Classics Banner.

There are several avenues one can take in trying to acquire a DVD or VHS copy of either film—the first being the public library. Your librarian can probably track down a copy and acquire it through interlibrary loan if your local branch does not carry it. Videos of the films may be ordered through studio Web sites or catalogs. The other option is to search the various Internet marketplaces set up through Ebay, Amazon, and the like. Numerous copies of both versions abound in these venues, though one must be careful to specify which version is desired. On more than one occasion, vendors assured me they had the 1957 version when what they were actually carrying was the 1932 one.

I personally enjoy the 1932 version of *Farewell.* There are elements of the book throughout, obviously. It can also hardly be denied that once things get going, vast sections of Hemingway's dialogue are employed rather conscientiously throughout the narrative. Yet at the same time, this movie really is an entity all its own—more of a distant cousin to the book than the direct relative it probably should be.

There are also a number of technical drawbacks, especially for students who are modern viewers and unaccustomed to the filming techniques of the period. Our students live in a culture where violence and warfare are daily news events—not to mention a frequent stomping ground for film. From the standpoint of war movies alone, any student who has watched *Platoon* or *Saving Private Ryan* has already been exposed to scenes far more violent and realistic than anything either version of *Farewell* even attempted to portray. In terms of the 1932 film, Frederic's involvement with the battlefield, as well as his own wounding, will be lost almost entirely on the students. There simply is not enough visual interest to draw them into that particular incident, especially when it is compared to what they witness daily on television. Students reading those passages will probably bring those scenes to life more vividly in their imaginations than the 1932 film can, since the filmmakers worked within the technical and stylistic norms of their time.

I do feel, however, that the 1932 version captures a mood that seems to be all but missing in the 1957 attempt. There is romantic chemistry between the film's romantic leads, despite the dated acting techniques. The 1957 remake of *Farewell* starring Rock Hudson and Jennifer Jones—the real-life spouse of producer David O. Selznick at the time—is as frustrating at times as it is beautiful. A good deal of the beauty is derived from the location in northern Italy and by the depths of the natural color captured and augmented by the period film stock.

The screenplay by Ben Hecht combined both the Hemingway novel and the stage play adaptation written by Laurence Stallings. As a result, those who watch the film after reading the book, or even during the reading process, may be taken aback. True, the 1932 version also butchered the book and added material at will. However, in the 1957 production, a much stronger attempt was made to stick to Hemingway's dialogue. As a result, even the slightest alteration rings strangely in the ear of the reader who has just finished reading the words on the page. I would not recommend screening either adaptation in its entirety for a class. However, I do think that some of the production can be used in the classroom and even presented in such a way as to facilitate an interesting discussion or two.

One area where these films may be helpful is in the discussion of sexuality and its portrayal in the arts of various decades. While both the novel and the films exercise a bit of sleight of hand in this area, Hemingway is keen in his insinuations regarding the early sexual rendezvous between Frederic and Catherine. Both films follow his cue in this endeavor, with varying degrees of success. In the 1957 version, the first romantic encounter during the rainstorm ends in a near-comical fashion. Once the act has apparently been committed, Jones suddenly rises into the frame while straightening up her hair. The smile on her face and the chirp in her voice are curtailed in such a manner that the viewer cannot be 100 percent certain if she and Hudson just had sex beneath the camera. For all the audience really knows, Jones could have just finished unpacking a picnic lunch or penciled in the final letters in her crossword puzzle. What went on off-camera could easily be taken in a number of ways, which was exactly the point.

In both films, the scenes are ambiguous because the societal norms of the times, as well as the censors hovering in the wings, would not permit further elaboration. Yet sexual relations were obviously required for Catherine's pregnancy—so the audience is made especially aware of the couple's marriage in the 1932 film. In terms of premarital sex, both movies simply do their best to step around the issue as smoothly as they can. A comparison between the book's handling of sex with the dual film portrayals (amazingly, the 1932 movie appears to touch on the initial sexual encounter more overtly than the later movie) could turn into an out-of-the-ordinary debate. This is especially true if the instructor poses the question of how such a scene would be handled if filmed today—an answer we arguably have already with the nudity presented in *In Love and War.*

Another option would be to delve into how effectively or ineffectively the students feel the screen actors in either version of the film have captured Hemingway's characters. What has been done well? What has not? Did any portrayal work better on screen than it did in the book? The same line of questioning may be applied in comparing various scenes or sequences in the book to their filmed counterparts. This could be an effective strategy whether individual portions or even the entire filmed versions are screened. In terms of the 1957 version, I personally feel a great deal of discussion can be generated simply by screening the first ten minutes of the picture. The students will immediately pick up on the fact that a couple of chapters are missing. They will also be confronted by the shifting of lines and condensing of events. And finally, the class will have a chance to evaluate the portrayals of Hudson, Jones, and Vittorio De Sica (who plays Rinaldi) in their spin on Hemingway's lead characters.

Each version has its strengths. True, the classic 1932 film is much more moody and distinctive, but the 1957 movie has a good deal more to offer in terms of spectacle. The Rock Hudson film, though large in scale, at times comes off as a glorified B movie. When it comes to the protagonists, the relationship between Hayes and Cooper—despite what we would consider a dated acting style—is far more believable in its context. The 1957 version—also dated in terms of the acting modern audiences are accustomed to—comes across as far more hollow. Instead of fretting too much over minor differences or detours between the novel and the screen versions, it is important to remember the big picture is what is important for our overall evaluation of either film's usefulness in a classroom setting.

## In Love and War

If, as legend has it, Hemingway himself could not even be convinced to screen the Selznick rendition of *Farewell,* one can hardly imagine what Papa would have thought of this attempt by Sir Richard Attenborough to visually re-create the World War I experiences of the writer's youth. Though beautifully shot, the movie is often melodramatic and simplistic in its presentation of the budding wartime love affair between young Ernest (Chris O'Donnell) and Red Cross nurse Agnes von Kurowsky (Sandra Bullock), whose letters and journal, collected in Henry Villard and James Nagel's *Hemingway in Love and War,* served as the film's basis. When the camera does linger on the unfolding attraction put on display by O'Donnell and Bullock, one gets the sense that so much more could have been done to reveal these largely one-dimensional characters to the audience. The story is intended to be a study of Hemingway's early life: the historical underpinnings for *Farewell;* the shift in Ernest's worldview from youthful idealism to dour pragmatism; and most importantly his failed romance with Agnes. However, save for a few concluding scenes, the typical audience member may not leave the film feeling that he or she knows much more about the inner lives or motivations behind these historically based characters than he or she did before the opening credits rolled.

Make no mistake, this is not a good movie. Yet as a tool for assisting students, especially when it comes to understanding certain character motivations in the novel, this film has a number of valuable attributes. It is a modern film, one they watch willingly—without my having to pull teeth, as tends to be the experience with the older *Farewell* films. The story line frequently touches on individuals whose life situations are reflected quite plainly in the written work the students are studying. Most importantly, an identification will instantly be made with the actors, whom almost all the students will probably recognize without a problem. This will help draw the pupils into the film's story line and leave them open for questioning—if not outright denouncing—the media material in the discussions following the screening.

Bullock, surprisingly, is actually quite good working with a flawed script. That said, I am not certain she has necessarily captured the real Agnes at all. Take, for example, the instance where she reads a passage loosely quoted from Agnes's memoir during a voiceover in the closing moments of the film. The narration consists of a description of her thoughts after she has left Ernest, alone and brooding in his cabin, where he is writing stories, for the very last time. The final encounter, a convention often employed by screenwriters to draw closure to the actions of their characters, apparently never took place. Historically, of course, this is quite problematic. Yet this is exactly the type of material that can succeed or fail based on the way it is framed to a group of students. If it is done so with an attitude stressing the fact that what is being shown is a *quasi-fictional* re-creation based loosely upon the lives of actual people, there is quite a bit to work with in the story line.

The real problem, however, is not with the fictionalization. What is at issue is the fact that what Bullock says during this final encounter completely contradicts what we know of the character she has just spent two hours of screen time portraying. What Bullock does seem to capture successfully is a particular attitude—one that I must admit is not very easy to pinpoint directly. It could almost be described as a beleaguered, world-weary savvy that she layers into the performance. It is a presence that is a good deal more nuanced and subtly come-hither than any she has managed to pull off in her screen roles either before or since. In other words, as a viewer, I had no trouble whatsoever believing that the young wide-eyed Hemingway of this film would have fallen for

Agnes as portrayed by Bullock. This is especially true in the scenes in which she sits by his bedside after his injury. I can also see this Hemingway eventually holding her up as an object of initial devotion. The filmmaker's portrayal of the Hemingway character's tour in Italy, when he fell for Agnes, makes Ernest's attraction to her apparent. It is also apparent that—in real life—the actual Hemingway seemed to venerate Agnes through the many female characters in which he alternately revisited, reviled, and at times religiously worshipped her memory in his later writings. At all times, the distinction between what is being portrayed in the film and what may have actually happened in real life must be emphasized for the students.

Ernest as portrayed by O'Donnell appears far too eager, especially in the early stages of the movie. It is only when his ambitious and electric energy has a focus to hone in on—Agnes—that the viewer gets a sense the actor may be somewhat closer to hitting the general mark. In fact, more often than not, I believe O'Donnell is dead on at showing at least one Hemingway trait aptly: Ernest's shift-on-a-dime temperament that allowed his mood to turn abruptly from charming to enraged. He also seems to have captured the way those emotional turns were apparently so often governed by the state of his current mood (bragging out of jealousy about sleeping with Agnes to a fellow patient—also wounded and smitten with Agnes—directly in front of the nurse herself while on a field trip, playfully and adventurously threatening to jump while still on crutches into a lake in order to get Agnes to pay more attention to him, etc.).

The main downfall in the performance comes from something that was probably not O'Donnell's fault whatsoever. Unfortunately, the film leaves too many gaps in the closing third of the story when it comes to Hemingway's sullen evolution. The more mature, brooding Ernest whom O'Donnell portrays in the film's closing scene represents his strongest acting in the feature, if not in his entire career—despite the implausibility inherent in this depiction of a final meeting with Agnes. However, since the last time the audience saw the character was only a few minutes earlier, and at the time he was crying like a baby and smashing things in his room after reading Agnes's "Dear Ernest" letter, the dramatic shift in characterization is a little too sudden. The young, broadly grinning Hemingway has held court on screen for too long by this point to be escorted so swiftly and shockingly from the narrative.

It is for these reasons, primarily, that any presentation of this film to students—either in part or whole—as any sort of a representation of Hemingway's life must be tempered heavily with strong guidance from the instructor. A good deal of time should be given to addressing the way things more likely unfolded (such as through the use of eyewitnesses accounts, like his sister Marcelline's memoir) so as not to absently allow the students to fall for the "facts" as Hollywood would have the audience believe them to be. With this in mind, a great final twist would be to read directly from the convivial correspondence between Hemingway and Agnes that took place several years later during Ernest's marriage to Hadley (excerpted in Kenneth Lynn's *Hemingway*).

Yet with the proper setup, I believe that *In Love and War* can be used quite effectively—again, with strong input from the teacher—as an introduction to the world of Hemingway the man. It can also pave the way for addressing some of the main concerns and themes of his work, as well as the myths, legends, and codes that ultimately grew around the public persona behind which he lived during the first half of the twentieth century. So many students come to us not having anything close to the amount of information on historical figures or events that we feel they should—or that we ourselves may have possessed in the later years of high school and college. With Hemingway, though, we have an advantage. Students may not know the name too well before they enter the classroom, yet most of them have had more than a passing interest in at least one major part of his life—his status as a celebrity. Youths of today are immersed in the culture of celebrity like no other generation in history. Hemingway's extraordinary celebrity could be an effective hook for drawing students in.

From a practical point of view, there is at least one more important point to take into consideration in deciding which scenes to show from the film: trench warfare. Though not *Gallipoli* by any means (as will be discussed later), the penultimate moment in which Hemingway is wounded while rescuing an Italian soldier from a bombed-out trench is full of possibilities for class discussion. Not only could it be used to talk about how World War I was fought, but it could also lead to an investigation of Hemingway's heroic code, which plays such a monumental role in the major written works of his career. The conversation he has with the soldiers in the trench about his own newspaper writing is also an excellent opening to the fascinating topic of Hemingway as a journalist; his continued influence on the written medium in which he developed his skills; and his clipped, staccato style.

Following the United States' second involvement in Iraq and the embedding of reporters with troops by news agencies through the Defense Department, I found a fascinating avenue of conversation suddenly available to me in the classroom. I would begin by playing the trench scene, move to talking about what Hemingway saw and experienced in the war, and then try to present Ernest's renderings of war in some of his stories, along with those in *For Whom the Bell Tolls* and *A Farewell to Arms,* as artistic works drawn partially from his own time as a Red Cross volunteer (and former *Kansas City Star* journalist) in

World War I. I then played a clip of some of the embedded American journalists as they reported from the battlefields of Iraq and waited for the connections to sink in.

My students had themselves seen the fear and uncertainty in Iraq through the eyes and cameras of those reporters during the weeks of nonstop broadcasts in March 2003. They had also witnessed some of the battles in progress and, in a few brief instances, carnage from both sides of the conflict. Though modern fighting technology may stand a million miles ahead of that used during trench warfare, the brutality of warfare obviously remained the same. The students' personal experiences of having seen the war in Iraq on television from a journalist's point of view gave everyone in the classroom instant insight into Hemingway and immediately helped to shed light on some of his possible motives as a writer. It ultimately seemed to provide them with a better understanding of why he may have presented the war-torn characters and situations in *Farewell* the way that he did.

## DRAWING ON OTHER MEDIA

Earlier, I mentioned that many forms of television programs or movies could be used to draw a reader into the elements of a story. There are not nearly as many films about World War I that are easily accessible to the general public as there are about World War II. Fewer and fewer have been made as the years have gone by and other conflicts have been featured on the silver screen. This plethora of movies about warfare in the latter half of the twentieth century, as opposed to stories about the Great War, is both a blessing and a curse to a teacher using visual media. It is a curse because it is difficult to find fictional representations of the two critical forms of combat from that conflict—early aerial combat and trench warfare. It is a blessing because one can also use clips from many different war films representing a variety of confrontations in order to prove a point: when it comes to the brutality of war, the more fighting technologies change, the more their deadly results remain the same. For aerial combat, I tend to rely on actual stock footage of battles found in historical documentaries—though crude and difficult to see—in order to give my classes a small visual taste of these earliest of dogfights. When it comes to trench warfare, however, the filmic ground is thankfully a little more solid.

Peter Weir's *Gallipoli* features Mel Gibson in one of his very first starring roles. It also showcases perhaps one of the most realistic depictions of trench warfare ever committed to film (aside from what is, despite a dreamlike quality, the most horrific portrayal of trench warfare I've ever seen, in Jean-Pierre Jeunet's formalistic yet frighteningly detailed meditation on World War I, *A Very Long Engagement*). The Turkish trench scenes that encompass nearly the final third of *Gallipoli* are especially brutal in their visual authenticity. It is difficult to watch those scenes and not be affected by the chaos, the confinement, and the sheer unjustifiable loss of life this type of ground-gaining strategy inflicted upon those engaged in such combat. It is almost impossible to imagine having to live that way under any conditions at all, let alone in a bloody battle zone. Classic films tend to feature murky trench scenes—albeit sometimes brief and not very realistic—from the dark, rainy European fronts. Both filmed versions of *Farewell* fit easily into this category, as does *In Love and War.* In *Gallipoli,* the action is all out in the sunny open. As a result, the audience is allowed to see and experience everything as it happens before them in plain view.

In Another modern production that tackles the subject of the Great War is *The Lost Battalion,* a made-for-television movie that premiered on cable in 2001. This feature is particularly adept at portraying battle chaos in an entirely different natural setting—the woodlands of the Argonne Forest. The scenery and even the combat styles differ from those depicted in *Gallipoli.* However, this movie is closer in setting to the fighting situations depicted in *Farewell* than those shown in *Gallipoli,* though this production may not at all times carry the resonance of the Mel Gibson picture.

In addition to these various visual suggestions, I also tend to rely on passages about the construction of *Farewell* written by an assortment of Hemingway's biographers. The writing of *Farewell* itself is described in detail in the Lynn biography, as well as in *Hemingway: The Critical Heritage,* edited by Jeffrey Meyers. A collection entitled *Hemingway on War* may be a good recommendation for students interested in continuing their study of the author's fascination with the theme throughout his career. This book was edited by his grandson, Seán Hemingway, and includes a preface by Hemingway's son Patrick. He delves into some observations about his father along these lines and also includes Hemingway's newspaper coverage of the Greco-Turkish War five years after World War I drew to a close, which may prove interesting to students for the glimpse it offers into how the author treated facts about a combat situation differently in his journalism than in his fiction.

Another good idea, depending on the students and the equipment available, is to try venturing into the world of e-texts with portions of the novel. Several typed text portions ranging in length from a page to a chapter (for example, Frederic's wounding) could be loaded in a program such as Microsoft Word, Publisher, or FrontPage. The students, in groups or as individuals, would then be asked to alter the font styles and colors, add pictures, or even create hyper-links to clip-art photographs that they feel evoke the spirit of the story.

Several of my colleagues recently explored the vast possibilities when such technologies are applied to classic texts in a project using William Faulkner's "A Rose for Emily." They were astonished by how involved their students became as they created and then read through each other's segments. The text and the images in the electronically augmented portions of the story ended up bring-ing new life and vitality to sections they might have quickly moved over during their initial reading assignment. My colleagues noticed that the e-text project enhanced creativity and drew the readers further into the deeper themes of the story. The students' interactions with the documents led to thoughtful, even emotional, discussions—and some of this occurred while the reading process was still taking place. Ultimately, after the e-text experience, they found their students kept running back to the original text in order to find more possible meanings beneath the surface of the author's original words.

And finally, I like to play for the students a recording of Hemingway's voice at least once over the course of the semester. There is a compilation available of Hemingway reading selections from his own works, including the Nobel Prize acceptance speech. The program, available on both audiocassette and CD, is entitled *Ernest Hemingway Reads*. Hemingway's voice was far different from how I was expecting it to be before I first heard the recording. I find this to be an interesting final note to add to the *Farewell* experience, as it allows the au-thor to speak for himself, in a sense.

I would like to draw this chapter to a close by making one assignment sug-gestion. It almost goes hand in hand that students who are not fans of reading are also not fans of writing. Part of this is due to laziness and poor training. Part of it is also because students are not often presented with topics they feel they can address adequately. A number may even feel that what they have to say will not matter or are embarrassed by the prospect of having another person read their work. I have three writing assignments that I administer during the sessions with *Farewell,* though two of them I slip under the radar as in-class assignments that are developed further at a later date. I do this to keep the stu-dents from becoming too apprehensive about their possible lack of spontane-ous writing skills.

Following discussion of a passage from the novel that I have found to be particularly lively, I ask the students to take out a piece of paper. The first de-bate of this type usually happens in the early stages of the reading assignment, and the topic tends to change from class to class. Without allowing them to refer to their books or to discuss the passage in question with anyone around them, I ask them to rewrite the scene in their own words. They are allowed to put it down on paper any way they see fit, as long as the core of the plot itself is not altered beyond recognition. Around this time, their faces are usually dropping, as they assume I am going to be collecting the papers at the end of class. While I do tell them that I will move through the room to make sure the assignment is being addressed, I also let them know that I will not be collecting or reading final drafts at the end of the day. Instead, I tell them that I will do so at the start of the very last class session of the semester.

The students, freed from the burden of judgment for the time being—yet aware that I am still looking over their shoulders, so goofing off is not an option—dive into writing. The room is blissfully silent, save for the scratching of pens and pencils across sheets of paper that only minutes before were painfully blank. When the class comes to an end, I tell the students to take their papers home. If they wish, I tell them, they may add to or edit any portion in the time before our next meeting as a group. I only ask that if they do so, they bring the original with them as well, so that a comparison may be made. Amazingly, even though I leave it as an option, the majority of my students have taken the time to rework and strengthen their passages. On the next day, I do collect the rough drafts and give them credit for the work done so far. However, I hand the passages back one week later—ungraded except for a mark of participation, along with the amending of any major spelling flaws.

A number of the students have continued to think about the written passage even after the papers had been turned into me. I tell them that I want them to hold onto the papers, adding that they may feel free to rework them as often as they like during the remainder of the semester. I then inform the class that there will be a modest section on the written portion of the exam from which they will be exempt if they continue to edit and add to their passages. I will grade their written work—as long as all versions are brought in, and the final version is typed or at least legible—as a substitute for that small portion of the exam. It has never ceased to amaze me just how far the writing of the students who bring in passages on exam day has advanced and developed when compared to their initial in-class scribbling.

Given time, a patient attitude, and incentive, the students put their minds to work in ways that astound me. Even better, it brings out a creative side to their skills that I know many of them doubted they even had. The alternate version of this assignment involves having the students describe a key scene from one of the films. Again, this tends to work best with a moment that was debated in class—something that brought about a stir of excitement or even a lively discussion among the students. Certain semesters, depending upon the class itself, I have even had them do this for both a novel passage and a film clip.

The main assignment I tend to offer in conjunction with the reading of *Farewell* is one I call the Eyewitness Project (see appendix). I have used this successfully in each setting in which I have taught *Farewell*. In fact, despite the work the students have to put into it, this project tends to be their favorite because of the interaction with others it requires, as well as the chance to take somebody else's experiences and then put them into their own words. The eyewitness portion of the project is easily tied to Hemingway. I talk about how as a young man, Hemingway not only saw but experienced the horrors of war firsthand. Afterward, as a young journalist, he was extremely adept at watching and asking questions in order to inform his articles. Those same skills were honed and applied to his own novels later on, when he took key instances and elements from his own life and used them as a framework for conveying his thoughts and beliefs about the world to those who read his books. This assignment allows the students to see an incident in history—one they were not alive to witness firsthand—from several points of view before synthesizing the information into their own dramatic accounts. As investigators, they, like the young Hemingway, will be searching for clues and data from both written sources and interviews that they conduct themselves. In addition to *Farewell,* they are required to read the introduction to the book *With Their Eyes: September 11th—the View from a High School at Ground Zero,* edited by Annie Thoms, along with several other passages from that text in order to gather ideas for how to translate the interviews into their own personal accounts.

I have but one hope following the reading of *A Farewell to Arms* and the assignments in support of that experience. It is for the students to carry that inquisitive, ever-questioning spirit they so often display during the media-inspired discussions and exercises we have concerning the book into the questions, judgments, and choices they make on a daily basis in their own lives.

## APPENDIX: Eyewitness Interview Project

History is storytelling. Every event that has ever been entered into a history textbook was at one time or another first witnessed, lived through, and documented by individual eyewitnesses. The aim of this project is for the student to interact with a historical event from the twentieth century in a slightly different way. This will be done through a combination of research, interview questions, and creative writing.

The project will begin with readings from *With Their Eyes* in conjunction with the assigned weekly chapters from *A Farewell to Arms.* Each student is responsible for reading the introduction to *With Their Eyes,* which explains the aim, purpose, and layout of the book. Students are also responsible for reading through three of the selections from the main text. The book is a collection of eyewitness accounts from 9/11. The information was gathered from a group of students who happened to be attending classes at a high school just down the street from the World Trade Center on the day of the attack. After a series of interviews, the testimony from each student was then translated into the short pieces that make up the book. The readings from *With Their Eyes* will be used as a basis for what each student will be expected to do for his or her own project.

First, each student will select an important event from the twentieth century—most likely one that took place within the last forty to fifty years. Next, students will look up two references regarding the events they have selected. One reference must be a historical source on the Internet. The other must be a history reference book in the library. Students should make photocopies of both articles for inclusion in the final project.

Each student will then select someone he or she knows who was alive during the event in question. This can be either a direct witness or a person who was alive during that time period and experienced it through the media. For example, someone who fought in the Vietnam War would be considered a direct witness to the conflict itself. He could comment on either the battles he experienced in general or a particular event—such as the fall of Saigon. A person who was alive at the time of the Kennedy assassination would be an indirect witness—unless she was actually in Dallas that day and saw the assassination herself. Such a person would therefore give her reaction to the situation as the event was portrayed to her through both the media and word of mouth.

Once students have selected their events and chosen the person they intend to interview, they should compose no fewer than seven questions to ask regarding what happened and how the interviewee experienced that moment in history. Where was he or she when the event occurred? What was that person's initial reaction? How did he or she respond? How did he or she feel? Students should devise some questions that are broad in scope, and others that are quite specific, and should try to get as many details as they possibly can from the responses. They should then record all their answers.

After reading up on the event and interviewing the subject, each student will then write a short piece in which he or she pretends to be the person interviewed and imagines that he or she is witnessing the event as it happens. In *With Their Eyes,* the authors of each piece do this in short poems. Poetry will not be required of students, unless that is how they choose to approach the assignment. Three or four narrative paragraphs written from a first-person point of view will be sufficient. The details and impressions given to students during the interview will prove invaluable for this portion of the project. Just as important, however, will be students' imaginations, as well as their creativity in approaching this narrative. However, creativity does not relieve any student from his or her responsibility to produce a strong, well-written, grammatically correct report. Students must always proofread their work before turning it in and should ask others to check their work for typos as well. After doing all these things, the student will reread the initial historical documents he or she found. Each student will then write a brief conclusion, in which he or she discusses how any impressions given by the potentially dry factual reporting from the texts may have been altered or enlivened had the writer discussed the event with an eyewitness.

The main portions of the project will be written in the following order:

*Introduction:* Talk about the event you wish to study, and give a brief introduction of the person you are going to interview. Be sure to tell what the person's relationship to you is (friend, family member, etc.) and his or her connection to the event.

*Historical References:* Discuss your Internet and text references. Talk about where and how you found them, and briefly describe their content.

*Interview:* Present the interview section by listing each question, using the exact words you plan to use. Follow this with a brief general summary of the answer given. Though you will want to take detailed notes of the answer at the time of the interview for use with the creative writing assignment, a short, broad sketch of each response will be fine for this part of the project. Repeat the process for every question you ask. The format of the question-and-answer section should be as follows:

Question 1: Where were you on the day the *Challenger* exploded?
Answer 1: John Smith stated that he was living in central Florida at the time of the *Challenger* disaster.

*Creative Writing:* Synthesize the information from the interview and the articles. Then, using your imagination, write about the event as if you were seeing it through the eyes of the witness to whom you spoke. Be as detailed and as creative as you can. Involve your senses—tell the reader what you see, hear, and even smell. You may give this portion a title, if you wish. This section must be a minimum of three to four full paragraphs.

*Conclusion:* Reread your references after you've written your eyewitness account. How has your impression of the event changed now that you have discussed it with someone who was alive to experience it? How could your interpretation of or reflections on other events from the past benefit from other firsthand reports? Is it wise to always rely on textbook accounts?

*Resources:* Attach copies of your photocopied references to the end of your project.

# Ernest Hemingway Presents: *A Farewell to Arms*

*Brenda G. Cornell*

Recognizing film as both a literary genre and an art form in its own right, freshman-level introduction to literature classes (otherwise known as English 1302: Composition and Rhetoric II) at Central Texas College frequently view film adaptations in order to supplement the study of a particular short story, play, or novel by comparing written and cinematic narrative forms, writing elements, and film composition techniques as methods for presenting ideas. Having inspired two film versions since the 1960s, a television miniseries in 1966, and the autobiographical film *In Love and War* in 1996, Hemingway's *A Farewell to Arms* offers challenges for nurturing students' critical thinking skills as well as their appreciation for novel and film renditions alike. My students read and study the novel scene by scene, as suggested by Hemingway's brief chapters. To discourage procrastination, we meet regular reading, discussion, and quiz deadlines over a six- to seven-week period, during which the study of the novel is interspersed with other readings in short fiction, poetry, and drama. As we read, we actually plan a film based strictly on what we read and on the application of basic cinematic techniques such as mise en scène and elongated moments.

The behavioral profiles and learning styles of Central Texas College students justify this type of study. As a typical community college population, students at CTC are visual learners. When a literary work is presented, a common question is: "Was that story a movie? Will we be able to watch it in class?" A basic part of their learning experience involves, then, a major attitude adjustment. Accustomed to the idea of a movie as a shortcut or escape from doing required assignments, many students surprise themselves as they discover a serious critical appreciation for the art of filmmaking. Further, the collaborative grouping plan gives confidence to the reluctant scholars; uncomfortable and overwhelmed in a traditional classroom with its authoritarian "the professor is the font of all wisdom" atmosphere, these students are very happy to learn from each other in a community ambiance facilitated by the teacher. Recent scholarship by Tom Angelo and K. Patricia Cross confirms the positive effects of collaborative learning in the community college setting. As they study the novel together, my small groups form a casting crew, a set crew, and a camera/film-editing crew in order to concentrate on the cinematic rendition of Hemingway's settings, characters, and action. Group presentations are made on the final day appointed for study of the novel. Since the earned grade is "the coin of the realm" (Angelo and Cross 1) and is thus shared by group members, everyone must have designated tasks. After the presentations, time permitting, we view one of the film versions and make comparisons in order to appreciate fully the artistic accomplishments of both Hemingway and the filmmakers. Despite Hemingway's reputed antipathy toward films inspired by his novels, he might have been more enthusiastic if filmmakers had actually solicited his input rather than simply paying royalties for the movie rights. In his study *Hemingway and the Movies,* Frank M. Laurence notes that it was not until 1958, in making the first film version of *The Old Man and the Sea,* that Warner Brothers, the same studio that had previously created two unsatisfactory versions of *A Farewell to Arms,* actively solicited Hemingway's contribution (11).

Appendix B offers suggestions for the group projects, which may range from the traditional (collaborative research reports) to the high tech (PowerPoint presentations) and the creative (dramatic readings or skits). Presentations from the spring 2004 classes evolved from the specialized talents of individual students. One group, having viewed the 1932 version of the film, staged and filmed their own video of three selected scenes: Frederic meets Catherine, Frederic seeks Catherine, and Catherine dies. Their culturally diverse cast included an already pregnant but lovely (and only slightly "showing") Catherine Barkley and a black female Major Rinaldi. Another group prepared a stunning playbill collage featuring Julia Roberts as Catherine Barkley and Jude Law as Frederic Henry, together with superimposed photos of World War I ambulances, battle scenes, and Red Cross nurses, based on Internet research. Still another group experimented with PowerPoint as a tool for presenting the major conflicts of the plot. As an added bonus, they discovered that PowerPoint's built-in security warning would not, in fact, allow them to save their presentations unless they credited their sources (somebody else was issuing cautions against plagiarism for a change). Not nearly so polished but equally impressive was the picture book created by another group: a gallery of anime-style caricatures and character sketches of all the major characters in the book.

During the fall 2004 semester, other fine projects included a time line showing parallels between the novel's events and Hemingway's life; a three-dimensional movie poster/shadowbox, complete with dolls and a wooden ambulance; and, one of my personal favorites, a photo album in which the group members, pretending to be Lieutenant Henry's grandchildren, found photographs from the Internet that, in their opinion, matched the experiences that Frederic and Catherine would have shared. The album had captions for each photo and was dedicated to "My Beloved Catherine." The students also included a group photograph of themselves, as the grandchildren, credited as illustrators, translators, and editors.

At the beginning of our study of the novel, I bring some projects from previous classes to show as examples. Each class feels the need to outdo previous efforts, and each semester brings more elaborate, creative, and stimulating projects than the ones before. The examples thus serve as visual attention-getting devices suggesting that the Hemingway novel unit will be something exciting and special.

Given the students' natural need to "see" as they read, it just makes sense to study Hemingway's novel with a visual focus. From the beginning of the semester, classes know the game plan and its rules (see Appendix A). In addition to complying with the class game plan, students promise to be open minded for the duration of our study, in return for my promise that we will view one of the films in class if there is time. *In Love and War* (1996) offers a good background. Again, time is a factor: when there is time, I show this film at the beginning of our study. When time does not permit a classroom viewing, I recommend it to the students as an out-of-class activity. I spend some time explaining how Hemingway felt, generally, about films adapted from his works and remind the students that our goal is to appreciate his contributions to the American novel. Since we devote a full six weeks to the study of the novel, and since our coursework also involves a research requirement, interested students are invited to pursue a research topic that compares certain aspects of the novel to one of its film adaptations—not exactly an assignment for those who want to rent the movie over the weekend, take a test on it, and write a book report or research paper of the cut-and-paste variety for Monday. Also, individual discussion groups are later invited to view one or both of the film versions in order to get ideas for their projects.

Our study of the novel begins with an overview of the elements of the novel and with an introduction to the language of film. We explore three elements of cinematography as explained in Roberts and Wallis's *Introducing Film*. Mise en scène, the French for "placed on stage," indicates specifically what is to be filmed (people, settings, props). It is one of the main elements shared by film and stage drama. The actual filming process, cinematography, goes one step further by visually actualizing what the written word imagines and what the stage drama enacts in terms of props, scenery, and costumes. Film editing, the third element, involves putting the scenes together in the interests of organization and coherence in storytelling. At this point, most students begin to appreciate the correlation between these film elements and those found in a novel, including elements of setting, point of view, characterization, and plot. Better yet, with their "movie glasses" on, they see that those traditional elements formerly restricted to academia suddenly become part of the more "relevant" areas of their everyday lives (the movies).

In studying the novel, each discussion group becomes one of three movie crews: a casting crew, which studies and analyzes characters; a set crew, which prepares meaningful settings; and a camera/film-editing crew, which selects meaningful focus points and plans how to present various scenes. This grouping is a starting point and offers student groups a focus for their major project assignments. The work begins with simple questions designed to elicit basic yet focal observations regarding Hemingway's mise en scène. In the novel's opening scene, for example, what do we see? Initially students will say that the setting for chapter 1 is boring or ordinary, or that Hemingway spends too much time describing the setting, but they should be reminded of the pivotal role that the physical, historical, and psychological setting often plays in fiction (at an early point in the semester, they will have read and analyzed "A Clean, Well-Lighted Place," in which setting plays a crucial thematic role). Like the author who carefully orchestrates his or her setting, the filmmaker places nothing in front of the audience by sheer accident. In terms of filmmaking, Roberts and Wallis note the importance of setting: "Whatever kind of setting is used in a film, even if it appears to be an everyday, ordinary apartment where the characters live, is important and worthy of analysis. It can provide us with information, not just about where the action takes place and when, but about mood, characters, type of story and the genre of the film" (4). After reading through the first section, the set crew makes a list of Hemingway's elements of setting, such as "a house in a village that looked across the river and the plain to the mountains" (*A Farewell to Arms* 3). For this initial exercise I provide cheap drawing paper or butcher paper and plenty of markers. Artistic talent is not important; what is important is the idea of setting given to us by Hemingway. Then there are a few questions to address:

1. List the physical items described (river, troops passing).
2. Is there a dominant mood intended here? Find supporting quotes (provide page numbers).
3. List the actions reported by Hemingway's narrator. Are they more important or less important than the setting, or are they part of the setting itself?
4. How do you think setting will affect the actions of the story?
5. Draw, in detail, the setting described in chapter 1.
6. Make a list of works cited using MLA format.

Later questions will explore options for costumes, appropiate to mood, theme, and how the characters see themselves, and lighting as a means of setting the mood for the story. The set crew keeps a book of visual impressions for books 1–5. We use the same basic guideline questions for each of the novel's five books.

The camera crew controls the way in which the viewer responds to the setting. Again, we use the drawing tablets or butcher paper, unless a computer lab and software (such as Microsoft Gallery or PowerPoint) are available for capturing and editing specific images. Students sometimes employ software for the final project even if the initial brainstorming is done on paper. In the literary performance, of course, the narrator is the camera crew, Hemingway's means of controlling the text and the audience response; the narration also provides guidelines for putting the story together. For example, here are some sample questions for the camera crew for chapter 1:

1. What type of camera lens would you use in order to film this first scene? Explain.
2. Is the camera static or moving? How do we know? Select appropriate transitional phrases from the book (provide page numbers).
3. Select appropriate shots (images that, in your opinion, Hemingway considers to be significant). Draw the images, using a separate sheet for each. Staple sheets together and flip for a moving picture effect. Selection is important here. Not all images may be equally important.
4. Make a list of works cited using MLA format.

Film editors will organize and edit the story for the screen. Their job is to select the main events, characters, and conflicts that Hemingway uses to make the story work. Since the first-person narrator is the main vehicle for telling this story, the film editors will also make decisions about the events of the narrative, the story line, and the plot contributions of each of the characters. Beginning with chapter 1, here are some of the film-editing crew's questions and tasks:

1. What happens in this chapter? Summarize the events in two or three sentences. Are conflicts foreshadowed?
2. How does Hemingway select and present the events?
3. What is the narrator's attitude toward the story he is telling? Find quotes in support of your answer (provide page numbers).
4. How much of the narrative in chapter 1 should be presented using the actual narration (voiceover), and how much should be presented by the camera?
5. Select a musical piece to be used as an overture for the story. Plan for sound effects.
6. Hold tryouts to decide who will provide the narration.
7. Make a list of works cited using MLA format.

Eventually, this group will also face the challenges of casting. Activities may include the following tasks:

1. Select the main characters based on their contributions to the plot and to the theme of the story.
2. Decide which actors would be best in these roles. Justify your choices by doing a bit of Internet research (past performances, film credits, etc.). Past choices include Jude Law or Tom Cruise as Frederic Henry, and Gwyneth Paltrow or Julia Roberts as Catherine Barkley. You may also choose classmates to portray the featured roles.

Student teams present their group project to the rest of the class. Evaluations are based on simple criteria, and peer evaluations are one-third of the grade (see appendixes C and D). Ultimately, after the final group presentations are done, my students (and I) are exhausted but satisfied. One or two students may still ask, "Do you think we still have time to see one of the movies as a group?" It is the end of the semester, and everyone is tired. There will be the inevitable groans and maybe a retort of, "Why? How could it be better than the way we did it?" Classes will come and go, but in the end, we've all had a great time, and it's a struggle for us to recall anything before or after Hemingway.

## APPENDIX A: English 1302 Study Unit for Hemingway's *A Farewell to Arms*

Please bear in mind the following tips for studying *A Farewell to Arms*.

1. On my course Web site, http://www.ctcd.edu/communications/bcornell/ ENGL1302_main.htm, you will find a short background PowerPoint lecture titled "Introduction to the Novel" under the link "Novel lecture." You will be expected to have read this material.

2. Everyone is expected to read the novel and to stay current with the assigned readings. Others in your discussion group are counting on you to make a contribution. In class, each person will be expected to be part of general discussions. If you skip class on the day discussion is scheduled, you will receive no grade for that day.

3. As we read Hemingway's novel, we will be planning a film based on the novel. As you read, try to see what Hemingway saw as he wrote the story. Keep a journal of your questions as you read.

4. Each group will produce a project (see handout suggestions) based on its interpretation of the novel and using at least one cinematic element as its foundation. Since the project will count for a significant portion of your grade, the group leader is responsible for keeping track of who does what. Group projects will be due the week before the final exam.

5. You will need to be able to answer questions (short answer and essay) dealing with the novel on the final exam.


## APPENDIX B: Suggestions for Group Projects for *A Farewell to Arms*

1. Poster depicting conflicts, themes, setting, or character types, with one-page explanation
2. Brief (ten slides or shorter) presentation using Microsoft PowerPoint (include selection of suitable music)
3. Oral presentation in which your group shares its findings with the class (use panel or forum format)
4. Mural depicting conflicts, themes, setting, or character types
5. Casting recommendations and justifications
6. Web page (three to four screens; use MS Word)

7. Collage representing group perspective and impressions
8. Cassette recording of a particularly significant scene or scenes (use all group members if you choose this option). Write an introduction for your script: create a context for the scene(s), and explain why these scenes are significant to the novel.
9. Movie poster advertising the class-generated film version of *A Farewell to Arms*
10. Essay comparing our version of the story to one of the Hollywood versions

Please remember that the group presentation is a major portion of your grade and that each group member is expected to pull his or her weight in the final project. Group leaders must keep a running account of who does what in the project notebook

## APPENDIX C: Peer Responses to *A Farewell to Arms* Projects

The peer response will consist of two groups of questions: the first deals with your critique of another group's presentation; the second deals with your response to your own group's project. Your feedback is important!

Response to Another Group
Group evaluated _____ Type of project _____

1. What did this group do especially well?
2. What suggestions do you have for improvement?
3. Did you learn anything new from this group's presentation?
4. What grade does this project deserve?

Our Group's Reactions
Group members _____
Type of project _____

1. What were the advantages of this assignment for you? How did it help you to appreciate the novel?
2. Were there difficulties? Explain.
3. What suggestions do you have for future semesters?

## APPENDIX D: Grading Criteria for *A Farewell to Arms* Group Project

1. Group followed all directions. _____
2. Project showed equal participation by everyone in the group. _____
3. Project showed a careful reading of the novel. _____
4. Project showed creativity and enthusiasm. _____
5. Project was well organized. _____
6. Visual aids were effective and creative. _____
7. Participants spoke clearly and distinctly. _____
8. Questions from the audience were handled well. _____
9. Group members seemed to work well together. _____
10. Overall, the presentation was effective. _____

# Works Cited

Allen, Woody. "A Twenties Memory." *Getting Even*. New York: Random House, 1971. 89–93.

*All the King's Men*. BBC Worldwide America. WGBH Educational Foundation. Distributed by Anchor Bay Entertainment, 2000.

"The Amazing Harkness Philosophy." Philips Exeter Academy. <http://www.exeter.edu/admissions/147_harkness.aspx>.

Angelo, Tom, and K. Patricia Cross. *Connecting CATs and CoLTs*. Starlink Teleconference. March 25, 2004. An Agency of the Texas Association of Community Colleges.

Baker, Carlos. *Ernest Hemingway: A Life Story*. New York: Scribner, 1969.

———. *Hemingway: The Writer as Artist*. 3rd ed. Princeton, NJ: Princeton University Press, 1963.

———. *Twentieth Century Interpretations of* A Farewell to Arms. Ed. Jay Gellens. Englewood Cliffs, NJ: Prentice Hall, 1970.

Bakewell, Charles M. *The Story of the American Red Cross in Italy*. New York: Macmillan, 1920.

Barbusse, Henri. *Under Fire*. 1917. Trans. Robin Buss. New York: Penguin, 2004.

Barlowe, Jamie. "Hemingway's Gender Training." *A Historical Guide to Ernest Hemingway*. Ed. Linda Wagner-Martin. New York: Oxford University Press, 2000. 117–53.

Barlowe-Kayes, Jamie. "Re-reading Women: The Example of Catherine Barkley." *Hemingway Review* 12.2 (Spring 1993): 24–35.

"Battles: The Battle of Caporetto, 1917." *First World War.com*. June 17, 2005. <http://www.firstworldwar.com/battles/caporetto.htm>.

Beegel, Susan F. "Conclusion: The Critical Reputation of Ernest Hemingway." *The Cambridge Companion to Ernest Hemingway.* Ed. Scott Donaldson. New York: Cambridge University Press, 1996. 269–99.

———. *Hemingway's Craft of Omission.* Ann Arbor: UMI Research Press, 1987.

Bell, Millicent, "*A Farewell to Arms:* Pseudobiography and the Personal Metaphor." *Ernest Hemingway: The Writer in Context.* Ed. James Nagel. Madison: University of Wisconsin Press, 1984. 107–28.

Benson, Jackson. *Hemingway: The Writer's Art of Self-Defense.* Minneapolis: University of Minnesota Press, 1969.

*The Big Parade.* Dir. King Vidor. Perf. Charles "Buddy" Rogers and Renée Adorée. MGM, 1925.

Booth, Wayne C. *The Rhetoric of Fiction.* Chicago: University of Chicago Press, 1961, 1983.

"Boston Police Bar *Scribner's Magazine.*" *New York Times* June 21, 1929: 2. <http://www.nytimes.com/books/99/07/04/specials/hemingway-scribners.html?_r=1&oref=slogin>.

Brasch, James Daniel, and Joseph Sigman. *Hemingway's Library: A Composite Record.* New York: Garland, 1981.

Brittain, Vera. *Testament of Youth.* 1933. New York: Penguin, 2005.

Broer, Lawrence R. *Hemingway's Spanish Tragedy.* Tuscaloosa: University of Alabama Press, 1973.

———, and Gloria Holland, eds. *Hemingway and Women: Female Critics and the Female Voice.* Tuscaloosa: University of Alabama Press, 2002.

Brooke, Rupert. "The Soldier." *British Poets of the Great War: Brooke, Rosenberg, Thomas: A Documentary Volume.* Ed. Patrick Quinn. Detroit, MI: Gale, 2000. 74.

Bruccoli, Matthew. *The Only Thing That Counts: The Ernest Hemingway–Maxwell Perkins Correspondence, 1925–1947.* Columbia: University of South Carolina Press, 1999.

Burgess, Anthony. *Hemingway: Grace under Pressure.* Princeton, NJ: Films for the Humanities, 1992.

Carothers, James. Comments to author. International Hemingway Conference. Stresa, Italy. July 2002.

Checchin, Giovanni. *Italiani sul Grappa: Documenti e fotografie inediti della Croce Rossa Americana in Italia nel 1918.* Asolo: Magnifica Comunità Pedemontana dal Piave al Brenta, 1984.

Comley, Nancy R., and Robert Scholes. *Hemingway's Genders: Rereading the Hemingway Text.* New Haven, CT: Yale University Press, 1994.

*Concise Dictionary of American History.* New York: Scribner, 1961.

Cowley, Malcolm. "Not Yet Demobilized." *New York Herald Tribune* October 6, 1929: 1, 6. *Ernest Hemingway: The Critical Reception.* Ed. Robert O. Stephens. New York: Burt Franklin, 1977. 74–76.

Crane, Stephen. *The Red Badge of Courage.* 1895. New York: Penguin, 1994.

Cummings, E. E. *The Enormous Room.* 1922. New York: Penguin, 1991.

DeFalco, Joseph. *The Hero in Hemingway's Short Stories.* Pittsburgh: University of Pittsburgh Press, 1963.

Donaldson, Scott. *By Force of Will: The Life and Art of Ernest Hemingway.* New York: Viking, 1977.

———, ed. *The Cambridge Companion to Ernest Hemingway.* Cambridge: Cambridge University Press, 1996.

———, ed. *New Essays on* A Farewell to Arms. Cambridge: Cambridge University Press, 1990.

Dos Passos, John. "Books." *New Masses* 5 (December 1, 1929): 16. *Ernest Hemingway: The Critical Reception.* Ed. Robert O. Stephens. New York: Burt Franklin, 1977. 95–97.

———. *One Man's Initiation: 1917.* 1920. Ithaca, NY: Cornell University Press, 1970.

———. *Three Soldiers.* 1921. New York: Penguin, 1997.

Dreiser, Theodore. *Sister Carrie: The Unexpurgated Edition.* Penguin Classics Edition. Ed. John C. Berkey et al. New York: Penguin, 1986.

Dunne, John Gregory. "The Horror Is Seductive." Rev. of *Jarhead: A Marine's Chronicle of the Gulf War and Other Battles,* by Anthony Swofford. *New York Review* May 29, 2003: 23–25.

Eksteins, Modris. *Rites of Spring: The Great War and the Birth of the Modern Age.* Boston: Houghton Mifflin, 1989.

Elkins, Marilyn. "The Fashion of *Maschismo.*" *A Historical Guide to Ernest Hemingway.* Ed. Linda Wagner-Martin. Oxford: Oxford University Press, 2000. 93–115.

Fadiman, Clifton P. "A Fine American Novel." *Nation* 129 (October 30, 1929): 497–98. *Ernest Hemingway: The Critical Reception.* Ed. Robert O. Stephens. New York: Burt Franklin, 1977. 83–84.

*A Farewell to Arms.* By Ernest Hemingway. Dir. Frank Borzage. Perf. Gary Cooper, Helen Hayes, and Adolphe Menjou. Adapt. Benjamin Glazer. Paramount, 1932.

*A Farewell to Arms.* By Ernest Hemingway. Dir. Charles Vidor. Perf. Rock Hudson and Jennifer Jones. Adapt. Laurence Stallings. Twentieth Century Fox, 1957.

Fenton, Charles. *The Apprenticeship of Ernest Hemingway: The Early Years.* New York: Farrar, Straus and Young, 1954.

Fetterley, Judith. *The Resisting Reader: A Feminist Approach to American Fiction.* Bloomington: Indiana University Press, 1978.

*Fodor's Europe.* New York: Fordor's Travel Guides, 2002.

Freud, Sigmund. "Why War?" *Character and Culture.* Trans. James Strachey. New York: Collier, 1963. 134–47.

Fromkin, David. *Europe's Last Summer: Who Started the Great War in 1914?* New York: Knopf, 2004.

Frye, Judith. *Living Stories, Telling Lives: Women and the Novel in Contemporary Experience.* Ann Arbor: University of Michigan Press, 1986.

Fussell, Paul. *The Great War and Modern Memory.* New York: Oxford University Press, 1975.

*Gallipoli.* Dir. Peter Weir. Perf. Mel Gibson. Paramount, 1981.

Graves, Robert. *Goodbye to All That: An Autobiography.* 1929. New York: Anchor, 1958.

*The Great War and the Shaping of the 20th Century.* Prod. KCET/BBC in association with the Imperial War Museum. 1996. Videocassette. PBS Video, 1998.

Grebstein, Sheldon Norman. *Hemingway's Craft.* Carbondale: Southern Illinois University Press, 1973.

Hammerton, J. A., ed. *The Great War Illustrated: A Pictorial Record of the Conflict of the Nations.* London: Amalgamated Press, 1914–19.

Hanneman, Audre. *Ernest Hemingway: A Comprehensive Bibliography.* Princeton, NJ: Princeton University Press, 1967.

Harmon, William, and Hugh Holman. *A Handbook to Literature.* 9th ed. Saddle River, NJ: Prentice Hall, 2003.

Hart, Albert Bushnell, et al., eds. *Harper's Pictorial Library of the World War.* New York: Harper, 1920.

Hawthorne, Nathaniel. *The Scarlet Letter: An Authoritative Text: Backgrounds, Sources, Criticism.* Ed. Seymour Gross et al. 3rd. ed. New York: W. W. Norton, 1988.

Heath, John B. "The Harkness System." *Phillips Exeter Bulletin* (September 1992): 56–58.

Hemingway, Ernest. *The Complete Short Stories of Ernest Hemingway: The Finca Vigia Edition.* New York. Simon and Schuster, 1998.

———. *Dateline, Toronto: The Complete* Toronto Star *Dispatches, 1920–1924.* Ed. William White. New York: Scribner, 1985.

———. *Death in the Afternoon.* New York: Scribner, 1932.

———. *Ernest Hemingway Reads.* Audiocassette and CD. Harper Audio, 1992.

———. *Ernest Hemingway: Selected Letters, 1917–1961.* Ed. Carlos Baker. New York: Scribner, 1981.

———. *A Farewell to Arms.* New York: Scribner, 1929.

———. *For Whom the Bell Tolls.* New York: Scribner, 1940.

———. *Hemingway at Oak Park High: The High School Writings of Ernest Hemingway, 1916–1917.* Ed. Cynthia Maziarka and Donald Vogel Jr. Oak Park, IL: Oak Park and River Forest High School, 1993.

———. *Hemingway on War.* New York: Scribner, 2003.

———. *Hemingway's Spain: Death in the Afternoon.* American Broadcasting Company Merchandising. McGraw-Hill Films, 1968.

———. *Hemingway's Spain: The Sun Also Rises.* American Broadcasting Company Merchandising. McGraw-Hill Films, 1968.

———, ed. *Men at War: The Best War Stories of All Time.* New York: Bramhall House, 1942.

———. *A Moveable Feast.* New York: Scribner, 1964.

———. *The Sun Also Rises.* New York: Scribner, 1926.

Herr, Michael. *Dispatches.* New York: Vintage, 1991.

Herrick, Robert. "What Is Dirt?" *Bookman* 70 (November 1929): 258–62. *Ernest Hemingway: The Critical Reception.* Ed. Robert O. Stephens. New York: Burt Franklin, 1977. 86–89.

Hewson, Marc. "'The Real Story of Ernest Hemingway': Cixous, Gender, and *A Farewell to Arms.*" *Hemingway Review* 22.2 (Spring 2003): 51–62.

Heyman, Neil. *Daily Life During World War I.* Westport, CT: Greenwood Press, 2002.

*History of World War I.* New York: Marshall Cavendish, 2002.

Holman, C. Hugh, and William Harmon, eds. *A Handbook to Literature.* 6th ed. New York: MacMillan, 1992.

Hurston, Zora Neale. *Their Eyes Were Watching God.* Harper Perennial Edition. New York: Harper and Row, 1990.

*In Love and War.* Dir. Richard Attenborough. Perf. Sandra Bullock and Chris O'Donnell. New Line Cinema, 1996.

*The Jazz Age: 1919–1929.* McGraw-Hill Films, 1955.

Jeunet, Jean-Pierre, dir. *A Very Long Engagement.* Warner Bros., 2005.

Jones, James. *The Thin Red Line.* New York: Dell, 1962.

Keegan, John. *The First World War.* New York: Knopf, 1999.

Kert, Bernice. *The Hemingway Women: Those Who Loved Him—The Wives and Others.* New York: W. W. Norton, 1983.

Kirby, Dan, Tom Liner, and Ruth Vinz. *Inside Out: Developmental Strategies for Teaching Writing.* 2nd ed. Portsmouth, NH: Boynton Cook, 1988.

Knodt, Ellen Andrews. "Teaching the 'Lost Generation' to the Current Generation through Active Learning." *Teaching Hemingway's* The Sun Also Rises. Ed. Peter L. Hays. Moscow: University of Idaho Press, 2003. 103–16.

———. "'Suddenly and Unreasonably': Shooting the Sergeant in *A Farewell to Arms.*" *Hemingway's Italy: New Perspectives.* Ed. Rena Sanderson. Baton Rouge: Louisiana State University Press, 2006. 149–57.

Knowles, Harvard V. "The Innocent Reader." Paper delivered at Ernest Hemingway Museum of Cuba, 2nd International Colloquium, Havana, Cuba, July 19–25, 1997.

"La Grande Guerra: The Italian Front, 1915–1918." The Great War Society. June 17, 2005. <http://www.worldwar1.com/itafront>.

Larson, Kelli A. "Stepping into the Labyrinth: Fifteen Years of Hemingway Scholarship." *Hemingway Review* 11.2 (Spring 1992): 19–24.

Laurence, Frank M. *Hemingway and the Movies.* Jackson: University Press of Mississippi, 1981.

Lawrence, D. H. *Lady Chatterley's Lover.* 1928. New York: Penguin, 1995.

Lewis, Robert W. *Hemingway on Love.* Austin: University of Texas Press, 1965.

———. A Farewell to Arms: *The War of the Words.* New York: Twayne, 1992.

Light, James F. "The Religion of Death in *A Farewell to Arms.*" *Modern Fiction Studies* 7 (1961): 169–73.

*The Lost Battalion.* Dir. Russell Mulcahy. Perf. Rick Schroder. A&E Home Video, 2001.

Lynn, Kenneth S. *Hemingway.* New York: Simon and Schuster, 1987.

Lyons, Michael J. *World War I: A Short History.* Englewood Cliffs, NJ: Prentice Hall, 1999.

MacDonald, Dwight. *Against the American Grain.* New York: Random House, 1962.

Marcus, Jane. "Corpus/Corps/Corpse: Writing the Body at War." *Arms and the Woman: War, Gender, and Literary Representation.* Ed. Helen M. Cooper, Adrienne Auslander Munich, and Susan Merrill Squier. Chapel Hill: University of North Carolina Press, 1989. 124–67.

Matthews, T. S. "Nothing Ever Happens to the Brave." *New Republic* 60 (October 9, 1929): 208–10. *Ernest Hemingway: The Critical Reception.* Ed. Robert O. Stephens. New York: Burt Franklin, 1977. 76–78.

"Memories from Stresa." The Ernest Hemingway Society. June 17, 2005. <http://www.hemingwaysociety.org/ members_pictures.htm>.

Mencken, H. L. "Fiction by Adept Hands." *American Mercury* 19 (January 1930): 127. *Ernest Hemingway: The Critical Reception.* Ed. Robert O. Stephens. New York: Burt Franklin, 1977. 97–98.

Messent, Peter. *Modern Novelists: Ernest Hemingway.* New York: St. Martin's Press, 1992.

Meyers, Jeffrey, ed. *Hemingway: The Critical Heritage.* Boston: Routledge & Kegan Paul, 1982.

"Milan." *ITWG.com.* June 17, 2005. <http://www.itwg.com/ct_00002.asp>.

Monkhouse, Francis John. *A Regional Geography of Western Europe.* Harlow, UK: Longmans, 1974.

Monteiro, George. "Ernest Hemingway's *A Farewell to Arms*—the First 65 Years: A Checklist of Criticism, Scholarship, and Commentary." *Bulletin of Bibliography* 53 (1996): 273–92.

Moreland, Kim. "Ernest Hemingway: Knighthood in Our Time." *The Medievalist Impulse in American Literature: Twain, Adams, Fitzgerald, and Hemingway.* Charlottesville: University Press of Virginia, 1996. 161–200.

Morselli, Mario A. *Caporetto 1917: Victory or Defeat?* Portland, OR: F. Cass, 2001.

*The Moving Picture Boys in the Great War.* Dir. Larry Ward. 1975. Videocassette. Image Entertainment, 2002.

Nagel, James. "Catherine Barkley and Retrospective Narration in *A Farewell to Arms.*" *Ernest Hemingway: Six Decades of Criticism.* Ed. Linda W. Wagner. East Lansing: Michigan State University Press, 1987. 171–85.

Oldsey, Bernard. *Hemingway's Hidden Craft: The Writing of* A Farewell to Arms. University Park: Pennsylvania State University Press, 1979.

Oliver, Charles. *Ernest Hemingway A to Z.* New York: Facts on File, 1999.

Ong, Walter J. "The Writer's Audience Is Always a Fiction." *PMLA* 90 (1975): 9–21.

Owen, Wilfred. "Dulce Et Decorum Est." *The Norton Anthology of Modern Poetry.* 2nd ed. Ed. Richard Ellmann and Robert O'Clair. New York: W. W. Norton, 1988. 541.

Paterson, Isabel. Review of *A Farewell to Arms. New York Herald Tribune* Sept. 27, 1929: 17.

*Paths of Glory.* Dir, Stanley Kubrick. Perf. Kirk Douglas. 1957. Videocassette. MGM, 1999.

Peele, George. "A Farewell to Arms." *The Oxford Book of English Verse: 1250–1900.* Ed. Arthur Quiller-Couch. Oxford: Clarendon, 1919. <http://www.bartleby.com/101/102.html>.

Phelan, James. "Distance, Voice, and Temporal Perspective in Frederic Henry's Narration: Successes, Problems, and Paradox." *New Essays on* A Farewell to Arms. Ed. Scott Donaldson. Cambridge: Cambridge University Press, 1990. 53–74.

Plimpton, George. "The Art of Fiction: Ernest Hemingway." Interview. *Paris Review* (1958): 60–89.

Rawls, Walton. *Wake Up, America! World War I and the American Poster.* New York: Abbeville Press, 1988.

*Reader's Guide to Periodical Literature.* New York: H. W. Wilson, 2006.

Remarque, Erich Maria. *All Quiet on the Western Front.* 1929. Trans. A.W. Wheen. New York: Ballentine, 1982.

Reynolds, Michael S. *Ernest Hemingway.* Vol. 2 of *Literary Masters.* Detroit, MI: Gale Research, 2000.

———. *"A Farewell to Arms:* Doctors in the House of Love." *The Cambridge Companion to Hemingway.* Ed. Scott Donaldson. Cambridge: Cambridge University Press, 1996. 109–27.

———. *Hemingway's First War: The Making of* A Farewell to Arms. Princeton, NJ: Princeton University Press, 1976.

———. *Hemingway's Reading, 1910–1940: An Inventory.* Princeton, NJ: Princeton University Press, 1981.

———. *The Young Hemingway.* 1986. New York: W. W. Norton, 1998.

Rickards, Maurice. *Posters of the First World War.* New York: Walker, 1968.

Rindfleisch, Norval. "Respecting the Pupil." *English* (February 1981): 10–19.

Roberts, Graham, and Heather Wallis. *Introducing Film.* New York: Oxford University Press, 2000.

Rogers, Barbara Radcliffe. *Exploring Europe by Boat: A Practical Guide to Water Travel in Europe.* Old Saybrook, CT: Globe Pequot Press, 1994.

Ruenzel, David. "Table Talk." *Teacher Magazine* (September 1992): 32–40.

Sandburg, Carl. "Chicago." *Norton Anthology of American Literature.* Ed. Nina Baym et al. 5th ed. Vol. 2. New York: W. W. Norton, 1998. 1161–62.

Scarry, Elaine. *The Body in Pain: The Making and Unmaking of the World.* New York: Oxford University Press, 1985.

Sedgwick, Eve Kosofsky. *Between Men: English Literature and Male Homosocial Desire.* New York: Columbia University Press, 1985.

Sellman, Roger Raymond. *An Outline Atlas of World History, with Notes.* New York: St. Martin's Press, 1970.

Shepherd, William R. *Historical Atlas.* New York: Barnes and Noble Books, 1973.

Sinclair, Upton. *The Jungle.* 1906. New York: New American Library, 1960.

Smaniotto, Pierino, and Thea Bekers. "Milano—Italia." June 17, 2005. <http://www.smaniotto.net/milano_index_it.html>.

Smith, Paul. "The Trying-Out of *A Farewell to Arms.*" *New Essays on* A Farewell to Arms. Ed. Scott Donaldson. Cambridge: Cambridge University Press, 1990. 27–52.

Spanier, Sandra Whipple. "Catherine Barkley and the Hemingway Code: Ritual

and Survival in *A Farewell to Arms.*" *Ernest Hemingway's* A Farewell to Arms.
Ed. Harold Bloom. New York: Chelsea House, 1987. 131–48.

———. "Hemingway's Unknown Soldier: Catherine Barkley, the Critics, and the
Great War." *New Essays on* A Farewell to Arms. Ed. Scott Donaldson. New York:
Cambridge University Press, 1990. 75–108.

"StresaOnline." June 17, 2005. <http://www.stresaonline.com/stresa_lakemaggiore.php>.

Svoboda, Frederic J. "The Great Themes in Hemingway: Love, War, Wilderness,
and Loss." *A Historical Guide to Ernest Hemingway.* Ed. Linda Wagner-Martin.
Oxford: Oxford University Press, 2000. 155–72.

Swofford, Anthony. *Jarhead: A Marine's Chronicle of the Gulf War and Other Battles.*
New York: Scribner, 2003.

Terry, Charles L. "Harkness Learning Is Still the News." <http://www.exeter.edu/
publications/exeter/fall_99/harkness1.htm>.

Thoms, Annie, ed. *With Their Eyes: September 11th—the View from a High School
at Ground Zero.* New York: Harper Teen, 2002.

Trevelyan, G. M. "Report." *Anglo-Italian Review* June 1918. Rpt. by Giovanni Cecchin,
*Hemingway, G. M. Trevelyan e il Friuli: Alle origini di Addio alle Armi.* Lignano
Sabbiadoro, Italy: Commune di Lignano Sabbiadoro, 1986.

Trogdon, Robert W., ed. *Ernest Hemingway: A Literary Reference.* New York: Carroll & Graf, 1999.

Trumbo, Dalton. *Johnny Got His Gun.* 1959. New York: Bantam, 1984.

Tucker, Spencer C. *The Great War, 1914–1918.* Bloomington: Indiana University
Press, 1998.

Tuttleton, James W. "'Combat in the Erogenous Zone': Women in the American
Novel between the Two World Wars." *What Manner of Woman: Essays on English
and American Life and Literature.* Ed. Marlene Springer. New York: New York
University Press, 1977. 271–96.

Twain, Mark. *Adventures of Huckleberry Finn.* 2nd ed. Ed. Sculley Bradley et al.
New York: W. W. Norton, 1977.

Villard, Henry Serrano, and James Nagel, eds. *Hemingway in Love and War: The
Lost Diary of Agnes von Kurowsky.* New York: Hyperion, 1996.

Wagner-Martin, Linda. "The Romance of Desire in Hemingway's Fiction." *Hemingway and Women: Female Critics and the Female Voice.* Ed. Lawrence R. Broer
and Gloria Holland. Tuscaloosa: University of Alabama Press, 2002. 54–69.

Waldhorn, Arthur. *A Reader's Guide to Ernest Hemingway.* New York: Farrar, Straus
& Giroux, 1972.

*War in Spain.* Prudential Insurance Company. McGraw-Hill, 1960.

Warren, Robert Penn. "Hemingway." *Kenyon Review* 9 (Winter 1947): 1–28.

Way, Brian. "Hemingway the Intellectual: A Version of Modernism." *Ernest Hemingway: New Critical Essays.* Ed. A. Robert Lee. London: Vision, 1983. 151–71.

Wood, Leonard, et al., eds. *The History of the First World War.* New York: Grolier,
1965.

Young, Philip. *Ernest Hemingway: A Reconsideration.* Rev. ed. New York: Harcourt,
1966.

Zakaria, Fareed. "The Birth of Modernity." *Newsweek* November 11, 1996: 91.

# Selected Bibliography of Works on
## *A Farewell to Arms*

Adair, William. "*The Sun Also Rises:* The Source of *A Farewell to Arms.*" *ANQ: A Quarterly Journal of Short Articles, Notes, and Reviews* 12 (Fall 1999): 25–28.

———. "Time and Structure in *A Farewell to Arms.*" *South Dakota Review* 13 (1975): 165–71.

Aubrey, James R. "Heller's 'Parody on Hemingway' in *Catch-22.*" *Studies in Contemporary Satire: A Creative and Critical Journal* 17 (1990): 1–5.

Baker, Carlos. *Ernest Hemingway: A Life Story.* New York: Scribner, 1969.

Balbert, Peter. "From Hemingway to Lawrence to Mailer: Survival and Sexual Identity in *A Farewell to Arms.*" *Hemingway Review* 3.1 (Fall 1983): 30–43.

Barlowe-Kayes, Jamie. "Re-reading Women: The Example of Catherine Barkley." *Hemingway Review* 12 (Spring 1993): 24–35. *Ernest Hemingway: Seven Decades of Criticism.* Ed. Linda Wagner-Martin. East Lansing: Michigan State University Press, 1998. 171–84.

Bell, Millicent. "*A Farewell to Arms:* Pseudoautobiography and Personal Metaphor." *Ernest Hemingway: The Writer in Context.* Ed. James Nagel. Madison: University of Wisconsin Press, 1984. 107–28.

Bloom, Harold, ed. *Modern Critical Interpretations: Ernest Hemingway's* A Farewell to Arms. New York: Chelsea House, 1987.

Brasch, James Daniel, and Joseph Sigman. *Hemingway's Library: A Composite Record.* New York: Garland, 1981.

Brenner, Gerry. *Concealments in Hemingway's Works.* Columbus: Ohio State University Press, 1983.

Cohen, Milton. "War Medals for Sale? Public Bravery vs. Private Courage in Hemingway's WWI Writing." *North Dakota Quarterly* 68 (Spring/Summer 2001): 287–94.

Cohen, Peter F. "'I Won't Kiss You. . . . I'll Send Your English Girl': Homoerotic Desire in *A Farewell to Arms.*" *Hemingway Review* 15.1 (Fall 1995): 42–53.

Comley, Nancy R., and Robert Scholes. *Hemingway's Genders: Rereading the Hemingway Text*. New Haven, CT: Yale University Press, 1994.

Davis, Judy. "Three Novels Mentioned in *A Farewell to Arms*." *Notes on Contemporary Literature* 19 (Sept. 1989): 4–5.

Dekker, George, and Joseph Harris. "Supernaturalism and the Vernacular Style in *A Farewell to Arms*." *PMLA* 34 (1979): 311–18.

Donaldson, Scott. "Censorship and *A Farewell to Arms*." *Studies in American Fiction* 19 (1991): 85–93.

———, ed. *New Essays on* A Farewell to Arms. Cambridge: Cambridge University Press, 1990.

Dow, William. "*A Farewell to Arms* and Hemingway's Protest Stance: To Tell the Truth without Screaming." *Hemingway Review* 15.1 (Fall 1995): 72–86.

———. "Hemingway's *A Farewell to Arms*." *Explicator* 55 (1997): 224–25.

Eby, Carl P. *Hemingway's Fetishism: Psychoanalysis and the Mirror of Manhood*. Albany: State University of New York Press, 1999.

Elliott, Ira. "*A Farewell to Arms* and Hemingway's Crisis of Masculine Values." *LIT: Literature Interpretation Theory* 4 (1993): 291–304.

Engelberg, Edward. "Hemingway's 'True Penelope': Flaubert's *L'Education Sentimentale* and *A Farewell to Arms*." *Comparative Literature Studies* 16 (1979): 189–206.

*A Farewell to Arms*. By Ernest Hemingway. Dir. Frank Borzage. Perf. Gary Cooper, Helen Hayes, and Adolphe Menjou. Adapt. Benjamin Glazer. Paramount, 1932.

*A Farewell to Arms*. By Ernest Hemingway. Dir. Charles Vidor. Perf. Rock Hudson and Jennifer Jones. Adapt. Laurence Stallings. Twentieth Century Fox, 1957.

Fetterley, Judith. "*A Farewell to Arms*: Hemingway's 'Resentful Cryptogram.'" *The Resisting Reader*. Bloomington: Indiana University Press, 1978. 46–71.

Finnegan, Robert Emmett. "Mirrors and Newspapers in Hemingway's *A Farewell to Arms*." *Durham University Journal* 86 (1994): 259–70.

Fleming, Robert E. "Hemingway and Peele: Chapter 1 of *A Farewell to Arms*." *Studies in American Fiction* 11 (Spring 1983): 95–100.

Gajdusek, Robert E. "The Oxymoronic Compound and the Ambiguous Noun: Paradox as Paradigm in *A Farewell to Arms*." *North Dakota Quarterly* 63.3 (Summer 1996): 40–49.

Gellens, Jay, ed. *Twentieth Century Interpretations of* A Farewell to Arms: *A Collection of Critical Essays*. Englewood Cliffs, NJ: Prentice Hall, 1970.

Gerstenberger, Donna. "*The Waste Land* in *A Farewell to Arms*." *Modern Language Notes* 76 (1961): 24–25.

Gradoli, Marina. "Count Greffi's Birthday Parties." *North Dakota Quarterly* 64.3 (1997): 56–59.

Graham, John. *The Merrill Studies in* A Farewell to Arms. Columbus, OH: Merrill, 1971.

Harrington, Gary. "Partial Articulation: Word Play in *A Farewell to Arms*." *Hemingway Review* 20.2 (Spring 2001): 59–75.

Hatten, Charles. "The Crisis of Masculinity, Reified Desire, and Catherine Barkley in *A Farewell to Arms*." *Journal of the History of Sexuality* 4 (1993): 76–98.

Haytock, Jennifer A. "Hemingway's Soldiers and Their Pregnant Women: Domestic Ritual in World War I." *Hemingway Review* 19 (Spring 2000): 57–72.

Herndl, Diane Price. "Invalid Masculinity: Silence, Hospitals, and Anesthesia in *A Farewell to Arms.*" *Hemingway Review* 21 (Fall 2001): 38–52.

Hewson, Marc. "'The Real Story of Ernest Hemingway': Cixous, Gender, and *A Farewell to Arms.*" *Hemingway Review* 22.2 (Spring 2003): 51–62.

Hill, William Thomas. "The Roads of the Abruzzi and the Roads of Earthly Paradise in Hemingway's *A Farewell to Arms.*" *Studies in the Humanities* 10 (1994): 25–43.

Josephs, Allen. "Hemingway's Out of Body Experience." *Hemingway Review* 2.2 (Spring 1983): 11–17.

Kautz, Elizabeth Dolan. "Gynecologists, Power and Sexuality in Modernist Texts." *Journal of Popular Culture* 28.4 (Spring 1975): 81–91.

Kleinman, Craig. "Dirty Tricks and Word Jokes: The Politics of Recollection in *A Farewell to Arms.*" *Hemingway Review* 15.1 (Fall 1995): 54–71.

Laurence, Frank M. "Death in the Matinée: The Film Endings of Hemingway's Fiction." *Literature Film Quarterly* 2 (1974): 44–51.

———. *Hemingway and the Movies.* Jackson: University Press of Mississippi, 1981.

Leff, Leonard J. "A Thunderous Reception: Broadway, Hollywood, and *A Farewell to Arms.*" *Hemingway Review* 15.2 (Spring 1996): 33–51.

Lewis, Robert W. *A Farewell to Arms: The War of the Words.* New York: Twayne, 1992.

———. "Manners and Morals in *A Farewell to Arms.*" *Hemingway: Up in Michigan Perspectives.* Ed. Frederic J. Svoboda and Joseph J. Waldmeir. East Lansing: Michigan State University Press, 1995. 157–65.

———, ed. *Hemingway in Italy and Other Essays.* New York: Praeger, 1990.

Lindsay, Clarence. "Consequential Identity in Hemingway's *A Farewell to Arms.*" *Midamerica: The Yearbook of the Society for the Study of Midwestern Literature* 24 (1997): 99–114.

Lockridge, Ernest. "Faithful in Her Fashion: Catherine Barkley, the Invisible Hemingway Heroine." *Journal of Narrative Technique* 18 (1988): 170–78.

———. "*Othello* as a Key to Hemingway." *Hemingway Review* 18 (Fall 1998): 68–77.

Lynn, Kenneth S. *Hemingway.* New York: Simon and Schuster, 1987.

Mandel, Miriam. "Ferguson and Lesbian Love: Unspoken Subplots in *A Farewell to Arms.*" *Hemingway Review* 14.1 (Fall 1994): 18–24.

———. "Headgear and Horses: Authorial Presence in *A Farewell to Arms.*" *International Fiction Review* 22 (1995): 61–66.

Martin, Robert A. "Hemingway and the Ambulance Drivers in *A Farewell to Arms.*" *Ernest Hemingway: Six Decades of Criticism.* Ed. Linda Wagner. East Lansing: Michigan State University Press, 1987. 195–204.

———. "Hemingway's *A Farewell to Arms:* The World Beyond Oak Park and Idealism." *Hemingway: Up in Michigan Perspectives.* Ed. Frederic J. Svoboda and Joseph J. Waldmeir. East Lansing: Michigan State University Press, 1995. 167–75.

Mazzaro, Jerome. "George Peele and *A Farewell to Arms:* A Thematic Tie?" *Modern Language Notes* 75 (1960): 118–19.

McIlvaine, Robert M. "A Literary Source for the Caesarean Section in *A Farewell to Arms.*" *American Literature* 43 (1971): 444–47.

McNeely, Trevor. "War Zone Revisited: Hemingway's Aesthetics and *A Farewell to Arms.*" *South Dakota Review* 22 (Winter 1984): 14–38.

Merrill, Robert. "Tragic Form in *A Farewell to Arms.*" *American Literature* 45 (1974): 571–79.

Meyers, Jeffrey. *Hemingway: A Biography.* New York: Harper and Row, 1985.

Miller, D. Quentin. "'In the Late Summer of That Year': The Problem of Time in *A Farewell to Arms.*" *Hemingway Review* 10 (Spring 1991): 61–64.

Monteiro, George, ed. *Critical Essays on Ernest Hemingway's* A Farewell to Arms. New York: G. K. Hall, 1994.

———. "Ernest Hemingway's *A Farewell to Arms*—the First Sixty-Five Years: A Checklist of Criticism, Scholarship, and Commentary." *Bulletin of Bibliography* 53 (1996): 273–92.

———. "Patriotism and Treason in *A Farewell to Arms.*" *War, Literature, and the Arts: An International Journal of the Humanities* 9 (1997): 27–38.

Nagel, Gwen L. "A Téssera for Frederic Henry: Imagery and Recurrence in *A Farewell to Arms.*" *Ernest Hemingway: Six Decades of Criticism.* Ed. Linda Wagner. East Lansing: Michigan State University Press, 1987. 187–93.

Nagel, James. "Catherine Barkley and Retrospective Narration in *A Farewell to Arms.*" *Ernest Hemingway: Six Decades of Criticism.* Ed. Linda Wagner. East Lansing: Michigan State University Press, 1987. 171–93.

Nolan, Charles J., Jr. "Catherine Barkley: Hemingway's Scottish Heroine." *Hemingway Review* 7.1 (1987): 43–44.

———. "Shooting the Sergeant: Frederic Henry's Puzzling Action." *College Literature* 11 (Fall 1984): 269–75.

Norris, Margot. "The Novel as War: Lies and Truth in Hemingway's *A Farewell to Arms.*" *Modern Fiction Studies* 40.4 (1994): 689–710.

Oldsey, Bernard. "Genesis of *A Farewell to Arms.*" *Studies in American Fiction* 5 (1977): 175–85.

———. *Hemingway's Hidden Craft: The Writing of* A Farewell to Arms. University Park: Pennsylvania State University Press, 1979.

Oliver, Charles M., ed. *Ernest Hemingway's* A Farewell to Arms: *A Documentary Volume.* Detroit, MI: Thomson Gale, 2005.

———. *A Moving Picture Feast: The Filmgoer's Hemingway.* New York: Praeger, 1989.

———. *Special Issue on* A Farewell to Arms. Spec. issue of *Hemingway Review* 9.1 (1989): 1–112.

Phelan, James. "The Concept of Voice, the Voices of Frederic Henry, and the Structure of *A Farewell to Arms.*" *Hemingway: Essays of Reassessment.* Ed. Frank Scafella. New York: Oxford University Press, 1990. 214–32.

———. "Distance, Voice, and Temporal Perspective in Frederic Henry's Narration: Powers, Problems, Paradox." *New Essays on* A Farewell to Arms. Ed. Scott Donaldson. Cambridge: Cambridge University Press, 1990. 53–74.

Phillips, Gene D. *Hemingway and Film*. New York: Frederic Ungar, 1980.

Pozorski, Aimee L. "Infantry and Infanticide in *A Farewell to Arms.*" *Hemingway Review* 23.2 (Spring 2004): 75–98.

Prescott, Mary. "*A Farewell to Arms:* Memory and the Perpetual Now." *College Literature* 17 (1990): 41–52.

Price, Alan. "'I'm Not an Old Fogey and You're Not a Young Ass': Owen Wister and Ernest Hemingway." *Hemingway Review* 9.1 (Fall 1989): 82–90.

Reynolds, Michael S. "*A Farewell to Arms:* Doctors in the House of Love." *The Cambridge Companion to Ernest Hemingway.* Ed. Scott Donaldson. New York: Cambridge University Press, 1996. 109–27.

———. *Hemingway's First War: The Making of* A Farewell to Arms. Princeton, NJ: Princeton University Press, 1976.

———. *Hemingway's Reading, 1910–1940: An Inventory.* Princeton, NJ: Princeton University Press, 1981.

———. *Hemingway: The American Homecoming.* Cambridge, MA: Blackwell, 1992.

———. *Hemingway: The Final Years.* New York: W. W. Norton, 1999.

———. *Hemingway: The 1930s.* New York: W. W. Norton, 1997.

———. *Hemingway: The Paris Years.* Cambridge, MA: Blackwell, 1989.

———. *The Young Hemingway.* New York: Blackwell, 1986.

Seed, David. "The Ravages of Time in Hemingway's *A Farewell to Arms.*" *Durham University Journal* 81 (June 1989): 265–69.

Slattery, William C. "The Mountain, the Plain, and San Siro." *Papers on Language and Literature* 16 (1980): 439–42.

Sloan, Gary. "*A Farewell to Arms* and the Sunday-School Jesus." *Studies in the Novel* 25 (1993): 449–56.

Smith, Paul. "Almost All Is Vanity: A Note on Nine Rejected Titles for *A Farewell to Arms.*" *Hemingway Review* 2 (Fall 1982): 74–76.

Spilka, Mark. *Hemingway's Quarrel with Androgyny.* Lincoln: University of Nebraska Press, 1990.

Stephens, Robert O. "Hemingway and Stendhal: The Matrix of *A Farewell to Arms.*" *PMLA* 88 (1973): 271–80.

Stubbs, John. "Love and Role Playing in *A Farewell to Arms.*" *Fitzgerald/Hemingway Annual 1973.* Ed. Matthew J. Bruccoli and C. E. Frazer Clark Jr. Washington, DC: Microcard Editions Books, 1974. 272–84.

Sylvester, Bickford. "The Sexual Impasse to Romantic Order in Hemingway's Fiction: *A Farewell to Arms, Othello,* 'Orpen,' and the Hemingway Canon." *Hemingway: Up in Michigan Perspectives.* Ed. Frederic J. Svoboda and Joseph J. Waldmeir. East Lansing: Michigan State University Press, 1995. 177–87.

Traber, Daniel S. "Performing the Feminine in *A Farewell to Arms.*" *Hemingway Review* 24.2 (Spring 2005): 28–40.

Tyler, Lisa. "Passion and Grief in *A Farewell to Arms:* Ernest Hemingway's Retelling of *Wuthering Heights.*" *Hemingway Review* 14 (Spring 1995): 79–96. *Ernest Hemingway: Seven Decades of Criticism.* Ed. Linda Wagner-Martin. East Lansing: Michigan State University Press, 1998. 151–69.

Vernon, Alex. "War, Gender, and Ernest Hemingway." *Hemingway Review* 22.1 (Fall 2002): 34–55.

Villard, Henry S., and James Nagel, eds. *Hemingway in Love and War: The Lost Diary of Agnes von Kurowsky, Her Letters and Correspondence of Ernest Hemingway.* Boston: Northeastern University Press, 1989.

Wagner-Martin, Linda. *Ernest Hemingway's* A Farewell to Arms: *A Reference Guide.* Westport, CT: Greenwood Press, 2003.

Waldhorn, Arthur. "Harold Loeb's 'Ants.'" *Hemingway Review* 2 (Fall 1982): 86–87.

Wexler, Joyce. "E.R.A. for Hemingway: A Feminist Defense of *A Farewell to Arms.*" *Georgia Review* 35 (1981): 111–23.

Whitlow, Roger. *Cassandra's Daughters: The Women in Hemingway.* Westport, CT: Greenwood Press, 1984.

Whittier, Gayle. "Childbirth, War, and Creativity in *A Farewell to Arms.*" *LIT: Literature Interpretation Theory* 3 (1992): 253–70.

———. "Clinical Gaze and the Erotic Body in *A Farewell to Arms.*" *Studies in the Humanities* 23 (June 1996): 1–27.

Wiener, Gary, ed. *Readings on* A Farewell to Arms. San Diego, CA: Greenhaven Press, 2000.

Williams, David. "The Politics of Impersonality in *A Farewell to Arms.*" *University of Toronto Quarterly: A Canadian Journal of the Humanities* 59 (Winter 1989–90): 310–33.

Wilson, Andrew J. "Bidding Goodbye to the Plumed Troop and the Big Wars: The Presence of *Othello* in *A Farewell to Arms.*" *Hemingway Review* 15.2 (Spring 1996): 52–66.

Young, Philip. *Ernest Hemingway: A Reconsideration.* Rev. ed. New York: Harbinger, 1966.

# Contributors

*J. T. Barbarese* is associate professor of English and creative writing at Rutgers University in Camden, New Jersey. He is the author of four books of poetry, most recently *The Black Beach* (University of North Texas Press, 2005) and a translation of Euripides' *Children of Herakles* (University of Pennsylvania, 1999). His poems and translations have appeared in *Atlantic Monthly, Boulevard, Georgia Review, Denver Quarterly, Cortland Review,* and *Poetry,* his short fiction in *Story Quarterly,* and his essays and journalism in *Tri-Quarterly, Georgia Review, Studies in English Literature, Journal of Modern Literature,* and the *New York Times.*

*Brenda G. Cornell* has been a community college teacher for the past twenty years (Texas State Technical College, 1987–2002; Central Texas College, 2003–2006). She earned both MA and PhD degrees from the University of Southern Mississippi, Hattiesburg, Mississippi, with specialties in the novel, recent American literature, and the works of William Faulkner. She has published essays on Eudora Welty and Faulkner, and her dissertation ("Barry Hannah: The Writer as Entertainer," 1990) is the first critical work on the novels of Barry Hannah. She lives in Waco, Texas, with Mr. Bagger Vance, her Turkish Van cat.

*Peter L. Hays* is a professor emeritus of the University of California, Davis. He is the author or editor of three books on Hemingway, the most recent being *Teaching Hemingway's* The Sun Also Rises (University of Idaho Press, 2003), as well as numerous articles on Hemingway.

*Jennifer Haytock* is associate professor of English at SUNY College at Brockport, where she teaches twentieth-century American literature. She has published *At*

*Home, At War: Domesticity and World War I in American Literature* (Ohio State University Press, 2003) as well as essays on Ernest Hemingway, Edith Wharton, and Willa Cather.

*Ellen Andrews Knodt* is professor of English and former division head of Arts and Humanities at Penn State, Abington. Winner of the prestigious all-University Atherton Award for Excellence in Teaching, she teaches undergraduate courses in writing and American literature and has published works in both areas. Her articles on Ernest Hemingway have appeared in the *North Dakota Quarterly,* the *Hemingway Review,* and in several essay collections.

*Amy Lerman* earned her MA and PhD from the University of Kansas, and her dissertation was on Hemingway and the feminist critique. Currently, she is a residential faculty member at Mesa Community College in Arizona, where she teaches classes in developmental English, composition, and literature. Besides Hemingway, she has presented and published on Samuel Beckett, Toni Morrison, Louis Owens, and Raymond Carver, and her current interests are popular culture (particularly food and culture and "chick lit") as well as twentieth-century American literature and pedagogy.

*James H. Meredith,* after twenty-five years of commissioned service, retired from the U.S. Air Force in September 2004. During his years of service, Jim was lucky enough to teach fifteen years at the U.S. Air Force Academy, where he rose to the rank of professor of English. He is now director of Academic Publications for Northcentral University. Jim currently holds the office of president of the Ernest Hemingway Foundation and Society and also serves on the F. Scott Fitzgerald Society Board. His most recent book is *Understanding the Literature of World War I* (2004), a companion to his *Understanding the Literature of World War II* (1999); both books were published by Greenwood Press. His long-awaited *Hemingway and War in His Time* (Kent State University Press) is forthcoming.

*Kim Moreland* is professor of English at George Washington University. Her articles on Hemingway have appeared in the *Hemingway Review, North Dakota Quarterly,* and *Southern Humanities Review,* as well as in several essay collections. Her book, *The Medievalist Impulse in American Literature: Twain, Adams, Fitzgerald, and Hemingway,* was published by the University Press of Virginia (1996). She has also published articles on other American writers of the nineteenth and twentieth centuries, notably Henry Adams, Jack London, and F. Scott Fitzgerald.

*Jackson A. Niday II* has taught English at the U.S. Air Force Academy for eleven years. His academic interests include rhetorical theory and war literature. In his professional life, he applies those academic interests in a number of arenas, including his work as an associate editor of *War, Literature, and the Arts;* as director of the USAFA Speech and Debate Team; and as director of the USAFA consultative program, *Writing for Leaders.*

*Charles M. (Tod) Oliver,* now of Charlottesville, Virginia, holds a PhD from Bowling Green University and is professor emeritus of English at Ohio Northern University, where he retired in 1992. He edited the *Hemingway Review* from 1970 to 1992 and the *Hemingway Newsletter* from 1979 to 2005. He spent twelve years (1980–1992) as secretary of the Ernest Hemingway Foundation and Society. Oliver is the editor of *A Moving Picture Feast: The Filmgoer's Hemingway* (Praeger, 1989) and *Ernest Hemingway's* A Farewell to Arms: *A Documentary Volume* (Thomson Gale, 2005) and the author of *Ernest Hemingway A to Z: The Essential Reference to the Life and Work* (Facts on File, 1999), *Critical Companion to Walt Whitman* (Facts on File, 2006), and *Critical Companion to Ernest Hemingway* (Facts on File, 2007).

*Mark P. Ott* teaches at Deerfield Academy in Massachusetts. His book, *Ernest Hemingway and the Gulf Stream: A Contextual Biography,* is forthcoming in 2008 from Kent State University Press. Ott has presented academic papers at international Hemingway conferences in Cuba, Oak Park, Bimini, Italy, Key West, and Spain, and his scholarship has been published in the *Hemingway Review.* He has been awarded grants from the Ernest Hemingway Society, the Ernest Hemingway Collection at the John F. Kennedy Library, and the Arts and Sciences Advisory Council of the University of Hawaii–Manoa.

*David Scoma* is professor of English in the General Education Department at the Orlando, Florida, campus of DeVry University. He has also served as an educational media specialist for the Orange County public school system. David holds a PhD from the University of Central Florida's Texts and Technology program.

*Gail D. Sinclair* is Scholar in Residence and Coordinator of the Colloquy on Liberal Education at Rollins College. She served as site director for the 2004 International Hemingway Society Conference and is a co-program director for the 2008 Hemingway conference. Her publications include essays in *Hemingway and Women: Female Critics and the Female Voice,* the *Hemingway Review, Studies in the Novel,* and *Mississippi Quarterly.* She is currently coediting a book on Hemingway and Key West and has an essay forthcoming on *The Great Gatsby* in *MLA's Approaches to Teaching Literature* series. She also serves on the board of directors for the F. Scott Fitzgerald Society.

*Thomas Strychacz* is a professor of American literature at Mills College, California, where he has taught for fifteen years. He is the author of *Modernism, Mass Culture, and Professionalism* (Cambridge University Press, 1993), *Hemingway's Theaters of Masculinity* (Louisiana State University Press, 2004), and many articles on American literature and culture. A new book, *Dangerous Masculinities,* is forthcoming from the University of Florida Press.

*Frederic Svoboda* is professor of English at the University of Michigan–Flint. He has chaired the Department of English and directed the Graduate Program in American Culture and recently served as senior advisor to the chancellor. He has published widely in American literature, including a book-length study of the composition of Hemingway's *The Sun Also Rises* and the edited essays from the Petoskey, Michigan, conference of the Hemingway Society, which he helped to organize. He currently serves as a director and treasurer of the Ernest Hemingway Foundation.

*Lisa Tyler* is professor of English at Sinclair Community College in Dayton, Ohio, where she has taught since 1990. She is the author of *Student Companion to Ernest Hemingway* (Greenwood, 2001) and more than two dozen articles in scholarly journals and edited collections. She also created and maintains Virtual Hemingway, a list on the International Hemingway Society Web site (www.hemingwaysociety. org) of hundreds of Hemingway-related Web sites.

# Index

Text and cover for

*Teaching Hemingway's* A Farewell to Arms

was designed and composed by Darryl ml Crosby

in 10/13.5 Minion Pro with display type in Meta bold;

printed on 55# Natures Natural stock

by Thomson-Shore, Inc., of Dexter, Michigan;

and published by

THE KENT STATE UNIVERSITY PRESS

*Kent, Ohio 44242*